Politics and Civil Liberties in Europe

FOUR CASE STUDIES

POLITICS
AND
CIVIL LIBERTIES
IN EUROPE

Four Case Studies

Edited by
RONALD F. BUNN
and
WILLIAM G. ANDREWS

Contributions by
GEOFFREY MARSHALL, *Oxford University*
JEROME B. KING, *Williams College*
RONALD F. BUNN, *Louisiana State University*
MICHAEL P. GEHLEN, *Purdue University*

D. VAN NOSTRAND COMPANY, INC.
PRINCETON, NEW JERSEY
TORONTO   LONDON

Van Nostrand Regional Offices:
New York, Chicago, San Francisco

D. Van Nostrand Company, Ltd., *London*

D. Van Nostrand Company (Canada), Ltd., *Toronto*

PRINTED IN THE UNITED STATES OF AMERICA

Preface

AMERICAN CIVIL LIBERTIES HAVE ATTRACTED INCREASING CONCERN
from the academic community in recent years, yet similar problems in other countries have received little attention. This collection of case studies is intended to help repair that gap. Also,
the editors hope that by focussing the studies on one relatively
narrow topic, the cases will be more readily comparable than if
the topics had varied more from country to country. Finally, a
determined effort has been made to keep the studies so brief that
the book can be used as supplementary reading in college comparative government courses without intruding unduly either on
the instructor's reading list or the student's budget.

Each contributor was asked to describe and analyze a civil
liberties incident and its political context in one of the four major
European countries usually covered in comparative government
courses. Each incident was selected to highlight a principal civil
liberties problem area and to illustrate the operation of the political
system in dealing with a concrete, controversial problem. The case
of the nuclear disarmers in Britain concerns the right of the people
peaceably to assemble in political demonstrations. The Canal
affair in France involved the right of a political offender to be
tried fairly. The *Spiegel* Affair in West Germany pitted an irate
administration against a powerful news magazine in a struggle over
the meaning of freedom of the press. The Sinyavsky-Daniel trial
was merely one episode in the long and continuing battle over
freedom of literary expression in post-Stalin Russia. Each case
describes another engagement in Man's eternal search for the
means and opportunity to give his spirit free expression. The issues,
the weapons, the style of combat, the outcome vary widely from
system to system. Their similarities and their variation shed light
both on the substance of the issues and on the machinery that
deals with them.

This book had its genesis in a study of the *Spiegel* case by one of the editors. The other suggested that the study be revised and included with similar studies on Britain, France, and the Soviet Union in a short casebook. Both editors solicited the other contributions and edited the completed manuscript. They are grateful to the contributors for responding so ably and willingly to their invitations and, especially, for their patience in seeing their work pass through the irksome, seemingly endless, and sometimes mutilating process of publication.

R.F.B.
W.G.A.

Contents

Contributors and Editors

WILLIAM G. ANDREWS is Professor and Chairman of the Department of Political Science, State University of New York, College at Brockport. He is author of *French Politics and Algeria* and editor of *Soviet Institutions and Policies*.

RONALD F. BUNN is Associate Professor of Government, Louisiana State University.

MICHAEL P. GEHLEN is Associate Professor, Department of Political Science, Purdue University and Visiting Associate Professor, Department of Political Science, University of California—Berkeley. He is author of *The Politics of Coexistence*.

JEROME B. KING, of Williams College, has been appointed Associate Professor of Government, University of Massachusetts (Amherst), and is currently working on a study to be called *French Courts and Free Speech*.

GEOFFREY MARSHALL, Fellow of the Queen's College, Oxford University, is author of *Parliamentary Sovereignty and the Commonwealth*.

Introduction

by Ronald F. Bunn

AT LEAST SINCE ARISTOTLE, A CENTRAL UNDERTAKING IN THE systematic study of politics has been the effort to generalize about the distinguishing features of political communities and, on the basis of these generalizations, to extract typologies by which political systems may be classified. Recent theoretical discussions of this ancient project, stimulated by the knowledge explosion that permits greater insights into exotic as well as the more familiar cultures, have pointed comparative politics in the direction of functional analyses that transcend, without necessarily rejecting, the traditional classificatory categories such as "democratic," "authoritarian," and "totalitarian."

In its broadest sense, a functional approach views political systems by looking beyond their apparent institutional and formal apparatus to the interconnections and interplay among politically relevant groups and phenomena, whether or not organized formally and whether or not "assigned" a formal role in the decision processes. Certain identifiable functions, the "functionalist" might suggest, are performed in all political systems, however "primitive" or "modern" by contemporary standards. The political scientist delineates the similarities and differences in the performance of these common functions and tries to formulate comparative frames of reference to permit generalizations that are less culture-bound and more universally valid.

One promising area for functional inquiry is provided by the two cultural tugs found in any political community: consensus and cleavage. Consensus represents the agreement upon which order and authority must ultimately rest; cleavage refers to the disagreement that exists within the consensual framework. The constant, sometimes dramatic and frequently routine, reconciliation of consensus and cleavage is a primary function of politics. Consensus, through time, permits stability and continuity in political development; cleavage, through time, encourages change, whether incremental or radical. The history of political communities reveals the unceasing intermingling and harmonization of consensus and cleavage and the occasional irreconcilability of the two culminates in periods of revolution and readjustment.

If in the reconciling of consensus and cleavage we find the primary function of politics, we may also conclude that it contains one of the great problems of politics. An "under-consensual" political system is disordered, ineffectual in grappling with fundamental political problems, and imminently in jeopardy of being jettisoned through the efforts of one or more dissident groups within the community. An "over-consensual" community may also, however, be functionally disordered, if for different reasons and in less dramatic form. The essential problem of the over-consensual political system is its tendency toward rigidity, accompanied by an insensitivity or sluggishness toward the need for innovation and modification. In its extreme condition this resistance to change may produce significant residues of permanent hostility which may inspire the alienated group to opt for destruction of the system. Even if a political community were perfectly consensualized, without any elements of dissent or cleavage—and we may assume the non-existence of such a society—the problem of encirclement and inundation by external developments would likely cause serious challenges to its continuance. The "proper" balance between consensus and cleavage, of course, defies precise measurement. Much depends upon the variables found within each political culture or sub-culture which shape the configurations of the agreements and disagreements. Moreover, distinctions would have to be made in the quality of the cleavage, in the intensity and fundamentality of the disagreements, before attempting to speculate about the requisite "balance" of consensus and cleavage within a community. But the tension between consensus and cleavage is at once both the explanation and the dilemma of politics.

Consensus and cleavage—two political cultural conditions—have their political functional counterparts in aggregation and articulation. This means that the groups (parties, bureaucracies, interest groups, communication systems, etc.) primarily involved in the political process—the reconciliation of consensus and cleavage—are called upon to perform a dual function. On the one hand they attempt to aggregate and bring together the diversities of views and interests into manageable alternatives or options upon which decisions finally will be based. Simultaneously they seek to define these diversities, to project them into the aggregative phase, and, in general, to articulate or expose the disagreements within the community. The tension created within the political system by the necessity and interdependence of consensus and cleavage finds its counterpart in the tension which may characterize these groups or sub-systems. Thus, a political party system which is "under-consensual" and ideologically fragmented evidences the functional disorder, on a smaller scale, of the "under-consensual" political system: it will tend toward indecisiveness with the resulting inability to mobilize the necessary degree of consensus upon which authority must rest. To take the reverse situation, the "over-consensual" party system may distort the political process toward rigidity and unresponsiveness to the pleas for change and innovations.

The consensus-cleavage dichotomy also has important implications for the stylistic qualities of the political process. Much here will depend upon the nature or root causes of the consensus. If, for example, a political system is heavily dependent upon a relatively well-defined and pervasive body of dogma for the creation and continuation of its consensus and if this body of dogma is acceptable over a period of time, we may conclude that the system contains many characteristics of the high-consensus system, strong in its aggregative function. Yet we could not identify this type of high-consensus system as stylistically "pragmatic," since ideology, real or imagined, constantly penetrates the decision process and fixes rather severe limitations on the freedom of the articulation function. The Soviet system seems to fit the general category of a strongly aggregative, high-consensus, and ideological system. In the British, and perhaps the West German, system we find an example of a high-consensus system, yet it differs markedly from the Soviet system in its stylistic approach. In the British model, for example, consensus is derived from sources which are less dependent on a rigidly defined body of dogma—although beliefs, values, and "ideologies" are still present—and subsequently the style of the system is highly pragmatic. A pragmatic system submerges ideological argument and shifts the political process away —but not entirely—from matters of ideology toward specific issues and policies in which pragmatic bargaining among the articulating and aggregating groups predominates. The French system provides still another example. Here we find neither high consensus nor strong aggregation. Stylistically the French pattern is tainted markedly with ideological overtones, but for reasons differing from those in the case of the Soviet system. In France we find evidence of ideological sub-systems, instead of the all-pervasive single ideology, so that political dialogue may continue to orient around basic ideological themes but simultaneously the boundaries to articulation are not so restricted as in the Soviet Union. Indeed, articulation has been a particularly strong feature of the French system. Whether the Gaullist innovations have permanently shifted the French system away from this pattern remains at the moment uncertain.

Perhaps enough, in any event, has been said to suggest the general framework within which the following cases might be considered. We believe that each case has something significant to offer in exploring the functioning of consensus and cleavage. The dimensions of the cleavages around which these cases focus, the manner in which these cleavages were articulated and aggregated, and the responses of the authorities to the challenges to consensus, —these and other facets of our studies seem relevant to the traditional task of discovering typologies of political systems.

Britain: The Case of the Nuclear Disarmers

by Geoffrey Marshall

POLITICAL PHILOSOPHY IS NOT MUCH DEBATED IN BRITISH COURTS of law. *Chandler*'s case was an exception. At the Old Bailey in London on February 12, 1962, six members of the Campaign for Nuclear Disarmament (C.N.D.)—Michael Randle, Trevor Hatton, Ian Dixon, Terence Chandler, Patrick Pottle, and Helen Allegranza—were charged with conspiring together to incite and commit an offense under the Official Secrets Act for a purpose prejudicial to the safety and interests of the State. How are the interests of the State to be defined and by what methods may they be opposed or contested? These were the issues raised by *Chandler*'s case and by the episodes which preceded it.

NUCLEAR DISARMAMENT IN BRITAIN

Throughout the 1950's questions of defense policy played a major part in the political struggle between and within the political parties. After the defeat of the Attlee administration at the General Election of 1951 disagreement within the Labour Opposition over, for example, the question of German rearmament led to dissension both in the party in Parliament and at the constituency level. The Conservatives, retaining office under the premiership of Eden after 1955 and Macmillan from 1957, presented to the electorate a relatively united front. The necessity of maintaining an independent British nuclear capacity to deter aggression remained a primary plank in Conservative election policy. Despite a series of expensive cancellations of weapon delivery systems and the satirists' jibe that the independent British nuclear deterrent, upon which safety and prestige allegedly depended, was not independent and not British and not a deterrent, the Conservative policy did not appear to be electorally unpopular.

The leadership of the Labour Party under Hugh Gaitskell (until his death in 1963), though it differed from the Conservative Government in many matters of defense strategy, was not opposed to nuclear armaments in principle to the extent of wishing to see Britain alone reject atomic weapons, though it favored "multilateral" disarmament if that could be achieved. It was the conflict between this "multilateral" position and advocacy of "unilateral" nuclear disarmament by Britain alone if necessary that opened up a vein of debate which from 1957 to 1961 threatened to split the Labour Party.

Pacifism has always been a strong though minority influence in British left wing politics. Throughout the 1950's opposition to nuclear tests had been a small-scale but persistent phenomenon. By 1958 a full-scale movement had begun to win adherents in local constituency Labour parties and within the trade unions, traditionally less militant than the constituency activists in Labour Party affairs. At the Labour Party conference of 1960 came a major clash between the policy of the parliamentary party and the unilateral disarmers. In debate on the issue the bloc vote of the Transport and General Workers Union was thrown against the leadership. The position of Hugh Gaitskell, who refused to accept the vote of the conference as binding upon the Parliamentary Labour Party, was placed in jeopardy and for a year the Party lived in an atmosphere of faction and constitutional crisis. Finally, at the 1961 Labour Party Conference the unilateral vote was reversed and the leadership's official policy endorsed. The defeat put an effective end to the hope that the objectives of the Nuclear Disarmament movement could be furthered from within the official parliamentary opposition. Attempts to secure the election of individual M.P.s pledged to nuclear disarmament were mooted but seen to be an ineffective method of major progress for the movement. In the British parliamentary system, dominated by the two disciplined parties, independent members with a minority program are virtually impossible to elect and, if elected, have little impact on the course of events. It was this palpable fact which diverted much of the energy of the C.N.D. into extra-parliamentary action and some of its members into civil disobedience.

POLITICAL DISORDER: THE BACKGROUND

Civil disobedience and political disorders are rare in twentieth century Britain. They are not contemplated by its theory of government and if they appear they are an embarrassment to it. For one thing they place a question mark against the assumption, which it normally and cheerfully makes, that law and order are non-political—that government and politics is one thing and the enforcement of law another. Such feelings are only possible, given a settled constitution and an agreement that the law which is enforced is generally acceptable.

These conditions have of course been present in the United Kingdom at least since mid-Victorian times. It is just about a hundred years since Mr. Gladstone became convinced that votes could safely be given to working men because they had adequately demonstrated their regard for law and established institutions. In 1863 he was greatly impressed by a deputation of trade unionists who came to see him. Their words, as reported by John Morley, were as follows: "Since the abolition of the corn laws we have given up political agitation; we felt we might place confidence in Parliament; instead of political agitation, we tried to spend our evenings in the improvement of our minds." [1] It is really for respectable persons of this kind that English civil liberties are specially designed. They are meant to fit the situation of the man who conducts himself peaceably on the whole and reasonably always. They are for the citizen who may write to the papers when his comfort or moral sense is disturbed, but who will move along quietly when asked to by the police.

Nevertheless on more than one occasion in the last fifty years, there have been groups who have failed to respect these conventions of behavior, and the resulting threats to public order and security have left their mark on the British constitutional machinery. One result has been the creation of statutory powers which police and public authorities did not possess in the nineteenth century when Professor Dicey frowned so authoritatively and elegantly on administrative discretion. Many of these provisions are bound to involve the exercise by public officers of discretionary—and one might even say political—powers, whose use and control have not been very much debated.

Not all powers for dealing with disorder are new. Some of them
are old ones put to new uses. One example is the common law
and statutory power of the justices of the peace. This was set in
motion during the suffragette disorders which occurred before the
first World War. Alongside the constitutional campaigners for
women's suffrage there had developed a body of militants who
favored direct action. They were not behaving at all like the
reasonable man of the common law and the police were having,
to say the least, some difficulty in moving them along. When imprisoned they frequently went on hunger strikes. The Liberal government of the day responded by passing the "Cat and Mouse Act"
as it was popularly known, a measure which provided for the release and subsequent rearrest of hunger strikers.[2] When the Bill
was before the House, one backbencher tried to have it amended
to provide for the deportation of suffragettes to St. Helena, but
even without that provision the legislation was looked on with
disfavor by many members of Parliament. Among these was Mr.
George Lansbury who lost his seat in 1912 fighting as an independent on the suffrage question. In the following year he was
committed to prison after making a number of speeches whose
gist was that suffragettes should attack and destroy property, since
private property was of less importance than the rights of women
and the lives of hunger-striking prisoners. At the Albert Hall he
said: "When Parliament betrays its trust you have a right to rebel.
Let all of us here stand shoulder to shoulder with the militant
women. Let them burn and destroy. For every leader that is taken
let a dozen more stand forth." [3]

The events in which Lansbury and the suffragettes were involved
provide a striking parallel to the attempts at civil disobedience
which have been made in the last decade by campaigners for nuclear disarmament. Lansbury in 1914, it may be noted, was not
prosecuted, as he perhaps might have been, for a seditious libel.
He was summoned on information laid before a magistrate that
he was a disturber of the peace and an inciter of others to commit breaches of the peace. He refused to give any undertaking
as to his future conduct and was sent to prison under the provisions of a statute originally passed in 1361. The procedure at
common law for binding over and the powers given to the justices
by this statute of Edward III to require sureties for good behavior

are in effect a measure of preventive justice. That very phrase appears to suggest a breach in the principle that punishment may follow only an actual and not a prospective breach of law. But if the law actually is that the Queen's subjects must promise in some circumstances not to break it, then the rule of law remains formally, though some might feel shakily, intact. In the House of Commons in 1913 Opposition members argued that the procedure could be used against those who might advocate strikes, or as one member said, to silence the advocacy of any doctrine whatsoever which those in power considered dangerous. Lansbury, it was said, had "refused to put his tongue in such a position that any magistrate may hold it for him." [4] In the High Court[5] it was argued unsuccessfully that no reliance could be placed on the statute of 1361 since the version which now appears had been mistranslated from the French of the original statute roll. It is clear from either version that the objects of the legislation and of the fourteenth century commissions of the peace were the control of those who, as it was said, had been "plunderers and robbers beyond the sea and were now returned and were likely to go wandering and threaten the peace of the king and his people." The adaptation of these disciplinary powers to meet the twentieth century needs of Mr. Asquith (and more recently of Mr. Macmillan) might be thought a remarkable illustration of British constitutional flexibility.

THE CAMPAIGN FOR NUCLEAR DISARMAMENT

In 1961 Bertrand Russell went to prison after the manner of Lansbury. Like Lansbury, he was summoned to be bound over to keep the peace. With several dozen members of the nuclear disarmament movement he refused to be bound over and was jailed for a week.

The nuclear disarmament movement, at various times, adopted a variety of tactics ranging from peaceful picketing of rocket and air bases through protest marches and attempts to persuade workers on nuclear installations to leave their jobs to tax refusal, violations of the Official Secrets Acts, and mass sit-down demonstrations. Its original sponsors (Canon John Collins, J. B. Priestley, Kingsley Martin, Bertrand Russell, and Michael Foot being the best known) were not in favor of illegal or, as it later became known, "direct" action. Russell, however, did join the advocates of civil disobedience in 1961. Formed in the aftermath of the revised British nuclear defense policy of 1957, the Campaign's program as set out in the following year was the securing of an unconditional renunciation of the use or production in Britain of atomic weapons. Its immediate objectives in pursuit of this aim were to halt nuclear testing and to bring about the removal of nuclear bases from British territory and a cessation of patrol flights of aircraft carrying atomic weapons.

Possibly the most successful of all the C.N.D. enterprises was the Aldermaston protest march from Trafalgar Square to the Aldermaston atomic research station. From 1958 the march provided a focus for a new style of resistance to the establishments of both major political parties.[6] From 1960 the direct action wing of the movement came increasingly into conflict with the police as they sat down on East Anglian rocket sites and at the Polaris submarine supply base in Scotland. In 1961 the direct actors formed themselves into a "Committee of 100" specifically dedicated to civil disobedience. Russell took an active part in the demonstrations. In February 1961 he led a sit-down outside the Ministry of Defence. In August he spoke at a rally in Hyde Park and was fined twenty shillings for contravening regulations forbidding the use of loudspeaker equipment. The magistrate on that occasion topped off the sentence with a sermon: "It puts me in mind," he said, "of the Book of Job—'Great men are not always wise, neither do the aged understand judgment.' That exactly describes Lord Russell." [7]

In this line the philosopher, now in his eighty-ninth year, was willing enough to compete. In September, while serving his seven day prison sentence, he dispatched a sermon of his own. He said:

> To all, in whatever country, who are still capable of sane thinking or human feeling: friends, along with valued colleagues. I am to be silenced for a time—perhaps for ever, for who can tell how soon the great massacre will take place? The populations of East and West, misled by stubborn governments in search of prestige and corrupted by official experts bent on retaining their posts, tamely acquiesce in policies which are certain to end in nuclear war.
>
> There are supposed to be two sides, each professing to stand for a great cause. This is a delusion. Kennedy and Khrushchev, Adenauer and De Gaulle, Macmillan and Gaitskell, are pursuing a com-

mon aim: the ending of human rights. You, your families, your friends and your countries are to be exterminated by the common decision of a few brutal but powerful men. To please these men, all the private affections, all the public hopes, all that has been achieved in art and knowledge and thought, and all that might be achieved thereafter is to be wiped out for ever.

Our ruined lifeless planet will continue for countless ages to circle aimlessly round the sun, unredeemed by the joys and loves, the occasional wisdom and the power to create beauty, which have given value to human life. It is for seeking to prevent this that we are in prison.[8]

Technically, what Russell and his colleagues were in prison for was a refusal to bind themselves not to engineer a breach of the Queen's peace on the following September 17 in Trafalgar Square. The prosecution illustrates a curious feature of the British system of government. Although it was commonly said that "the authorities" had taken action against the nuclear disarmers, the authorities in the shape of the Home Office appeared to disclaim responsibility. "Both the Home Office and ministerial circles went to some lengths yesterday," *The Times* reported, "to dissociate Mr. Butler the Home Secretary and the Government generally from the action of the police." [9] That the Government has in the normal run of things nothing to do with prosecuting offenders is of course true. It is unlikely, however, that the police in this case acted spontaneously and alone. Almost certainly the Metropolitan Police Commissioner consulted the Director of Public Prosecutions and the responsibility for much of the official activity in September 1961 must lie with them. It was not on the whole well received by political commentators of Left or Right. The right wing *Spectator* thought that the prosecution would "have made both those inside prison and those outside it ten times as determined to carry on their dangerous and illogical campaign as they were before." The *New Statesman* spoke of the Government's "elephantine prosecution," which many would interpret as a calculated attempt to silence the mounting criticism of nuclear weapons.

It is just possible that what was in the Metropolitan Police Commissioner's mind was something more in the nature of a calculated attempt to silence the mounting potential criticism of the London constabulary whose leave was being regularly cancelled to supervise weekend demonstrations. At all events sizeable efforts were made to forestall the Committee of 100's activities on Sunday the 17th. With the consent of the Home Secretary, who could no longer disclaim accountability, the Metropolitan Commissioner made an order prohibiting them from holding any public procession in the central London Area.[10] Under the Metropolitan Police Act, 1839, directions were also issued to constables to request persons in the specified areas of Central London not to remain in the streets. Failure to comply was an offense under the Act. A chief inspector of police visited the office of the Committee of 100 with a copy of the Public Order Act and told them that it would be invoked.

The aim of the Committee and its supporters had been to march from Trafalgar Square to Westminster. On the day of the demonstration a number estimated at 12,000 people gathered in the Square. Four thousand police were on duty and cordoned off the exits to Whitehall. Prevented from marching, many of the demonstrators sat. Between 800 and 1,000 were arrested and charged with disobeying the orders of the Police Commissioner.

The behavior of the police was the subject of a number of complaints on this occasion. Allegations were made that at midnight when a decision was made to clear the Square the remaining demonstrators were handled with unusual ferocity. Eye-witnesses later alleged that demonstrators had been dragged head downward across the Square, that a number of them had been thrown into the fountains, and that television cameramen had been threatened and prevented from filming the proceedings.[11]

Apart from rallies, sit-downs, and marches the C.N.D. conceived a number of other devices legal and illegal for the irritation and embarrassment of authority. For a short period they operated a private broadcasting station which invaded the British Broadcasting Corporation's television frequency after the evening closedown. Another, though later, development was the "Spies for Peace" Movement which developed in 1963. Its purpose was to ridicule the Civil Defense preparations made by the Government by publishing details of the plans for dealing with the aftermath of a nuclear attack on Britain, together with confidential information from the report of a NATO military exercise held in 1962. Some of the unpublished administrative details of the civil defense plans were protected by the Official Secrets Acts, in particular the scheme for regional government to be organized after a nuclear attack from a number of underground regional headquarters or regional seats of government which had been prepared but whose locations had not been announced.

In April 1963, on the eve of the annual Aldermaston march, the Spies for Peace distributed a pamphlet and a large number of leaflets giving, with details and a sketchmap, the location of the secret R.S.G.6 or regional seat of government for the south of England. Aldermaston marchers were invited to break their journey and visit the site. Though the disclosures were not of any great importance the authorities treated them with solemnity and irritation. As many as possible of the leaflets were confiscated and D (for Defence) notices[12] were issued to prevent their appearance in the newspapers. Since the contents were published in the French press and broadcast over Prague Radio, the efficacy of this action was open to doubt. C.N.D. demonstrators took to writing the name of R.S.G.6 on walls and it was reported that one had been apprehended by the police for singing the forbidden geographical location.

In Parliament the Opposition made the most of the Government's embarrassment. On April 23 Prime Minister Macmillan explained the purpose of the regional seats of government and defended the retention of the D notice prohibition on the ground that it covered more than the location of the R.S.G.6 bunkers. That the defense was an implausible justification for forbidding the publication of the pamphlets may perhaps be concluded from the dialogue between Mr. Harold Wilson and the Prime Minister.

> *Mr. Wilson.* While we understand the general position on D notices, since in this instance the information is now known to about half the country—the information in this document, including this rather disturbing revelation of the Fallex operation—to all overseas governments, what is the purpose of keeping on the D notice in respect of individual items contained in this document?
>
> *Mr. Macmillan.* I doubt very much whether this is known to half the country, and I think that if the right hon. gentleman were to weigh his words a little more carefully . . . (Opposition cries of protest). Are you really saying that one out of every two people in England could tell you the location of the regional headquarters? Of course not. It is not so.
>
> But the D notice covers more than the location—the communications system, the physical characteristics, and all kinds of details. I

repeat, I am grateful to the press for so loyally keeping to the requests made to them.

Mr. Wilson. Weighing my words with a great deal less frivolity than the Prime Minister has shown, is he aware that all the details in this document have been broadcast on Prague radio, and a lot of what Prague radio said has been published in one British newspaper.

Conservative Members. How do you know?

Mr. Wilson. I read *The Daily Telegraph* which printed what was said by Prague radio.

Since so much of this has come out, and so much of it is known to overseas governments, to the British press, and to a considerable number of people in this country, would the Prime Minister say why he has to keep on the D notice the information contained in this particularly reprehensible document?

Mr. Macmillan. "Half the people of this country" has now sunk to "a considerable number of people". I do not believe that half the people of this country listen to Prague radio—at least I hope they do not.

The only question for the right hon. gentleman or anybody who considers the duty of the Government is whether, as a result of this matter leaking out, it is our duty to publish every detail—all because of that. Not at all.

I think we had far better stand at the position where we are, and I see no reason why we should give all these details, nor is there any demand, so far as I know, from the press.

Captain Kerby (Arundel and Shoreham, C.) asked the Home Secretary how many copies of the "Spies for Peace" document, R.S.G.6, had been impounded to date by the Metropolitan Police force and what was his estimate of the number of copies still in public circulation in the United Kingdom.

Mr. Brooke. By the Metropolitan Police, 16: several thousand are probably now in circulation.[13]

As a specimen of an authenticated British official secret the Spies for Peace revelation is not without its interest. It ran (in part):—

The Government has established a secret network of Regional seats of government, covering the whole country. One you will have heard of—RSG 6—at Warren Row, nr. Reading. . . . The post-nuclear government at RSG 6, Reading, has offices at the RSG centre, government at RSG 6, Reading, has offices at the RSG centre, among the civil service buildings in White Knights Park. But RSG 6 is really at a subterranean bunker 8 miles from Reading at Warren Row village near Wargrave, less than a mile from the A4. RSG 6 is disguised as the Home Office Underground Factory, Warren Row, and kept up from the Ministry of Works office in Buckingham Ave.

Slough. RSG 6 lies inside the hill, a comfortable war grave for the Southern Region military government. RSG 6 is not a Civil Defence centre but is for military government. It is the HQ of the regional Commissioner, who will have supreme power over the 3,000,000 bodies in his region. Civil Defence plays a minor role in this HQ. All the officials have been already appointed. Virtually every important Government department is represented. Special workers will be conscripted by members of the RSGs. . . . The whole thing is a perfect example of military government. RSG 6 has been activated several times; most recently in exercises Parapluie & Fallex & Mammoth which was last Sunday & the greatest failure of the lot. In Oxford only 30 out of 165 casualties meant to be evacuated by lunch were in fact removed. All three exercises resulted in millions of totally unnecessary deaths, in complete administrative breakdown & ultimate chaos. These exercises proved once & for all that there is no defence against nuclear war. The fact that the government has prepared so extensively (although ineffectively) for nuclear war shows that not even it has faith in its own deterrent defence policy. It is scandalous that the government should spend our money on post-nuclear attack arrangements while upholding to the country the infallibility of its deterrent policy. This government is not competent to organize our policies & should not be entrusted with our lives & our money.

In *The Times* correspondence columns various semantic and substantive issues were taken up. One letter to the editor asked: "Sir,—Are we not in danger of using 'secret' as a synonym for what was formerly known as 'official'? Another suggested that the public was entitled to know the precise method by which they were to be governed after a nuclear attack and the identities and qualifications of those who were to exercise authority:

If the revelation is to be delayed until after any attack, I can imagine the hoots of derision from the sadder and wiser remnants of the population at the announcement by one of the 14 Regional Governors of his appointment as one of the chosen few who will lead us out of this new valley of darkness.

Considered as a tactic of civil disobedience the publication of minor official secrets had clear merits. It brought to bear a large amount of dissident force on a small corner of authority without major risk to the participants. The sit-downs on the other hand sometimes ran the risk of reversing that situation and exposing small numbers of known leaders of the movement to superior official forces. That was in fact the end result of the attempts in

1962—to demonstrate a token opposition to nuclear warfare by temporarily immobilizing airfields from which aircraft carrying atomic weapons were known to operate. The attempt ended in jail sentences for six C.N.D. leaders (one of whom later committed suicide) and a legal victory in the House of Lords for the Crown and its prosecutor.

The Wethersfield Demonstration

In November 1962, the Committee of 100 prepared a plan for mass demonstrations at air bases throughout the country. The bases at Brize Norton and Wethersfield, Russell announced, were the moral equivalents of Buchenwald and Auschwitz. A sit-down demonstration at the Royal Air Force station at Wethersfield, Essex, was scheduled for December 9. On the 6th, special branch officers raided the London office of the Committee and took away documents. It was announced that any incursion on to the airfields would be treated as an offense under the Official Secrets Act. Notices were posted declaring the bases prohibited places under the Act.

On the 9th, none of the demonstrators succeeded in their object. The buses on which many of them had planned to travel were withdrawn as the result of police persuasion. Although a total turn-out of 50,000 had been hoped for, only five or six thousand arrived at the various airfields. Several roads were blocked, a number of scuffles took place, and eight hundred or so arrests were made; but no aircraft were prevented from taking off. Conspiracy charges under the Official Secrets Act of 1911 were then brought against six of the Committee's organizers and they were sent for trial at the Old Bailey. The trial and its two appeals are worth detailed attention. They produced an unwontedly heavy mixture of legal and moral theory, uneasily contained in the traditional mould of an English criminal trial.

Regina v. Chandler[14]

Section 1 of the Official Secrets Act 1911 provides that

If any person for any purpose prejudicial to the safety or interests of the State (a) approaches or is in the neighbourhood of, or enters any prohibited place within the meaning of this Act; . . . he shall be guilty of felony . . .

The six nuclear disarmers were charged with "conspiring together to incite divers persons to commit and conspiring together and with others to commit a breach of section 1 of the Official Secrets Act 1911, namely for a purpose prejudicial to the safety or interests of the State to enter a Royal Air Force Station at Wethersfield", which was a "prohibited place" under the Act.

The chief witness called for the prosecution was a Royal Air Force Officer, Air Commodore Graham R. Magill, Director of Operations at the Air Ministry. Air Commodore Magill gave evidence that on December 9, Wethersfield air base was occupied by squadrons of the United States Air Force, assigned to the Supreme Commander, Allied Forces in Europe. The squadrons were vital to the defenses of Britain and Western Europe. They were combat ready and at constant alert, prepared to take off at any moment.

The six defendants all pleaded not guilty and their counsel, Mr. Jeremy Hutchinson, Q.C., stated that their defense would be that in seeking to immobilize the air base they were not actuated by a purpose which was prejudicial to the interests of the State. They wished to put before the jury the plea that it was not in the interests of the State to have aircraft armed with nuclear bombs and that their purpose in being at Wethersfield was in fact beneficial to the State's interests.

Here Mr. Justice Havers intervened. Suppose, he said, that the evidence showed conclusively that the intention of the defendants was to block the airfield and prevent aircraft from taking off, could it then be held in view of the Crown's evidence about the necessity of the airfield to the national defense that that was not a purpose prejudicial to the national interest? That question, Mr. Hutchinson said in reply, was precisely the question which the jury would have to decide. It would be for the jury to decide whether it would be better for the aircraft to remain on the ground, and whether the purpose of attempting to ensure that they did so was or was not prejudicial to the interests of the State. To establish that proposition he would wish to cross-examine the Crown's witness and to call expert evidence on behalf of the defendants. To this course the Attorney General, Sir Reginald Manningham-Buller, objected. It could not be competent, he suggested, for the defense to lead evidence of this kind. If that were possible, it would be equally possible for a communist spy charged under the Act to say that he was entitled to be acquitted if he genuinely believed that his activities on behalf of countries behind the iron curtain were, properly considered, in the country's best interests and in the interest of peace. It was no answer for the defendants to put forward what their beliefs might have been or to argue that these beliefs were reasonable.

On these points the entire trial and the subsequent appeals were to turn. There were three major and distinct questions to be determined. First, in what sense were the subjective intentions or beliefs of the defendants admissible as evidence of the "purpose" of their acts, as that term was used in the Official Secrets legislation? Secondly, were their acts in fact prejudicial to the interests of the State? Thirdly, what meaning should be given by the courts to the phrase "interests of the State"?

At the Old Bailey it was primarily the first two questions which were argued upon the admissibility of the defendants' proposed evidence. On the second day of the trial Mr. Justice Havers ruled that defendants' counsel could not be permitted to call military or scientific experts on nuclear warfare or on the effects of nuclear explosions or on the radar system, or any other evidence designed to establish that it would be beneficial to the interests of the State to give up nuclear armaments. As to cross-examination of the Crown's witnesses, it was difficult, Mr. Justice Havers conceded, to lay down rulings in advance. In general, however, he would not allow questions about whether bombs were likely to go off, whether they had a highly explosive effect, or whether it was good or bad for the country to have them.

Under these general rules the trial proceeded. Hutchinson, who was appearing for five of the accused, did not succeed in putting any of his proposed questions to Air Commodore Magill. The sixth defendant Patrick Pottle conducted his own case. The following dialogue took place.[15]

> *Pottle* (to Air Commodore Magill). Have you read all the facts of the nuclear bombs on Hiroshima and Nagasaki?
> *The Judge*. Do not answer that.
> *Pottle*. Is there any official order from the Government that you could not accept?
> *The Judge*. He is an officer in her Majesty's Forces.
> *Pottle*. So there is no decision that you would not accept?

Air Commodore Magill. It is my duty to carry it out.

Pottle. Would you press the button that you know is going to annihilate millions of people?—If the circumstances so demanded it, I would.

Pottle. You would slit the throats of all the two-year-old children in this country?—It is the same as saying he would press the button to explode a nuclear bomb.—The following is a statement made by Sir Winston Churchill in the House of Commons . . .

The Judge. To quote from a document is not cross-examination.

Pottle. Sir Winston Churchill said: "We must not forget that by creating atomic bases in East Anglia we have made ourselves the target . . . of any Soviet attack."

The Judge to Air Commodore Magill. Do not answer that.

Pottle. What do you consider to be an emergency? What is this emergency you are talking about? Would it be beneficial to the state and the people of this country to send off bombers carrying nuclear weapons against whoever is attacking us? Would this be beneficial to the state and are the people going to gain from this?

The Judge (to the air commodore). You must not answer that question.

Pottle. Do you agree with the statement of the Attorney General in his opening speech that those who are responsible for the national security must be the able judges of what the national security requires?

The Judge. You cannot ask him whether he agrees with what the Attorney General has said.

Pottle. Do you agree with the statement made by Mr. Duncan Sandys in 1957 when he was Minister of Defence when he said: "Bases cannot defend people"?

The Judge. Do not answer.

Pottle. You have said that you would accept any order from the state that was given to you. Eichmann's defence was . . .

The Judge. You cannot mention him in this case.

Pottle. Would you consider a Soviet attack on Britain in the interests of the Soviet state?

The Judge. Do not answer.

Pottle. As the Attorney General has mentioned international law perhaps it would be appropriate for me to quote from the United Nations Charter?

The Judge. No.

Pottle. There is a document *Defence Outline of Policy* issued by the British Government. Perhaps I can quote from this and put a question to the Air Commodore about the nuclear deterrent. . . . "It must be frankly recognized that there is at present no means of providing adequate protection for the people of this country against the consequences of an attack with nuclear weapons. In the event of war the fighter aircraft of the R.A.F. could unquestionably be able to take heavy toll of bombers but a proportion would inevitably get through. Even if it were only a dozen they could, if loaded with megaton bombs, inflict widespread disaster."

The Judge. It is quite irrelevant. Do not answer. I rule the question inadmissible.

Pottle to Air Commodore Magill. Do you agree with Mr. Harold Macmillan when he said in Moscow in February, 1959: "It is impossible to hide from ourselves the dangers of a war by miscalculation or by muddle?"

The Judge. Do not answer that question.

Pottle. I ask if you will reconsider your ruling. There are six people in the dock and the only way we can defend ourselves is to cross-examine witnesses that the Attorney General has put into the box. Every question asked is ruled out of order so we are left with no defence.

The Judge. If I am wrong the Court of Criminal Appeal will put it right.

Similar difficulties occurred in counsel's examination of the defendants themselves. One of them, Michael Randle, was examined by Mr. Hutchinson about the purpose of his action.

> *Mr. Hutchinson.* Did you agree to enter that airfield for any purpose prejudicial to the safety or interests of the state?—No. Did you ever incite other people to do so?—No.
>
> *Sir Reginald Manningham-Buller,* Q.C., the Attorney General. That is for the jury to determine.

Continuing, Randle said there were a number of reasons for holding the demonstration at Wethersfield—blocking the base by simultaneous walk-on, grounding aircraft and a demand for the reclamation of the airfield for civilian purposes. The long-term object was to bring home to the people of the country that millions could be killed by nuclear weapons and thereby try to prevent the massacre of millions of people.

> *Mr. Hutchinson.* The jury has got to decide whether this young man (Randle) is worthy of credence.
>
> *The Attorney General.* I am not suggesting that there is any lack of sincerity in this witness's beliefs. The reasons on which he bases those beliefs are irrelevant. If the beliefs are inadmissible then the reasons for them are equally inadmissible.
>
> *The Judge.* I cannot allow you to continue on this line of examination, Mr. Hutchinson.
>
> (Cross-examined by the Attorney General, Randle agreed that the committee's purpose was to embark upon a campaign of civil disobedience.)

The Attorney General. To embark upon a course of breaking such laws as you thought fit?—Yes, as we thought fit.

The Attorney General. One reason for breaking the law was to draw attention to your views?—Yes.

The Attorney General. A further object of breaking the law was to impede the manufacture and use of nuclear arms?—That is correct. From an early stage you had considered the possibility of interfering with the use of the Atomic Weapons Research Establishment?—Yes.

So we may take it in embarking upon these actions of civil disobedience and deliberately intending to flout the law you were appreciative of the consequences to yourself?—We were aware that the consequences might involve imprisonment and were content about it.

At the conclusion of the trial the jury, after retiring for four hours, found all six accused guilty of the offenses charged. Five were sentenced to eighteen months imprisonment and one to twelve months imprisonment. All gave notice of appeal and the second hearing was set down for April.

Regina v. Chandler[16]

The major grounds of the appeal were that Mr. Justice Havers was wrong in law to exclude the evidence which the defendants wished to give as to the facts on which their purposes were based and as to whether their purpose was in fact prejudicial to the interests of the State. For the Crown the Attorney General argued that evidence of the appellants' intentions was rightly excluded and on the question of prejudice to the State's interest the evidence given on the Crown's behalf must, if given in good faith, be treated as conclusive. In reply Hutchinson asserted that Parliament had laid down in the Act the terms under which an individual might be convicted of a crime and all the elements of the crime had to be proved before a jury in the normal way. It could not be the position that all the Crown had to do was to call a Government official of some kind to say "That act is prejudicial because I am the only person who knows" or "This is a Government decision" or "It is a Government base or a Government dockyard and therefore any interference with it must be prejudicial." The Crown was in no different position from anybody else. They must produce evidence and be cross-examined on it. If that were not so the function of the jury under section 1 of the Official Secrets Act

would be entirely removed and it would be impossible for anyone to put up any defense at all once the competent or proper
officer had given evidence. It was not for the court to decide that
a defense was ridiculous. It was for the jury to decide that. Here
the prosecution had clearly been giving expert evidence to the
jury and by being prevented from cross-examining it or putting to
the Crown's witness the opinion of other experts the appellants
had been deprived of providing the jury with the necessary facts
upon which they could come to a proper decision.

After questioning counsel for both sides the Lord Chief Justice
announced that the court had decided to dismiss the appeals and
would put their reasons into writing.

On April 11, 1962, Lord Parker, C.J., delivering the judgment,[17] stated the facts and reviewed the judge's rulings in the
lower court. Those rulings and the Attorney General's contentions
they considered to be plainly right. It had been open to the defense
to cross-examine on the question whether the acts committed by
them would in fact prejudice the operational effectiveness of the
airfield and those questions going to that issue had been properly
allowed. But all questions as to the policy of the Crown in having
an air base at Wethersfield and using it for the purpose of carrying out a policy of nuclear deterrence had been properly dis-
allowed. In that matter the Crown had had complete discretion,
as it had to declare any particular place a prohibited place within
the meaning of the Act. At common law the prerogative of the
Crown acting on the advice of Ministers gave it unfettered control
over the disposition and use of its armed forces, and the manner
of the exercise of such prerogative powers could not be inquired
into by the courts whether in a civil or a criminal case. As was
said in the case of *The Zamora* [1916] 2 A.C. 77, 107

> Those who are responsible for the nation's security must be the sole
> judges of what the national security requires. It would be obviously
> undesirable that such matters should be made the subject of evidence
> in a court of law or otherwise discussed in public.

The appeal therefore was dismissed. Since, however, the decision,
in the opinion of the court, raised a point of law of general public
importance, the court would so certify and grant leave to appeal
to the House of Lords.

Chandler v. Director of Public Prosecutions[18]

At the end of May the points of law raised by the appellants were argued before the final tribunal by John Foster, Q.C. and Basil Wigoder. In questioning counsel, Lord Devlin raised for the first time a point which had not hitherto received much attention. What as a matter of law was to be understood by "the State"? If it meant simply "The Government," was it not the case that once the Government had decided rightly or wrongly to have an army, navy or air force, anything which injured the army, navy or air force was prejudicial? To this counsel replied that "state" did not mean "government," for if it did, what happened if the government changed between the commission of the offense and the trial? If a government of nuclear disarmers came to power, would the accused still be guilty of the offense? "State" he suggested meant the numerical collection of inhabitants in a geographical area. As to the meaning of "purpose" he insisted that it meant what the defendants intended to bring about. Lord Russell as the founder of the organization knew all about its purpose and his evidence ought to have been given weight. The purpose was to make the facts of nuclear warfare known. The blocking of the airfield was only an incidental means to that end.

On July 12, 1962, the law lords delivered their speeches. All five read an opinion. All were for dismissing the appeals.[19]

Lord Reid took the point made in the Court of Appeal by the Lord Chief Justice that the disposition and use of the armed forces under the prerogative could not be questioned in the courts. Whether they should be used in a particular way was, he thought, a political question with which the criminal system was not fitted to deal and a way should be found of reading the statute which avoided the raising of such issues. The 1911 Act had been passed at a time of grave misgiving about the German menace and "it would be surprising and hardly credible that the Parliament of that date intended that a person who deliberately interfered with vital dispositions of the armed forces should be entitled to submit to a jury that government policy was wrong and that what he did was really in the best interests of the country."

The second opinion was that of Viscount Radcliffe. It began: "My Lords, the evidence in this case left no room for doubt as to what the appellants had intended to do, what they had done and why they had done it." In effect they were saboteurs and not the less so because of what they hoped their actions would ultimately achieve. The trial judge had rightly distinguished between the immediate purpose and the long range purpose. Although "motive," "intention," and "purpose" were overlapping concepts there was no great difficulty here. The ultimate aims of the appellants did not constitute a purpose within the meaning of the Act. If the direct purpose was prejudicial then the offense had been committed. The issue in the form proposed by the appellants was not justiciable in a court of law.

Lords Hodson and Pearce spoke to similar effect. Lord Devlin, though he reached the same conclusion as his brethren, adopted a somewhat different attitude. He did not think that the issue of what was prejudicial to the state was a question of law. It must be a question of fact for the jury, though he found it difficult to see how a jury could have found actions designed to obstruct the policy supported by the majority of the population to be otherwise than prejudicial to the state. The appellants' long range objects and intentions could not properly be ruled out if the question had simply been one of prejudice to the interests of the country. But for the purposes of the 1911 Act the prejudice to be considered was that to the state understood as the "organs of government of a national community" and in the United Kingdom (at least in relation to the armed forces) that organ was the Crown. About the interests of the Crown, the Crown could give evidence and there was nothing to suggest that the evidence given in the present case was exaggerated or given in bad faith. There was no other conclusion (he thought) than that the appellants had committed the offense of which they were accused and the appeal should be dismissed.

A Comment on the Decision

Quite apart from its impact on the Campaign for Nuclear Disarmament the *Chandler* case is a remarkable one from the point of view of English jurisprudence. It also furnishes an apt illustration of the attitude of the judiciary to the process of statutory interpretation and the consideration of executive policy. In his essay "The Crown as Corporation" [20] F. W. Maitland once remarked that the notion of " 'the State,' though it might govern political thought and on rare occasions make its way into the preamble of a statute . . . was slow to find a home in English law books." Indeed it was "a person whose personality our law does not formally or explicitly recognise." Yet in the Official Secrets Act, 1911,[21] the "State" makes an undisputed appearance and its interests and safety are protected. But are those interests to be construed as the interests of the Crown? Or are they those of Ministers? Or of the electorate or community?

In August, 1911, when the Official Secrets Act was rushed through all three stages in the Commons it is perhaps unlikely that these conceptual distinctions were very vividly present to the minds of members of Parliament. Nor perhaps had it occurred to anyone that spies or saboteurs might try to advance the argument that what they were about was really for the greater good of the realm and beneficial to its interests. Indeed it is an odd feature of the drafting of section one of the 1911 Act, that Parliament did not simply forbid unauthorized entry of a prohibited place within the meaning of the Act. Alternatively, they might have made danger to the national interest dependent by some subjective formula on the opinion of a Minister. Instead, the section required an objective state of affairs to be established to the satisfaction of a jury before the offense was committed. At one stage in the *Chandler* case Lord Devlin appeared to be conceding this implication,[22] but by a swift equation of "Crown" and "State" and by allotting the Crown a privileged role, he was able to concur in the majority view. In the end all their Lordships treated the arguments of Lord Russell and his followers roughly in the way that Dr. Johnson treated the views of Bishop Berkely. "We disprove it thus." Or as the Attorney General said, "The thing speaks for itself."

One principle clearly requiring further examination is the view that the prerogative powers involved in the disposition and armament of the forces of the Crown may not be inquired into by the courts, and that the manner of their exercise should not be the subject of evidence or be otherwise discussed in public. This was said to follow from the decision of Lord Parker in *The Zamora*[23] and a similar conclusion was drawn (in the House of Lords by Lord Reid) from *China Navigation Co. Ltd. v. Attorney-General*.[24] Neither of these cases is precisely in point. The internal management of the Crown's forces under the prerogative is certainly discretionary. And, as the *China Navigation* case illustrates, the Crown cannot be compelled to make any particular use of armed force for the benefit of subjects outside the realm. But the disposition and use, as distinct from management, of armed force within the realm, is distinguishable and could conceivably conflict with the rights of subjects in ways which might require judicial arbitrament. The Crown's prerogative hardly provides a very exact guiding light for the interpretation of statutes in which the legislature has attempted to regulate what is required by the national interest.

Lord Reid's judgment makes three concessions to the appellant's case. There was, he agreed, no general rule that the government or a minister must always have the last word about the public interest or about what is and is not prejudicial to the safety of the state. Secondly, "state" did not mean "the Government or the Executive," (nor the majority of the people but "the organized community"). Thirdly, he was "prepared to start from the position that when an Act requires certain things to be established against an accused person to constitute an offence, all of those things must be proved by evidence which the jury accepts unless Parliament otherwise provides." If the words of the Act necessarily led to the conclusion that accused persons were entitled to be acquitted if a unanimous verdict could not be obtained, as to whether what they had done was or was not in the best interests of the country, then it was no answer that it was inconceivable that Parliament should have so intended. Nevertheless, Lord Reid must have believed such a state of affairs to have been inconceivable since the issue which the Act appears to have left open to the jury to decide was one with which, he thought, our criminal system is not devised to deal. It would be, he suggested, a "political question—a question of opinion on which anyone actively interested in politics, including jurymen, might consider his own opinion as good as that of anyone else."

Lord Radcliffe's judgment refines upon the nature of "political" questions. A court, he thought, was not debarred from adjudicating or admitting evidence upon a question because it was "what is ordinarily known as political" provided that the issue presented itself in a triable form.[25]

Lord Radcliffe could think of few issues which presented themselves in "less triable form." "The more one looks at it," he said, "the plainer it becomes . . . I do not think there is anything amiss with a legal ruling that does not make this issue a matter for judge or jury." The trial judge had even, he thought, been overfavorable to the appellants in appearing to leave as an open issue to the jury the question whether the purpose of obstructing an airfield was prejudicial to the safety and interests of the state. The issue was not open in any general sense.

On these points there was inconsistency and disagreement. Lord Devlin, for example, thought it to be no justification for the judge's exclusion of evidence to say, as Lords Reid and Radcliffe did, that the validity of the disputed issues was a matter of opinion. Opinion he suggested must be based on fact, and opinion, on such matters as the likelihood of accidental explosions and mistakes on radar, is expert opinion which the law treats as a species of fact. "Hard facts where they can be ascertained and expert opinion where they cannot would be the proper bases for the verdict of a jury on such an issue." The offense charged, he went on, was drawn in the widest terms. Acts harmless in themselves were made criminal if done for a purpose prejudicial to the safety and interests of the state. It had not been suggested that what was prejudicial to the state was a question of law, and it was the jury and not the judge who must pronounce on all questions of fact. A judge was not entitled to direct the jury how to answer a question of fact, however obvious he might believe the answer to be.

Lord Devlin's judgment, in effect, rejects the major reason given by Lords Reid and Radcliffe for dismissing the appeal and turns entirely upon the narrow construction, already mentioned, which he places on the words "state" and "interest." ("State" interest did not mean the "national" interest and safety, but "the organs of government of a national community" and in this context the Crown.) This, it may be observed, is a different and narrower concept than Lord Reid's "organized community" [26] which, since there are many forms of organization including political parties and established churches, must mean little less than the whole people or community considered from a political point of view. Similarly "interests" is defined by Lord Devlin as "objects of state policy." His argument here deploys several analogies to support the view that "interest" most naturally means that which a person sees as his object. "A man is entitled to decide for himself how he should govern his life . . . and when the decision is taken it dictates what his interests are." It does not, however, follow from the fact that people are generally conceded the right to make their own decisions as to what their interests are, that "interest" *means* that which is decided by them. If anything, linguistic convention inclines to an objective sense of interest in which people (and governments) may be mistaken about their own interests. But given a subjective definition of interest and a narrow definition of "state" it must follow that the Crown is alone able to give authoritative evidence as to the interests of the state. Lord Devlin concludes that "the Crown's opinion as to what is or is not prejudicial in this case is just as inadmissible as the appellants'. The Crown's evidence about what its interests are is an entirely different matter. They can be proved by an officer of the Crown wherever it may be necessary to do so." But it is hard to see how these two questions can, on Lord Devlin's view, be entirely different matters. If the Crown can define its interests it can thereby determine what is to count as prejudicial to them. "The servants of the Crown . . . are capable," Lord Devlin concedes "of formulating a policy *ad hoc* so as to prevent the citizen from doing something that the Crown does not want him to do" and it is the duty of the courts "to be alert now as they have always been to prevent abuse of the prerogative." But the appellants, he thought, had been rightly convicted because in this case there was nothing to suggest that the crown was exaggerating the peril to its interests or abusing the prerogative. The presumption in favor of its evidence as to its interests was not in principle irrebuttable. So it may be possible for blatantly inappropriate applications of the Act to be contested (as, for example, if the Conservative Central office were to be declared a prohibited place). In the *Chandler* case it seems highly unlikely that the jury would have acquitted even if the disputed evidence had been given. But in the light of the majority of the judgments, and *dicta* such as "those who are responsible for the national security must be the sole judges of what the national security requires," it becomes unclear in what circumstances powers conferred under this particular legislation may be challenged in the courts.

Parliamentary Reactions

Some further reflections may be suggested by the *Chandler* case. As an example of the British judicial process in operation, it displays a patent and typical reluctance of the bench to embark upon criticism of executive policy unless compelled to do so by the clear wording of statutes. This attitude is normally defended by reference to the proposition that government policy is intended by the sovereign legislature, to be controlled by Parliament and by no one else. That is what the doctrine of ministerial responsibility to Parliament is all about. Admittedly this doctrine has had some hard knocks from critics, during the last twenty years, who have pointed out that governments usually wield a solid majority vote in the House of Commons, and that the sanction of dismissal for ministers who are thought to have misused their powers is unlikely to operate in a twentieth century legislature dominated by two major political parties.

But even if one leaves aside this difficulty (for on issues of justice and civil rights which do not cut along party lines, the House of Commons can often bring effective control to bear on ministers) there remain some matters of public concern in which neither the courts nor the legislature exact a clear answerability from executive officials. Law enforcement is one such matter. When, as in the case here discussed, the application of the law to what are essentially political offenses is in issue the difficulty may become acute. It is not easy to discover, in Britain, whether a decision to invoke the Public Order Act or to issue a series of warrants under the Official Secrets Act has stemmed from ministers and government policy or who can properly be held responsible to Parliament for these actions, if indeed anybody can. The boundary here between routine law enforcement and political policy becomes vague. It cannot be known whether a particular matter was discussed in cabinet or whether ministers have acquainted the Attorney General and the Solicitor General with their views. The conventions affecting the independence of these officials vis-à-vis their political colleagues are not entirely clear.[27] The advice given by the law officers to the cabinet is certainly treated as confidential by the rules of the House of Commons, and a direct question as to that would not be in order. Nor can questions be put which may reflect on the decision of a court of law or prejudice a case under trial or awaiting an appeal hearing.

These constitutional oddities of the British parliamentary system make it difficult if not impossible to give clear answers to questions which naturally arise about the series of prosecutions of nuclear disarmers. Did the Government as such, or individual ministers, play any part in the process or in any way influence the prosecuting authorities in what were undeniably prosecutions with highly political results? The answer is probably that in a direct sense they did not. It would in the first place be denied that these were political prosecutions. They were all for straightforward petty or less petty offenses—obstructing the highway or the police, disobeying local bylaws or regulations, refusing to be bound over to keep the peace, being on prohibited property. Moreover, it is in a sense true that the Government never has a hand in any prosecution. Most prosecutions in Britain are, in theory, private prosecutions brought by policemen as individuals. The Government does not start and cannot stop summary proceedings. A number of serious crimes cannot be prosecuted without leave of the Director of Public Prosecutions or the Attorney-General, but when these officers give leave for the bringing of a prosecution, or when a serious prosecution is taken over by the Director of Public Prosecutions, the decision is taken as an officer of the Crown. The Director of Public Prosecutions acts under the general directions of the Attorney General, but the Attorney General does not act under the authority of the Government.

Though the exact formulation of the unwritten convention is, as already mentioned, unclear, and its justification debatable, it is true that all the Law Officers appointed in the last forty years have professed the principle that they must, in executing their functions, act upon an independent view of public policy and decline to receive instructions from the Cabinet, Prime Minister, or any other politically elected person. This view of the matter was endorsed by Mr. Harold Macmillan in the House of Commons in 1959 and it seems unlikely, therefore, that any direct initiative in C.N.D. prosecutions was taken by ministers collectively, or by the Home Office (which is not in any sense a Ministry of Justice in the European sense). All that can be suggested or suspected is that the Law Officers' views of public policy are those of men whose general convictions are similar to those of their colleagues in office, and they are entitled to attach weight to these views in reaching decisions on matters affecting public order. There is clearly a degree of discretion involved as to the choice of prosecuting procedures. The use of the Official Secrets Acts carrying severe penalties, rather than prosecuting for ordinary obstruction or breach of the peace, may be criticized in Parliament and the press, but the armor of quasi-judicial immunity which surrounds the process of prosecution in Britain, both immunizes from undesirable political pressure and inhibits what may on occasion be justifiable political criticism.

Many of these difficulties were apparent in the parliamentary discussion of the nuclear disarmers case. The Labour Opposition was anxious and willing to attack what it considered to be a government prosecution, to secure clemency for the imprisoned demonstrators and to debate the amendment of the Official Secrets Act. On February 22, 1962, Mr. Parkin put down a question to Home Secretary, R. A. Butler, to ask if he would immediately advise the exercise of the prerogative of mercy to respite the sentences passed on the previous day at the Central Criminal Court. Since this was before the hearing in the Court of Criminal Appeal, the Home Secretary and the Attorney General were able to postpone their accounting to the House.

Mr. Butler (Saffron Walden, Conservative). No. (Ministerial cheers.) It is open to the persons concerned to apply to the Court of Criminal Appeal for leave to appeal against their sentences.

Mr. Parkin. In asking the Home Secretary to have second thoughts, will he bear three things in mind? Firstly, this was a symbolic political trial of half a dozen people arbitrarily selected, among thousands of people who consider themselves equally technically guilty. . . .

The Speaker. The hon. member cannot in a question criticize the conviction of a court.

Mr. Parkin. I was hoping to avoid any reference to the proceedings of the court.

This is a case for the exercise of the prerogative on these grounds: the real conflict here was not between the State and its power to protect itself against illegal activities, but between the image of Parliamentary and democratic processes and those who are half convinced that those democratic processes are no longer adequate to deal with the issues before the nation.

The Speaker. I have no authority from the House to allow the hon. gentleman to make some speech in the guise of a question. We must have some regard to the rules of the House.

Mr. Parkin. I am not attempting to make a speech. (Ministerial cries of "Oh".)

The Speaker. The hon. gentleman appears to be very unsuccessful in avoiding doing so. (Laughter.)

Mr. Eric Fletcher (Islington East, Lab.). Is the Home Secretary aware that there is great public concern at the fact that the Official Secrets Act, which was designed expressly and only for the security of the State, is being used as a vehicle for the suppression of freedom of political opinion? (Opposition cheers.)

Mr. Butler. I am not prepared to comment upon the proceedings in court. It is open to the persons concerned to apply for leave to appeal within 10 days of their conviction. In the meantime it would not be right for me to comment on the case.

Mr. Frank Allaun (Salford East, Lab.). Is the Home Secretary aware of the deep sense of injustice felt that such savage sentences should be imposed?

The Speaker. That is clearly out of order.

Mr. Paget (Northampton, Lab.). The Official Secrets Act is designed to protect this country from a foreign enemy. It is not designed to protect us against political disturbance. We have legislation with regard to public nuisance. This was a public nuisance, and a nuisance to the police. Is it not an abuse of procedure to have used the Official Secrets Act?

Mr. Butler. I must absolutely refuse to comment on the case while the right of appeal lies open.

Mr. Sydney Silverman (Nelson and Colne, Ind. Lab.). While it would be improper for the House, or the Home Secretary to comment on the actual case or its conduct, or the result, under the Official Secrets Act such a prosecution cannot be instituted without the leave of the Attorney General. When are we to have an opportunity of calling the Attorney General to account for what many of us believe to be an abuse of his powers?

The Speaker. The right hon. gentleman rose to a point of order; there just is not one in that.

While the appeal was pending the government refused facilities for debate on any motion relating to the remission of the sentences. The Opposition then turned its attention to the Official Secrets Act itself. On March 15, 1962, Mr. Leslie Hale moved for leave to introduce a Bill amending the Act of 1911, to make clear that its provisions were intended to be confined to the punishment of spies. The original Act of 1889, he said, had been amended for that purpose in 1911.

When the Act was introduced in 1911 Lord Haldane put forward the somewhat infelicitous explanation for the necessity of Section I, saying that a mysterious gentleman had been found on a secret service station and he had explained that he was listening to the birds. As it was mid-winter, his ornithological enthusiasm was doubted, but it could not be positively disproved. (Laughter.)

If one found at a secret station a gentleman looking like Mr. Erich von Stroheim, with a dachshund, an Anglo-German phrase book, a camera, and a sword stick, one's suspicions might be aroused. (Laughter). It would be difficult to bring positive evidence of his real intentions, and this was the dilemma.

But most positive undertakings were given to the House that this section related to espionage—and to espionage only—and would not be used for any other purpose. Sir Gordon Hewart, then Attorney-General, said in 1920 that it could never be contended that in a Bill to amend the Official Secrets Act, 1911, and clearly referring to Section I of the Act, the words "purposes prejudicial to the interests or safety of the State" referred to something of a different character from that which was being dealt with in the 1911 Act, which was spying.

His amending Bill provided that anyone prosecuted under the Act, if he could establish there was no connexion with spying, should have a defence to prosecution.

By 196 votes to 70 the Government's majority (predictably) refused leave to introduce Mr. Hale's Bill.

At last, on April 5 the House of Commons had its opportunity to examine the Attorney General and to exercise its prerogative as the Grand Inquest of the Nation. In the words of *The Times* parliamentary report for that day:

The Speaker took the Chair at half past two o'clock.

Mr. Driberg (Barking, Lab.) asked the Attorney General if he would state the principles which guided him in deciding whether or not to authorise prosecutions under the Official Secrets Act.

Sir Reginald Manningham-Buller (South Northants. Conservative). I authorise prosecutions for offences under the Official Secrets Acts in those cases where having regard to the relevant facts, I consider it to be in the public interest to institute proceedings.

So the Official Secrets Acts remain unsullied and available for governmental use, though their application outside the realm of espionage is subject to a growing volume of criticism.[28] The Committee of 100 has, so to speak, retired hurt, but with its footnote to constitutional history guaranteed. In the history of political philosophy too, there is an unwritten chapter into which it and other twentieth-century resisters to established authority have still to be fitted. At this time there is more to be said about the logic and morals of disobedience to defective laws than was said by Aristotle and the oddity is that so little more has yet been said.

NOTES

1. Morley, *Life of Gladstone*, Vol. 1, p. 568 (1908 ed.).
2. The Prisoners (Temporary Discharge for Ill Health) Act, 1913.
3. 56 H.C. Deb. 5s. col. 2508.
4. 51 H.C. Deb. 5s. (1913) col. 2344.
5. *Lansbury* v. *Riley* [1914] 3 KB 229.
6. The march and its minstrelsy are described in detail by Christopher Driver in *The Disarmers* (1964). Two verses of a representative composition ran (to the tune of John Brown's body and without acknowledgment to the Duke of Wellington)

"Macmillan and the Tories are out to wait and see
They think the great deterrent will secure the victory
I don't know if they scare the Reds; by God they frighten me
If they won't ban the H. Bomb now.

"We're going to stop the loonies and preserve the human race
We're going to save our country, for we like the dear old place
We're going to stuff a rocket up Mr. Dulles' base
If they don't ban the H. Bomb now."

(Driver, pp. 61-62)

7. *The Times*, September 14, 1961.
8. *The Times*, September 14, 1961.
9. *The Times*, September 14, 1961.
10. This power is exercisable under the Public Order Act 1936 s.3. by which the Commissioner may, to prevent serious public disorder, prohibit all public processions for any period, not exceeding three months.
11. A debate on the Trafalgar Square demonstration took place in the House of Lords on 19 October. (See 234 H.L. Deb. 19 October 1961.) On March 1, 1962 the Home Secretary stated in the House of Commons that senior police officers had investigated all complaints received. A few police had misbehaved but inquiries had failed to identify the particular officers (654 H.C. Deb. 5s. cols. 1537-8). This episode was one of a number which has led to demands for independent investigations of complaints against the police. See Marshall, *Police and Government* (Methuen, 1965), Chap. 8.
12. The D notice system is operated by a committee, the Press, Services and Broadcasting Committee, composed of Government officials with newspaper and broadcasting representatives. Notices are issued to newspapers detailing matters which in the Government's view ought not to be printed in the interests of national security. The sys-

tem is voluntary in that it is not an offense to disregard a D notice, but prosecution under the Official Secrets Acts might follow refusal to be guided by them.

13. 676 H.C. Deb. 5s. col. 24 *et seq.*

14. At the Central Criminal Court, before Mr. Justice Havers and a jury.

15. *Times Law Report,* February 14, 15, 1962.

16. In the Court of Criminal Appeal, before the Lord Chief Justice, Mr. Justice Ashworth, and Mr. Justice Hinchcliffe.

17. See [1962] 2 *All England Reports* 314.

18. In the House of Lords, before Lord Reid, Viscount Radcliffe, Lord Hodson, Lord Devlin, and Lord Pearce.

19. See [1964] A.C. 787-814.

20. Maitland, *Selected Essays* (Cambridge University Press, 1936), p. 113.

21. 1 & 2, Geo. 5, Ch. 28.

22. E.g. [1964] A.C. 763 at p. 811 where he says "The fact to be proved is the existence of a purpose prejudicial to the State—not a purpose which 'appears to the Crown' to be prejudicial to the State."

23. [1916] 2 A.C. 77, 107.

24. [1932] 2 K.B. 197.

25. Lord Reid though had presumably intended to use the word "political" in such a way that it necessarily implied "not in a triable form." If its ordinary sense is "being of political importance" or "affecting the fortunes of politicians or parties or the public" then it could hardly be doubted that issues tried in the courts may be political.

26. Cf. Lord Pearce "I cannot accept the argument that 'the interests of the state' in this context mean the interests of the amorphous populace without regard to the guiding policies of those in authority." The phrase must mean ". . . the policies of the State as they are, not as they ought in the opinion of a jury to be."

27. See J. Ll. J. Edwards, *The Law Officers of the Crown* (Sweet and Maxwell, 1964) and Marshall and Moodie, *Some Problems of the Constitution* (Hutchinson, 1961), pp. 172-180.

28. Three recent publications have drawn attention to the potential danger of Official Secrets Act powers: H. Street, *Freedom, the Individual and the Law* (Pelican 1963); D. G. T. Williams, *Not in the Public Interest* (Hutchinson, 1965); *The Law and the Press* (A Report by Justice and the British Committee of the International Press Institute, 1965). See also *Report of the Privy Councillors appointed to inquire into the Interception of Communications,* Cmnd. 283 (1957) and *Security Procedures in the Public Service,* Cmnd. 1681 (1962).

France: The Canal Affair and the OAS Cases

by Jerome B. King

Military justice is to justice what military music is to music.
GEORGES CLEMENCEAU

ANDRÉ CANAL PLAYED A RATHER DIFFERENT PART IN MODERN
French history from the one he intended. His 1962 trial, as a major
participant in an extensive but unavailing effort to overthrow the
Fifth Republic, raised some thorny constitutional problems. The
immediate background of *l'affaire Canal* was the formal settlement
of the crisis in relations between France and Algeria. Most Frenchmen once considered Algeria as much a part of France as Paris.
This settlement, which provided for total Algerian independence,
created among many a feeling that President de Gaulle had be-
trayed France treasonously. Some consequently thought any means
needed to bring his Fifth Republic down would be justified.

Canal's career as a subversive was not long. Sent from Algeria
into metropolitan (continental) France to organize violence
against the regime in 1961, he was arrested in May 1962, tried
and condemned to death in September, reprieved by President
de Gaulle in November, and virtually lost to public view by the
Spring of 1963. His legacy to the institutions of the Fifth Republic was a new court, called the Court for State Security,
which did not, however, try Canal himself. The manner in which it
was brought into being and the purposes for which it was formed
provide commentary on the political life of the Fifth Republic, and
perhaps a moral as well.

The *affaire Canal* is a clear departure from the rule of law that
Americans hold so dear. One should not leap hastily to a moral

judgment, however. Law and politics will not remain separate in either theory or practice. Legal questions always involve policy; policy always involves law.

This has been evident in American history. Many fashions in constitutional interpretation have come and gone, fashions that were clearly linked with political and social life. It has been even more true in France. Her history has been far more full of alarms and excursions, and the needs of her national defense have much more often demanded national psychological unity with consequent pressure on her political institutions. Through all this, French society has remained basically revolutionary. Americans tend to think that law is a friend upon which their political and social institutions must be built. The slow change of the law suits the slow sense of change which is associated with sound progress. The French experience has been different. The proponents of the 1789 Revolution believed that the very basis of law had to be changed, that their laws were so closely associated with royal tyranny and a wrong way of life that they had to be destroyed and replaced. Those who opposed the Revolution saw in such beliefs the dissolution of all social bonds and the loosing of anarchy upon France.

This contradictory legacy of the Revolution in attitudes toward law is still felt today. Those psychologically attuned to the Revolution and those alienated from it came to an uneasy compromise, which found formal expression in the French constitutional doctrine of the separation of powers. According to this doctrine the legislative, judicial, and executive functions must always remain clearly and distinctly separate. None must ever encroach upon the others.

The difference from the traditional American theory of separation of powers is notable. Our system provides for a certain number of derogations from this principle on the basis of a competing one, that of checks and balances. One obvious consequence of this mixture has been the practical inseparability of law and politics in American practice.

But the French have been inclined to regard a strict separation of law and politics as indispensable to good government. The lawyers and the judges have their own distinct realm, they say, into which political considerations should never intrude. Statutes lay down general rules which the legal system applies fairly and squarely to the individual citizens. But the legal profession must not modify these general laws by precedents, because it inevitably speaks for the interests of *particuliers*, or private citizens, and no true system of law can be built on the limited perspectives and selfish interests of private citizens.

In French Revolutionary doctrine the realm of politics was reserved to the legislature, which by virtue of its popular election and its procedures of organized debate, spoke for the "general will." What the general will decreed through statute, the legal profession was duty bound to apply to the solution of disputes between citizens.

To put this theory into practice, the Revolutionary legislatures instituted a system of dual jurisdictions. One branch, the so-called ordinary or regular courts, dealt with disputes between private citizens. The other branch, which we call the administrative courts today, dealt with disputes between the State and private citizens. By this means, the Revolutionaries hoped to insure that the interests of the State, which they equated with the public interest, would always supersede those of individuals. Equal justice for all individual citizens and assurance of the superiority of public interests over private was their aim.

It is a principle of this dual court system that only ordinary courts have jurisdiction over crimes, even so-called "political crimes." These are offenses that appear to affect the security of the state. Since World War I, for example, a variety of laws defining such crimes have been enacted in the United States "to frustrate subversive activity before it constitutes an unmanageable threat to the political institutions," seeking, especially "by the use of the conspiracy concept or other devices, to reach conduct that is not immediately injurious but which is deemed *potentially* dangerous." [1]

In France the threat of subversion has been of longer standing than in the United States, and has often taken more serious and potentially successful forms. Monarchists no longer constitute a real threat to the Republic, but their place has sometimes been filled by Communists on the Left and a variety of groups on the Right. President de Gaulle himself supported more than one scheme to undermine the Fourth Republic, and this fact has hardly helped him establish the legitimacy of his own regime in the face of its many diverse opponents.

In 1958, one such Gaullist scheme, combined with other circumstances in which he had no hand, pushed the Fourth Republic into oblivion and brought him back to Paris as a national savior once again. The Fourth Republic had failed on the very ground where it was supposed to have been unassailable: its negative consensus broke down through inability of its "rational-legal" machinery to protect every important social group from those who opposed it. The issue was the Arab rebellion in Algeria. The parliamentary system of offering some protection to every group collapsed when a substantial one—the Arabs of Algeria—felt that it had never been included in the system at all.

De Gaulle thus came back to power on the basis of a new kind of appeal for national unity. The national interest, as he defined it, was going to prevail. No longer would the chicaneries of the parliamentary game interfere with political vision.

Much of the spirit of 1789 was recaptured in his views of history and politics. The contemporary *ancien régime* of the parliamentary system, which catered to the conflicting and incoherent wishes of every political and economic group, was replaced by a quasi-revolutionary movement destined to give France new laws and new political institutions in keeping with the needs of the age. But history may be repeating itself again. Will future historians find upon looking back at this new France that many of the habits and practices of the *ancien régime parlementaire* managed to survive beneath the surface of the new regime?

An apocryphal story about French constitutions circulated early in the Fourth Republic. On being asked for a copy of the constitution, a Paris bookseller replied haughtily that he did not deal in periodical literature. The purpose of our study here is to determine whether there may be elements of a constitution beneath the periodical literature—elements which tell us more than can documents about the nature of French political life today and tomorrow.

We know that the Fifth Republic is based largely on the popular appeal of its president, and that his ability to combine ancient wisdom about the grandeur of France with the requirements of a rapidly changing world characterize this popular appeal. But what then of the "rational-legal" element in the Fifth Republic?" Superficially relegated to an unimportant place in the new regime, has it in fact disappeared altogether, to be replaced by a kind of "revolutionary justice" to which only President de Gaulle has the key? *L'affaire Canal,* if it does not answer the question conclusively, nevertheless contains evidence that the ideal of the old law is not yet dead, perhaps not even in the heart of the man who seems to have wanted so much to kill it.

THE BACKGROUND OF L'AFFAIRE CANAL

Who is André Canal? Few Frenchmen had heard the name before his arrest in April 1962, and probably not many more could now remember what he did, what he stood for, or the consequences of his acts. *L'affaire Canal* has its own importance in the history of the Fifth Republic, but it has little of the emotional aura of *l'affaire Dreyfus.* Canal was hardly an innocent figure unjustly condemned by a social elite determined to protect its special privileges. Constitutions do not always depend on the fate of honorable men.

Canal was born in Niort, a small French town, 47 years before his trial. Though not a *pied noir,*[2] he had nevertheless spent most of his adult life in Algeria. Even a month before his arrest in 1962 the police did not know his real name. They had captured some Secret Army Organization (OAS) documents referring to *"l'homme au monocle noir,"* but this *nom de guerre* was their only clue to his identity until March 1962. Then the arrest of three of Canal's lieutenants enabled the police to determine his name. The black monocle was a black patch he wore over a glass eye.

His arrest in Paris about seven o'clock in the evening of May 7, took place in the best musical comedy style.[3] The police had discovered his general whereabouts by means of tracing letters to his various aliases. But not sure of his exact address, they stationed three policemen, two in plain clothes and one dressed as a carpenter, in a square near his hideout. When Canal emerged from an apartment and began to cross the square, the three policemen cornered him against the grill fence of a churchyard in the center of the square. Though small in stature Canal proved an able fighter, and the three policemen were far from subduing him when a small crowd from the nearby café gathered to watch with curiosity, but with no intention of intervening in what it apparently took to be a private fight.

At this point one policeman called for help to a large truck-driver who had just parked at the scene and he, believing Canal to be having an epileptic fit, threw himself bodily on the smaller man. This allowed one policeman to draw his pistol, whereupon Canal calmed down. No sooner was the struggle over, however, when a squad car with three uniformed policemen of the local precinct arrived. They had been called by a passer-by who believed that the struggle was a kidnapping. Only after considerable argument and much study of the plainclothesmen's identity cards could the uniformed police be convinced that the supposedly kidnapped victim was in fact a criminal. As the newspapers were quick to re-mark, the arrest took place almost under the windows of Police Commissioner Clot, the very officer who, when head of the criminal brigade, had first identified André Canal only a few months before. In fact, this same Commissioner appeared to have been the object of some of Canal's earlier attentions, as two plastic bombs had blown the front off the florist's shop on the ground floor under his apartment.

Plastic bombs were one of Canal's trademarks. Not that he ac-tually placed the bombs himself. The police inquiry and the trial showed that Canal had had more of an administrative role in the OAS,[4] and that he was not entirely new to administrative func-tions. In Algeria, prior to the insurrection, he had been director of a company producing nonferrous metals. His career as an active subversive began late in 1961 when he was sent on ex-general Raoul Salan's orders to France to undertake the organization of the OAS' metropolitan mission.

This mission differed in aim, if not in means, from that which the OAS had earlier been carrying on in Algeria. The turning point in the life of the OAS had been the failure of the "generals' putsch" in April 1961. Four French generals—Salan, Jouhaud, Challe, and Zeller—had tried to take over direction of what they conceived to be France's task in Algeria. They acted desperately, and in retrospect seem to have had little chance of success. But they were desperate, or more correctly, perhaps, they had become the principal leaders and spokesmen for a largely desperate group of people—Algerians of European origin.

The failure of the April 1961 putsch did not end their activities. Unable to translate the political support of the European diehards —and apparently nearly the whole of the European community fell into that category at the time—into a movement capable of blocking the rule of Paris in Algeria, many of them increasingly turned their attention to the problem of overthrowing the Fifth Republic in Paris. What had begun as a policy to maintain Algeria as French territory ended as a policy to bring down President de Gaulle's regime. Various means were used in this attempt, but the principal ones were propaganda, terror, and assassination. Since no man more literally incorporated the regime than de Gaulle, the OAS assumed that assassinating him would do more than any other act to destroy the Fifth Republic.

André Canal's association with the OAS was clearly documented during his trial. His death sentence probably struck most French people as essentially reasonable, or at least understandable. To crimes of passion they may give the benefit of doubt. But crimes coldly organized, by a man who employs others for their execution, garner very little public sympathy. At stake in the Canal case was not so much the fate of the accused himself, but rather the means used to punish him. Death might well be appropriate for Canal the man. But did the regime use legitimate means to arrive at this verdict?

Dispute over the answer to this question symbolized in late 1962 and early 1963 the major problem facing de Gaulle's governmental system. This problem can be summed up by asking to what extent the legitimacy of a government should derive from its institutional structures and the formal relationships of one to another, and to what extent it should derive from the popular support of its leader. There was no question in anyone's mind—President de Gaulle's included—that the Fifth Republic was based primarily on the latter. Many of the critical acts of his presidency can be interpreted in terms of his intention to emphasize and re-emphasize the personal character of the regime. But the results of the *l'affaire Canal* suggest that the "personalization of power" has its limits even in de Gaulle's France. Before we can sense what these limits may be, we must know something of the background of André Canal's trial.

An outsider might validly ask why he wasn't tried on murder

and criminal conspiracy charges before an ordinary court. But such a question asked in France during 1962 had political overtones. And these overtones overshadowed, in the minds of most Frenchmen, the formal legal aspects of the matter.

Canal was obviously not simply a murderer conspiring with other criminals for private gain. His crimes were politically motivated and as such both the French authorities who brought him to trial and the French public believed that the political nature of his activities, like those of his nominal boss in the OAS, General Salan, should be made a part of the legal process and not simply an item of evidence introduced in passing.

The political charge against Canal and his associates lay in the fact that these men stood for a defeated policy in 1962. Their hope had been to keep Algeria French. But the Evian Accords of March 1962 were a death sentence to such hopes. These Accords provided for a vote of self-determination in Algeria on July 1, 1962, and the inevitable outcome was Algerian independence. The French public had already indicated massive acceptance of this policy in the referendum on April 8. Algeria was going to have a government of her own, which meant, in fact, a government of Arabs, by Arabs, and for Arabs.

To the European community of Algeria such a result seemed both a public disaster and a personal betrayal. For more than seven years the better part of the French army had been fighting to keep Algeria French and to protect French interests against those of an Arab rebel leadership and guerrilla army which, until recently, even the Paris government had thought little more than a group of terrorists. And now the Europeans' worst fears were suddenly realized. From having been treated as outlaws, the rebel Arabs had made the leap to becoming a legitimate government with which the authorities in Paris were prepared to deal.

The change appeared to be more than a *volte-face* to the *pieds noirs*. It was nothing less than treason to the whole direction and purpose of French history, as they saw it. The original white settlers may not have gone very far back in time in North African history, but their descendents believed their claim to the land as good or better than that of the Moslem inhabitants. They thought of themselves as having made the desert bloom and as having brought the civilization of France to a cultural backwater of the

Arab world. They believed their moral claim to the land to be complemented by a legal claim guaranteed by the whole force of the French nation itself.

The French conquest of Algeria had not gone beyond its military phase when great numbers of white settlers began to move in. In order to reassure the new settlers, Algeria was not made a colony or protectorate, like the provinces of Indochina acquired in the same epoch, but rather an integral part of France herself, with the same political and administrative relationship to Paris as any section of metropolitan France.

Perhaps not quite, for special allowance was made for the native Arab population. To give Moslems French citizenship appeared impossible. It seemed better to let the Arabs continue to live according to their own ways, disturbing their lives as little as possible. The natives were given a special legal "status" of their own, in which their political influence was kept at a minimum. This solution led, through almost fatal stages, not only to the subjugation of the Arabs, but also to the belief of the Europeans that such subjugation was natural, permanent, and morally justified.

France's collapse in 1939 and the need of de Gaulle's provisional Government to get established in 1943 in friendly surroundings in North Africa meant that Arab leaders saw the possibility of changed relations with metropolitan France. French recognition of Tunisian autonomy in 1954 was the last of the catalysts needed to set off an organized movement seeking Algerian independence. The major factors in the upheaval were the rapidly deteriorating breakdown in communications between the two communities after World War II, and the illusions both nourished as to their respective places in the life of Algeria.

On the side of the Europeans, these illusions fostered the growth of the Secret Army Organization. But the OAS would surely not have attained its importance if it had not attracted influential support throughout France. Undoubtedly the most dangerous support came from members of the military officer corps, some of whom had already helped overthrow the Fourth Republic.

The French Army's association with France's colonial enterprises had always been close. As the world's second largest, this empire had long been dependent on military services. The connection between the Army and the overseas territories developed into more than one of conquest and administration. Particularly after World War I a kind of psychological association became increasingly important, for the Army had learned not only that it had an important role to play in France's *mission civilisatrice,* but that the defense of France's metropolitan frontiers was in some measure dependent on the capacity of the military services to enlist and incorporate colonial troops into the home army. At a recognizable population disadvantage with respect to her hereditary enemy Germany, France came to count on counterbalancing this disadvantage by calling on the human as well as the physical resources of her colonies and overseas territories. The valor of native troops in the trenches from 1914-18 helped to foster the myth that the French empire was the modern counterpart of the Roman: one in which all citizens were really equal, regardless of color and native soil, one in which all were for one and one was for all.

The collapse of France in 1940 gave a curious turn to this myth among the military services. Casting about for those guilty of what appeared then as an ignominious defeat, the officer corps developed a theory of the malfeasance of the parliamentary system. Had the Third Republic been able to provide a consistent foreign policy, firm in the face of Hitler's aggressions? Had it been willing to vote the taxes and the military credits necessary for rearmament? Had it shown courage enough to demand of the people the sacrifices which would have been necessary to meet the German challenge successfully? Had it been willing to sacrifice politics as usual in times of crisis? To all these questions the officer corps was inclined to answer "no." For many of them, these inclinations became convictions in the postwar period.

Sent first to fight a "dirty war" in Indochina and later an even dirtier one in Algeria, the professional officers came more and more to resent the twists and turns of parliamentary policy-making. The failure to win the war in Indochina they again attributed to the unwillingness of the parliamentarians to demand the necessary sacrifices from the public. The 1954 Geneva settlement released from Far Eastern duty a substantial number of officers embittered by what they considered to have been doublecrossing by an incoherent and dishonest political system.

But these same officers's long experience with guerrilla warfare meant that they would be assigned to Algeria. Given the Fourth

Republic's inability to provide direction in the conduct of this new war, and the rapid turnover of governments in Paris, it is hardly surprising that some officers sought ways to go beyond tactics and strategy to policy-making itself. The goal of their policy came to be to keep Algeria French.

Certainly a majority of French people was in favor of retaining Algeria during at least the first three years after the outbreak of the rebellion in November of 1954.[5] This majority apparently be-lieved that retention of French control over Algeria was essentially a military problem, and that a sufficiently large and well-directed French Army could protect both the white population and the politically unsophisticated natives, who supposedly asked nothing better than to be left alone to live in their age-old ways under benevolent French guidance. The rebellion was seen in France, officially, as the work of a small group of terrorists, mostly ex-tremist and of Communist sympathies. The officer corps expected that the Army could count on a blank check to pursue a generally agreed-upon and supposedly well-defined goal. But by late 1957 the temper of political opinion in France with respect to the Al-gerian problem was beginning to change. The majority, in favor of keeping Algeria French, began to lose whatever convictions it may have had on the subject when those "last fifteen minutes of pacification," promised by the Socialist Government of Prime Min-ister Guy Mollet in the spring of 1956, seemed endless, while rumors of expanded military needs and less savory military methods began to drift back to France. The French military began to lose touch with civilian sentiments at home. The officer corps found that what they had hoped was a blank check to proceed with a complete military mop-up in Algeria was, in fact, a limited check in the first place, and increasingly less likely of being honored at all in any political or psychological sense by the home popula-tion. The last National Assembly of the Fourth Republic became very sensitive to this "softening" of the home front. In the corri-dors of the *Palais Bourbon* and the political counting houses of the capital, more and more rumors about a negotiated settlement with the FLN began to be heard.

When these rumors reached the French fighting forces in Al-geria, some of the professional soldiers found that all those nerve endings which had been rendered sensitive by the Indochina fiasco and by memories of the failure of the parliamentary system in the 'thirties were inflamed. Where could the Army turn to find sympathy for its tasks and firm political guidance for its tactical and strategic activities?

One place was to the civilian European population of the big cities in Algeria, who were becoming increasingly unhappy. Their leaders perceived the handwriting on the wall. In response, they called not for calm but rather, in the old Jacobin tradition, for the people to rise in arms. They believed that the political hacks in Paris were about to sell out not only the interests of the local European population and the faithful Moslems, who asked nothing more than to work dutifully and admiringly for their white mentors, but even the best interests of France herself. France without Algeria would be nothing but a truncated set of provinces, surrounded by hostile Communist and Communist-sympathizing states, weakened at home by the presence of a large Communist party, with a governmental system little more than a game of musical chairs for a handful of party hacks. Her fall could be only moments away unless something were done with force and dispatch.

A certain part of the professional Army now found itself in accord with the Europeans in Algeria. France must be saved from herself. Her political system must be cleaned up, her institutions reformed, morals and idealism re-established to the high place they once had in France's earlier and more glorious days. The key to the whole reform was saving Algeria. L'Algérie Française became more than a political rallying point. It was raised to a metaphysical principle. The Forum in front of Government House in Algiers became the scene of great popular rallies addressed by patriotic citizens and officers, and the neighboring streets resounded with the sympathetic honking of automobile horns.

But the Army needed a leader as well as a supporting environment. Who else could this leader be than Charles de Gaulle?

On May 13, 1958, the people of the Forum in Algiers chose a new form of government for the people of France. They had some help, of course, and their choice was not entirely free. Limitations had been set by the French Army in Algeria, the indifference of the great majority of the metropolitan population to the fate of the Fourth Republic, and the skill with which de Gaulle had played his role of oracle. Charles de Gaulle returned to power on a wave of popular enthusiasm on the south shore of the Mediterranean, which stirred the muddy waters of politics on the north shore. Since he had already brought the disparate elements of French society through the long travail of the Fall, Occupation, Resistance, and Liberation, who better could possibly reunite France now? Had he not already shown in both word and deed that he combined profound respect for the principles of the Republic without being blind to the limitations of the Republic's anarchic political institutions?

To the Europeans of Algeria the Fifth Republic appeared determined to pick up the fight which had lagged under the previous regime. With a firm military hand at the helm, a man infinitely conscious of France's prestige and natural spirit mobilizing the people, how could victory now elude the grasp of a military machine nearly 500,000 strong, armed with the best theories and the best military technology of the Western world? But many of these failed to note that although de Gaulle had ridden to power on the strength of the Army and the emotions generated in the European community of Algeria, his first commitment was, and had to be, to metropolitan France. And many people there had accepted his return to power, not because they wanted him to remake France, but because he seemed to them the only bulwark against a proto-fascist, military dictatorship. To all intents and purposes, one man had taken over the representative functions of the parliament which, like its equally discouraged counter-part under the Third Republic, had voted itself out of a job. The question remained whether, as representative of the whole people, de Gaulle could develop a freedom of maneuver with respect to Algeria which the parliamentary system had not enjoyed.

If he had come to power a few years earlier perhaps he would have been able to develop such freedom; his first year or so in power was marked by attempts to gain it. But as the fighting went on in Algeria, more and more articulate persons in the metropole began to oppose it. Although they probably did not reflect a particularly solid core of public opinion, these voices were supplemented by a growing public unwillingness to keep up the fight. Scruple combined with lassitude to reduce the will of the metropole far below that level would have been necessary to bring the war to a diplomatic success. Furthermore, France's major allies had never been happy about the struggle and, as it wore on, their spoken reservations became less restrained. Criticism from the newer African states, from the very nations which France had released from colonial bondage herself, also found its mark. So even as the French military effort in Algeria was reaching a peak, de Gaulle began to pronounce the fatal words of self-determination, as though they were an option to be given consideration.

The *pieds noirs* and the officer corps could hardly believe their ears. For what other possible reason had they brought de Gaulle to power if not to swing the nation around to their side? The idea of self-determination appeared officially in a Presidential speech of September 1959; citizens of Algiers took a trip to the barricades in January 1960.

Although this trip unquestionably had some tacit military support, it was largely a civilian operation. It is hard to say exactly what its organizers hoped for—perhaps to force the Army to choose between its divided loyalties, and to demonstrate to Paris that any policy which contemplated negotiation, leading toward self-determination, would end in civil strife among Frenchmen and not just between Frenchmen and Arabs. The barricades stayed up a week—rather longer than Paris hoped they would—and their dismantling was brought about after practically all the shooting had come from those behind the barricades. An almost amicable agreement between insurrectionists and paratroop contingents was arranged. Whatever other interpretation could be put on this first abortive putsch, if that is what it was, it was certain that the Fifth Republic could hardly count on its military forces to maintain order and discipline among the European community in Algeria.

Yet the events of that January confirmed the worst suspicions of the Algerian French. When the civilian leaders of the operation were arrested and then allowed to go free while awaiting trial, several of them took the occasion to depart for Spain to set up the conspiracy which soon became known as the OAS.

The remaining leaders were brought to trial in November 1960, before a regular military court. The leniency of the verdicts, reached after nearly four months of legal maneuver and publicity for the defendants' cause, gave little encouragement to the regime that similar insurrections in the future would be either effectively or promptly punished by ordinary judicial means.[6] But even as these conclusions were drawn, they were made irrelevant by new events. The "generals' putsch" was about to begin.

The timing of the 1961 revolt caught Paris by surprise. Rumors of trouble had been coming in for several days prior to the uprising, but Paris assumed that, if trouble came at all, it would be primarily the work of the OAS and that nothing would happen before May in any case. On Saturday morning, April 22, however, General Zeller, in the name of a "high command" constituted of four retired generals—Challe (who had been in command during the trouble at the barricades in January 1960), Jouhaud, Salan, and himself—seized the Algiers radio station, all official buildings, telephone and telegraph offices. They also arrested Governor Morin, general delegate of the Government in Algeria, and General Gambiez, formally in command.

The metropolitan public was at first surprised, but not particularly alarmed. It was getting used to rumblings in Algeria. But complacence turned rapidly into bewilderment and fear after a broadcast appeal of Prime Minister Debré at 1:30 p.m., Saturday, April 22:

> The government has decided to make the nation's will respected . . . I demand of all those who are in positions of responsibility . . . not to get engaged in an adventure which can only have the most tragic future consequences for the Nation. It is not only to loyalty and duty which I appeal, it is also, it is first, it is above all, to the respect of the fundamental interests of the Nation.

Meanwhile, President de Gaulle made known to his closest associates his intention of invoking Article 16 of the 1958 constitution, which would allow him to govern solely by decree, without the advice or consent of Parliament. On the 23rd, the Constitutional Council approved the use of Article 16 on learning that the Government considered that the four generals had entered "into open rebellion against the public powers," had as their goal the seizing of "the whole of the country's power," and that "by virtue of these acts of subversion, the institutions of the Republic are threatened in a serious and immediate manner, and the constitutional Public Powers cannot function in a regular fashion." [7]

Sunday afternoon, de Gaulle himself addressed the nation by radio and television. Viewers were surprised to see their President in the uniform of an army general as they had come to expect him to emphasize the civil rather than the military aspect of his regime. But his words were very much those of a general at war. The struggle to restore the Republic and re-establish independence after June 1940 and to continue the work of national recovery since 1958 risked being

> in vain, on the very eve of success, because of the odious and stupid adventure undertaken by the insurgents in Algeria. Behold the State mocked, the Nation defied, our power shaken, our international prestige debased, our place and our role in Africa compromised. And by whom? Alas! Alas! Alas! By men whose duty, whose honor, whose very reason for existence it was to serve and to obey.
>
> In the name of France, I order that all means—I say all means— be employed to block the path of those men, until they are defeated. I forbid all Frenchmen and, firstly, all soldiers, to carry out any of their orders . . . The future of the usurpers must be that alone which is determined by the rigor of the laws.
>
> In the face of the misfortune which has overcome the fatherland, and the threat which weighs on the Republic, . . . I have decided to bring Article 16 of our Constitution into play. Beginning today I shall take, if need be directly, such measures as will appear to me to be required by the circumstances. By this act I affirm in myself, for today and tomorrow, the French and republican legitimacy that the Nation has conferred upon me, that I will maintain it, whatever happens, until the end of my mandate or until either strength or life fail me, and that I will take the measures necessary to insure that it will last after I have gone.
>
> Frenchwomen, Frenchmen! See where France now is in danger of going in comparison to what she was on the way to becoming again.
>
> Frenchwomen, Frenchmen! Help me! [8]

Three hours after the Presidential speech, rumors began to circulate in Paris to the effect that dissident parachute troops were preparing to embark in Algeria for Paris. Underlying these rumors was the general belief both inside and outside of government circles that the best to be expected of the military services was that they would remain passive while waiting to see the outcome of the struggle between the regime and the activists, who on the military side were made up largely of a parachute regiment and some Foreign Legionnaires. Sunday evening the disarray of the government below the Presidential level was displayed by the tragi-comic broadcast appeal by Prime Minister Debré urging the public to go en masse to the airfields, as soon as sirens were heard, "in order to convince these mistaken soldiers of their grave mistake. Good sense must come from the popular soul and everyone must feel himself to be a part of the nation."

In retrospect neither national unity nor the loyalty of the military services themselves appeared so weak as was widely believed in the heat of events. Throughout Monday, April 24, the government received signs that the greater part of the Army and virtually the entire Air Force and Navy remained at least passively loyal to Paris and that the draftees, who constituted the larger part of the forces in Algeria, were not going to follow orders from mutinous officers. By Tuesday evening the revolt was clearly finished. Only one life had been lost—that of a non-commissioned officer loyal to the government who was killed by paratroops seizing an official building on the first day of the insurrection.[9]

Of the four generals, Challe gave himself up on the spot, Zeller surrendered some weeks later, and Jouhaud and Salan fled, having been deprived of rank and authority by governmental declaration and by the force of events.

The general's revolt was over. But its consequences beset the Fifth Republic for many months.

The Government's response to what de Gaulle soon called simply an "incident" was not of one piece. On the one hand, the government clearly attempted to minimize the seriousness of the affair, in order to reduce the role of the various organized manifestations of public opinion which contributed substantially to the rapid dissolution of the insurrection. Always scornful of these "intermediaries" between himself and the Nation, he was not going to pay any debts of gratitude for their support in time of need. To admit such a debt would be to open the door to the policy-making process to groups over which he had no direct influence.

On the other hand, the Government was anxious to show that the institutions of its regime had been able to surmount a considerable threat, and that only institutions of the type then existing could be expected to triumph over such threats in the future. The generals' putsch was a challenge to France; France could parry such challenges only by committing more power to the President's hands. Furthermore, apparently de Gaulle took the putsch seriously enough to believe that it necessitated personnel changes in critical branches of his administration. Military and civil officers

were put out to pasture, new ranks were created and new men
appointed to them. Various courts, military and otherwise, worked
overtime to bring perpetrators and accomplices of crimes against
the state to the bar of justice.

The President was clearly convinced that summary justice was
the best way to deal with threats against state security. As far as
his regime was concerned, the "trial of the barricades" had displayed all the evils inherent in the more or less regular judicial
procedures. It had dragged on for four months, giving defendants
admirable opportunities to use the prisoner's box as a platform
to attack the Fifth Republic in one of its most vulnerable spots:
its faithlessness to the Army and the European community in Algeria. To surmount these difficulties with the new crop of defendants nurtured in the generals' putsch the regime set up a new
court to deal with defendants even more expeditiously than the
ordinary military courts could.

The *ordonnance* of April 28, 1961, establishing the so-called
High Military Tribunal, therefore by-passed some of the traditional
procedures of French law, especially with regard to the naming
of magistrates, the bringing of indictments, and the rights of the
defense. Five professional civilian judges and three general officers
of the armed services, all named especially for the occasion, made
up its bench. Arraignment was by decree on the written order of
the Minister of Justice, dispensing with the ordinary methods of
inquiry by *juge d'instruction*. The defense lawyers were warned
beforehand that the bench would not permit them to call endless
witnesses nor to challenge the authority or jurisdiction of the
Tribunal which had constituted effective measures of delay in
other trials.

Under these new judicial arrangements the Challe-Zeller trial
ran like clockwork. Only three days elapsed from the opening
declarations of the defendants to the handing down of the verdicts.
There almost seemed to be a tacit agreement between bench and
bar that the defendants' best case would result from a thoroughly
dignified procedure, as befitted the rank of the accused. Each was
convicted and sentenced to 15 years and expulsion from the Legion
of Honor.

Meanwhile, the Government stepped up its administrative and
military "purification," arresting suspects without warrant and

holding them incommunicado for 15 days, as allowed by the new regulations issued under Article 16 of the Constitution. It searched and seized documents and newspapers of both the Right and the Left to protect itself against further attack and to convince most Frenchmen that it was truly a regime of the Center, equally severe against all the nation's enemies.

Whether these activities were relevant to the new threat which soon faced the Fifth Republic is open to question. Within 24 hours after the collapse of the April putsch, OAS tracts were again circulating in Algiers.

The day after the Challe-Zeller verdict was handed down, a special police investigator in Algeria was murdered. Throughout the months following the April putsch the anxieties of the European population grew. The police stepped up searches and uncovered new caches of arms. Their action, combined with the rumors received concerning Paris' negotiation with the FLN leaders at Evian near Switzerland, convinced the Europeans that they were on the point of being abandoned to the tender mercies of the Arabs.

The OAS was doing what it could to keep up European morale. One of its tracts in the summer of 1961 assured them that "the command headquarters of the metropolitan wing of the OAS Resistance to de Gaulle is getting organized and developed in all regions and in all segments of the metropolitan population," and gave a list of groups against the regime, which included the "army, veterans, students, journalists, union members." It concluded with a list of bombings and thefts that it claimed it had committed.

Indeed, the OAS did open a theater of operations in the metropole during 1961. The extent of its networks and the importance of the sum of the people who worked for it were revealed constantly by new arrests. By September OAS terrorist activities swung into high gear. The first night of that month it exploded bombs at the homes of Jacob Kaplan, first rabbi of France, and Geoffroy de Courcel, secretary general at the *Elysée*. But bigger things were in store. On September 8, an attempt was made on the life of President de Gaulle as he was travelling between his home at Colombey-les-Deux-Eglises and Paris. A homemade device of plastic and some other type of explosive had been laid across the road and caught fire as the presidential convoy sped by at its usual 80 mph.

Apparently, the OAS had concluded that the failure of the military *coup d'état* proved that the regime was too solidly based on popular support to succumb to that kind of overthrow. In what way was it then most vulnerable? The answer emerged clearly from the very notion of obvious relationship between the President and people. The ties between them might well be the strongest of their kind in modern French politics. But their very personal nature meant that the regime could be no more enduring than the life of the President.

The OAS did not base its entire policy on the assassination of de Gaulle. The mind of the public also had to be prepared for that eventuality, and since the regular news media were hardly available to the OAS, a new form of communication to the public had to be devised. The plastic explosive, mixed with various robberies, extortions, kidnappings, and murders, all backed by the fascinated horror and fear of the public, became the key to their operations.

These operations did not take place in political isolation. The capacity of the OAS to recruit, collect funds, to carry on its terrorism—all depended on the sympathy of an important minority of even the metropolitan population. In any comparison between the OAS and the Fifth Republic, most Frenchmen clearly preferred the latter. But the important thing was that even in expressing such preference the leading spokesmen for organized political life in France outside the immediate circle of power seemed to argue that it was a choice between evils, and not a choice between good and evil.

The legitimacy of the Fifth Republic was thus at stake in the minds of many of the very people who could be most counted on to support it. They agreed with the general orientation of many of its policies, they admired its president as a great leader, a great patriot, and a unique figure in 20th century politics. But they could not shake off the feeling that it was an interim regime, put together for a passing crisis in history, without real roots in the life of the nation.[10]

For those who supported de Gaulle in 1961 and 1962, as well as for those who were against him, this was a vulnerability of his regime which, although linked to his "personalization of power," went beyond it to illuminate a vulnerability at the very heart of French social life. The political reflection of this vulnerability showed up in the nature of the relations between the people and authority. De Gaulle was not immortal, as he himself admitted. But the legitimacy and strength of the Fifth Republic appeared to nearly everyone to be directly proportional to the strength of de Gaulle's public support, as expressed in the various referenda, which seemed, in 1962, to be becoming more and more characteristic of the regime. What steps, if any, was de Gaulle taking to assure a certain continuity in government after his reign? Was the regime itself taking on an institutional aspect which, like all institutions, would develop a certain momentum of its own, to guide the ship of State after its builder was forced to relinquish the helm? This continues to be the critical question about the Fifth Republic and it is one on which *l'affaire Canal* may throw some light.

THE TRIAL OF ANDRÉ CANAL AND POLITICAL JUSTICE UNDER THE FIFTH REPUBLIC

By the time of André Canal's arrest on May 7, 1962, France had begun to discover that to vote for peace and to establish peace were two very different things. The Evian Accords had won the approval of over 90% of those who voted in the referendum on April 8, but the events of the months immediately following indicated that the Algerian affair had been settled on paper only. Far from being immediately free of the Algerian burden by granting independence, the regime found that the burden had only changed its character. The enormous military expense was over, but the problem of legitimacy had become sharper than ever.

L'affaire Canal showed at least two things: that the political parties "of old" were not the only "intermediaries" to oppose the means of the Fifth Republic; and that certain "intermediaries" were indispensable to that strengthening of the institutions of the republican State which de Gaulle had always made one of his major goals. These non-partisan intermediaries were principally agents of the civil and military administration, including especially the courts. De Gaulle's ambition has been to have this type of intermediary express the popular will only after it has been interpreted by the Head of State himself. To attain this goal he has tried to create an administrative hierarchy in which every agent feels himself directly linked to the Head of State through a formal chain of command, and in which the psychological satisfactions of the job come not so much from a feeling of collegiality with one's fellow civil servants as from a sense of an almost mystical participation in the task of renovating France. But the success in this goal did not come easily where the administration of justice was concerned.

De Gaulle clearly expected the administration of justice under the Fifth Republic to serve his purposes and policies first. In the struggle with the OAS it was particularly desirable that judgments against OAS agents not only deter others from participating in the OAS, but convince the people generally that the institutions of the law were on the side of the established regime. The Government seemed to want to show that only it could fight effectively against subversion. The people might collectively bring their general will to the fight through voting in referenda, but as individuals they were to be discouraged from organizing their own defense.

During the late 1961 and early 1962 when OAS depredations were reaching new heights, the "former" political groups, not yet ready to abandon their representative function in favor of the Head of State, reacted with increasing bitterness—bitterness which the Government reciprocated. When, despite an official ban against all street demonstrations, various trade union leaders organized a massive showing of popular sentiment against the OAS in Paris on February 8, 1962, the police troops used considerable force to break it up. The balance sheet of three hours of struggle counted more than eight dead and 100 injured among the demonstrators, while 10 police were hospitalized. The Government promptly blamed the demonstrators, and argued that the disorder had been planned by Communists.

Only a month after this popular demonstration the OAS set off a car of explosives in front of the town hall of Issy-les-Moulineaux, a Paris suburb in the so-called Red Belt. Three passers-by were killed and 47 injured. With public indignation over this crime at an all time high, the Government announced the arrest of General Jouhaud, second in command of the OAS operation. Thus began the first of the four major trials dominating *l'affaire Canal*.

The prosecution demanded the death penalty

in the name of the Nation which has just approved the Evian Accords and by that act said "no" to the OAS. It is the nation, upset and torn asunder, which asked you to pronounce the sentence it expects of you without weakness.

For the defense, Maître Charpentier recalled that the OAS was also a victim, since

vengeance always calls forth vengeance . . . I ask you in our name, in the name of our country: take the first step which will lead on the road to amnesty. I ask it for the France of truth, liberty, and justice.

After two hours of deliberation the Tribunal found Jouhaud guilty, without extenuating circumstances, and condemned him to death. Women in the courtroom fainted; cries of "Long live Jouhaud," *"Algérie française"* and "We respect you, *mon général"* were heard.

Shortly after Jouhaud's verdict the Government announced the capture of the biggest fish of all, General Salan, living under a false name, false hairpiece and unaccustomed whiskers, at the apartment of his latest mistress in Algiers. His trial from the 15th to the 23rd of May was the great public event of the month.

The defense raised a critical political issue immediately: Could a special court made up of judges, even professional ones, appointed for the occasion, render a judgment truly independent of politics? It was made perfectly clear that the attack was not directed at the judges personally, but rather against the system which had brought them together on the bench of a new court.

General Salan's part in the trial was confined to the reading of a declaration which lasted 45 minutes. The theme of his declaration was familiar: "I am not a leader of a band but a French general representing the victorious army, not the beaten army . . . When one has known the France of courage he can never accept the France of abandonment."

After two and one-half hours of deliberation a majority of the Tribunal convicted Salan, but with extenuating circumstances, and sentenced him to life imprisonment. While the courtroom crowd sang *la Marseillaise* and the principal defense lawyer fervently embraced General Salan, questions about the future were already arising. Jouhaud, the second in command of the OAS, had been condemned to death, while its admitted leader was spared. In one month the opinion of the High Military Tribunal had changed.

Whatever the judges' reasons, their opportunity to try other members of the OAS was about to be cut short.[11]

The verdict was reached on May 25, 1962. On May 27, an *ordonnance* published in the *Journal Officiel* dissolved the High Military Tribunal, whose original establishment on April 27, 1961, had been prolonged on September 23 for the purpose of trying all those associated with "the events of Algeria." It had rendered 16 judgments in its life of 14 months, and its abrupt demise was only too obviously due to President de Gaulle's anger over the latest one. Though the Government and the Communists at last had something in common—disgust over a verdict they considered iniquitous—much public opinion expressed shock at the Tribunal's sudden disappearance. To these sentiments President de Gaulle replied on May 30, that "despite the fluctuations which the events of the past week have followed, the effects of which public opinion may have felt, the line laid down with respect to Algerian policy is and will be maintained."

The first step toward maintaining this line in the judicial realm was taken at the same meeting of the Council of Ministers. A new tribunal was created by the *ordonnance* of June 1, 1962. This so-called Court of Military Justice was given essentially the same jurisdiction as the defunct High Military Tribunal. But its membership was wholly different in character: five officers and five noncommissioned officers, none necessarily of previous legal experience. Yet like those of the High Military Tribunal, the verdicts of this new court were to be final. No appeal was to be allowed except to the mercy of the President himself. The question of appeal soon became the key to *l'affaire Canal*.

The Government's stated reason for abolishing the High Military Tribunal and replacing it with the Court of Military Justice fooled no one. In effect the Government said that, with the trial of General Salan, all the big fish of the OAS were deposed. The need for such an important court as the High Military Tribunal was now over. The cases of the lesser fry of subversion, coming up as the police caught them, could be taken care of handily by a court with less prestige. Only a matter of efficiency was involved in substituting one court for the other.

But for the legal profession and for all those who were worried about the authoritarian character of the Fifth Republic, this substitution of courts was a culminating point in a series of official acts, and it directed their attention particularly to the role of the judiciary in de Gaulle's regime.

The establishment of special courts for the trial of cases arising essentially out of sharp differences of political opinion was not new to France. The Revolution had brought about a substantial revamping of the law to bring it into line with the ordinary citizens' outlook rather than that of the monarchy and the privileged classes. Revolutionary legality was substituted for the *justice retenue* at the disposal of the royalty and the lawyers' justice at the disposal of the *Parlements* composed of the notables in the big towns. Yet the Revolutionaries' experiences from 1789 to 1815 suggested that law cannot be created out of whole cloth without reference to the definitions of rights provided by earlier law and still claim general obedience.

The theory according to which law requires only the sanction of the State through its police and its courts to effect obedience became especially attractive in French politics because of the rapid shift in forms of government: *régime d'assemblée* succeeding monarchy, military dictatorship succeeding *régime d'assemblée,* constitutional monarchy succeeding military dictatorship, and so on through much of the 19th century. Each of these regimes hoped to use the courts to impose its will on fractious citizens, and to give the authority of law to its own administration. But each in turn discovered that the existing courts, which it had necessarily inherited from the previous regime, had established modes of procedures for dealing with the cases brought before them which often operated to protect the very people the existing regime considered most dangerous to social stability, and sometimes even to its own survival.

The legal history of early 19th century France is consequently marked by the sudden appearance and equally abrupt disappearance of special courts, set up by the regime then in power to persecute its political enemies. In spite of the Revolution, or perhaps, rather because of the way it finally worked its way out, the institution of a "loyal opposition" never took root: distinctions between opposition and subversion were too fine to become the basis of stable institutions, and those who "opposed" the existing regime might, if they did so with effective publicity, find themselves before some bench of judges especially selected for the purpose, to answer for their temerity.

French experience with these "political" courts led eventually to a general disgust for them. By the time the Third Republic was set up in 1875, virtually all shades of political opinion agreed on one thing: that the use of political courts must be kept to a minimum and that "political crimes" must either be defined in terms of the ordinary criminal code and tried before the ordinary criminal courts or not be considered crimes at all. The only political court provided for under the Third Republic was Parliament itself, authorized to try crimes of high treason of which members of the Government were accused.

The coming of the Second World War brought the first derogation in principle from these rules. A decree of July 29, 1939, empowered military courts, which previously had tried only members of the armed services according to the Code of Military Justice, to sit in judgment of civilians accused of crimes against the so-called "external security of the State" in times of peace, as well as in war.

The criminal code had always distinguished between internal and external security of the State, and this distinction now became important from the procedural point of view. The external security of the State involved such matters as the sale of information and military secrets, the distribution of enemy propaganda, dealing with enemy agents, and so on. Internal security, on the other hand, concerned such matters as trying to get members of the armed services to disobey their officers, inciting French citizens to arm themselves against one another or against State authorities, and so on. Since the customary procedures in the ordinary courts went much further in protecting the interest of the defendant than did those of the military courts, it became a matter of importance whether the accused had to answer for his acts before the former or the latter.

The Algerian crisis, beginning in 1954, eventually effected a general shift in jurisdiction from the ordinary courts, first in favor of military tribunals in Algeria, then in France, and finally in favor of special courts such as the High Military Tribunal and the Court of Military Justice. Though this change began with parliamentary approval in the form of decree-laws, military disobedience and civilian subversion prompted de Gaulle to strengthen "the institutions of the State" by extending the jurisdiction of special and military courts through executive order.

Beginning in October, 1958, all crimes involving "direct or indirect aid to the rebels in Algeria" were brought under special jurisdiction. And by the executive *ordonnance* of June 4, 1960, which substantially revised the Criminal Code, the distinction between internal and external security of the State was abolished. Two other decrees of 1960 (February 12 and June 3) restricted the "rights of the defense" where "events" in Algeria were involved.

Thus, the "Trial of the Barricades" resulting from the 1960 Algiers uprising took place before a *Tribunal permanent des forces armées,* in spite of the fact that all the defendants were civilians. And we have already seen how the "generals' putsch" of April 1961 led to the establishment of the High Military Tribunal, an act which was formally undertaken by the Government on the basis of the virtually unlimited emergency powers accruing to it, under Article 16 of the Constitution, which de Gaulle invoked on April 24, when the crisis was at its height.

So when this High Military Tribunal received, in the words of Bâtonnier Charpentier, its own death sentence for failing to hand down Salan's death sentence, many segments of the public had already been rendered sensitive to the issues involved.

Legally speaking, these issues fell into four categories, all with the utmost importance to the accused man. First, when was a crime part of the "events in Algeria" and thus subject to a special jurisdiction? Second, in what way would such a crime be brought to the attention of the court—through the traditional procedures involving a magistrate authorized to carry out a complete preliminary inquiry (i.e., by a *juge d'instruction*), and the hearing of witnesses for all sides in the matter, or simply by decree of the Minister of Justice, who was obviously a partisan in the cause? Third, what would be the composition of the bench—professional judges, military officers, or both? And if the latter, of what rank? (Obviously, officers of the highest rank and nearest retirement age would be less subject to political influences than men of lower rank with much of their career still before them.) And finally, what procedures for hearing witnesses, for cross-examination, for appointing defense lawyers, and for lodging appeals to a higher or another court, would be used? [12]

The bench which was to try Canal in September 1962 was notably deficient in all these matters. It was only too obviously born under a cloud. Its personnel was less prestigious than that of the High Military Tribunal it replaced. Under the authority of the Ministry of Armed Forces rather than the Ministry of Justice, its jurisdiction was defined in even broader terms—anything from theft, to breach of promise, to murder—so long as it was an "infraction committed in relation with the events of Algeria." The procedures, both of inquiry and cross-examination were little short of summary: the defendant could be brought to trial within 48 hours of his accusation, while at the time of his accusation he might well have been held by the police incommunicado for any period up to fifteen days. If the accused failed to procure a lawyer, the court would appoint one on the spot, without giving him time to prepare his client's case. The president of the court could order additional hearings to give "greater certainty to the results" or cut them short at his own discretion. He could also exclude the public from the courtroom and forbid the publication of any part or all of the transcript of the trial. Finally, absolutely no appeal was allowed from any verdict the Court might render.[13]

The first president of the new Court was General de Larminat, a loyal personal admirer of General de Gaulle. His suicide at the end of the Court's first month of operation, though probably not due to a struggle of conscience, nevertheless augured poorly for the Court's future. Also, in June, the first actual executions for OAS activities—those of Dovecar and Piegts, who had murdered a French police officer in Algiers—raised new doubts about the validity of the special courts and their diverse verdicts. How could Dovecar and Piegts be executed simply for carrying out orders given them by General Salan? [14] And the fact that General Jouhaud's execution was continually postponed suggested to some that the regime was military at heart, incapable of rendering equal justice.

But who could deny the regime's ability to get things done, even in the realm of law where "due process" governs? On September 2, the *Journal Officiel* contained new revisions of the code of criminal procedure, already revised once in 1959, to circumvent the dilatory measures so often resorted to by lawyers responsible for the defense of OAS activists. The essential change concerned the indictment process, vastly strengthening the authority of the *juge d'instruction* to send the accused before the Court of Assizes (the normal court of first instance in France for all felonies) at his own discretion, and reducing the functions of the *Chambre de mises en accusation*, which had been responsible for putting criminal charges on a formal basis. Thus, the procedures which had first been used by the special courts dealing with crimes relating to the "events of Algeria" were now being generalized to cover all criminal procedures throughout France.

The great French criminal lawyer, *Maître* Garçon, member of the *Académie française*, argued that these new procedures were a "violation of the rights of defense" and in effect reinstituted a system once current under the Second Empire, by virtually discarding a law of 1897.[15] Just as important was the centralization of discretionary power in the hands of a given individual, which put the political authorities in a better position to exercise moral suasion on the *juges d'instruction*.

Public opinion probably would have shifted more against the special courts and legal manipulations of the regime if the OAS had not undertaken its spectacular assassination attempt against President de Gaulle on August 22. On the road to the airport to emplane for Colombey-les-Deux-Eglises, the President was caught in a crossfire from two vehicles parked near an intersection at Petit-Clamart, south of Paris. About 150 rounds were fired, seven of which hit the Presidential vehicle. Of these seven, one passed within a few inches of the President's head.

While reprobation of the attempt was expressed from nearly every side, Petit-Clamart raised once more the paradoxical character of the regime. With public anxiety about the future of the regime at a new high, General de Gaulle took up a revision of the Constitution which had first been rumored in April. His plan was to institute direct popular election of the President of the Republic, thus replacing the system of indirect election provided for in the 1958 Constitution. The ostensible purpose of the proposal was to provide an orderly means of succession to give a new President substantial popular backing, should the highest office become vacant through assassination. The "old" political parties immediately raised an outcry. Whatever their differences on other matters, they could agree that any system of election which assured the continuation of "personal" power was anathema to their traditional representative functions.

In this atmosphere of new tensions, Canal's trial began on September 15, before the Court of Military Justice, sitting at Fort-Neuf in Vincennes. It had been combined with that of one of his principal lieutenants, a former law student, Jean-Marie Vincent, accused of taking an active part in bombings in the Paris region. The link between the two men was made clear during the proceedings: Canal paid Vincent his maintenance and provided him and his group of activists with arms, bombs, and ammunition.

Although the differences between the two men were immediately obvious—Canal was calm, precise and clear in his preliminary declaration, while Vincent was excited, passionate, ranting—their basic argument was one that had already been made familiar by a now long line of earlier OAS defendants at other trials. "It would be vain," Canal declared,

> to evoke once again a defeat in comparison with which Dienbienphu was a tragic little game in the countryside . . . No one is interested in that. We undertook a campaign of "legitimate defense." But we were beaten by the very ones who were supposed to save us . . . The magnitude of our disaster gives the measure of the treason.

Canal found the "end of Algeria" comparable to the "extermination of the Warsaw ghetto and the crushing of Hungary."

The principal themes of the defense lawyers revolved around the accuseds' love of Algeria and the fact that the FLN leaders had not only been amnestied but allowed to form a legitimate government. The prosecution charged both Canal and Vincent with undertaking a civil war: "You bring on your country the greatest misfortune which can happen to any nation." It did not demand the death sentence for Vincent because of his youth (22 years). But Canal, like Salan, bore the greatest responsibilities. "The public prosecution (*ministère public*), which is indivisible, asked death for Salan. I ask it for Canal."

The bench, after an hour and a half's deliberation, granted the prosecutor's request: death for Canal, life imprisonment for Vincent.[16] Canal thus became the fifth OAS member condemned to death. Three had already been executed. Jouhaud was still waiting for the results of his lawyer's appeal to the Court of Cassation concerning the procedures used by the High Military Tribunal.

Since a direct appeal to the Court of Cassation was forbidden by the very *ordonnance* establishing the Court of Military Justice, Canal's principal defense lawyer Maître Martin-Martinière decided on a more subtle move. If the legality of the Court of Military Justice's procedures could be questioned as elements of an administrative rather than legislative decision, at least one court (the Council of State), known for its strong interest in individual rights, could get jurisdiction. If it could claim jurisdiction, it might find something improper about the Court of Military Justice. For although it is an established principle of French law that no legislative act can be challenged on the ground of its constitutionality before any court, it is equally well established that no administrative decision or ruling has the character of a legislative act. All administrative decisions and rulings can be challenged before the Council of State, France's highest administrative tribunal, on the question of their legality. The critical point, then, for Canal was whether the basis of the court which condemned him was legislative or administrative.

That this question could be asked at all suggests that President de Gaulle had been too clever when he replaced the special High Military Tribunal with another court. For the credentials of the High Military Tribunal undoubtedly would have made its verdicts invulnerable to the kind of legal maneuver undertaken on Canal's behalf. Its basis was as good as legislative, because it had been established under Article 16 of the Constitution, which grants the Head of State authority to take any measure which he deems necessary, virtually at his own discretion. Although Parliament does not lose its right to make laws when Article 16 is in force, the executive clearly gains the right to make laws in Parliament's place. Parliament's continuance in session, while Article 16 is in effect, only gives further authority to the measures taken by executive decree, even though the legislators may have no power over them. One of de Gaulle's first acts after the application of Article 16 in April, 1961, had been to set up the High Military Tribunal for the trial of all those connected with the Algerian events. And the High Military Tribunal's duties were extended, again by executive decree, on September 23, 1961, just before de Gaulle terminated his own emergency powers, effective October 1, 1961.

The establishment of the Court of Military Justice, however, could hardly be referred to the President's emergency powers under Article 16. Those had ended eight months previously. The *ordonnance* establishing this special court on June 1, 1962, had to be based on the Law of April 13, 1962, which in turn found its source in the referendum of April 8. The referendum of April 8 had asked the voters to approve all "measures to be taken on the subject of Algeria on the basis of the [Evian Accords]." What more republican basis could an executive decision have than a law passed on the basis of a popular referendum? This, at any rate, was the argument advanced by the Government.

The hope drawn from the apparently bleak prospect facing Canal was a tribute to the subtlety of French legal thinking. Yet more than legal principles were involved. Five conservative senators who opposed the regime and the Algerian settlement promptly associated themselves with Canal's appeal to the Council of State, thus emphasizing the political character of the decision the Council was being asked to make.

As framed by Canal's lawyer, the appeal took the form of three requests. The first asked an affirmation of the Council of State's jurisdiction over the contents of the June 1 *ordonnance,* setting up the Court of Military Justice. The second asked the Council to declare Article 2 of the Law of April 13 unconstitutional because of the broadness and vagueness of its delegation of power from legislative to executive hands. The third asked that the establishment of the Court of Military Justice be declared illegal outside of the delegation of powers so made.

The Plenary Assembly of the Council of State met Friday, October 19, 1962, to hear the arguments.[17] The Council of State's own *Commissaire du Gouvernement,* although expressing his reservations about the character of the Court of Military Justice and its summary procedures, nevertheless concluded against the Council of State's jurisdiction. He argued that the *ordonnance* of June 1, setting up the Court of Military Justice, did fall within the delegation of powers consented to by the referendum of April 8, and the Law of April 13, because of the violent nature of the opposition to the application of the Evian Accords. But the Plenary

Assembly refused to follow his line of argument. It decided late Friday evening against the legality of the procedures, which the Court of Military Justice had used to condemn André Canal. The key passages of the *arrêt* were:

> Considering that it does not result from the hearings, given the extent and the gravity of the attacks which the *ordonnance* in question makes against the general principles of criminal law, especially insofar as concerning the procedure . . . excluding any method of appeal, that the creation of such an exceptional court was necessitated for carrying out the [Evian Accords], the appellants are therefore well founded in maintaining that the said *ordonnance,* which exceeds the limits of the delegation of power consented to by Article 2 of the Law of April 13, 1962, is tainted with illegality (*entachée d'illégalité*) . . .

The Government was not long in replying. Saturday afternoon, less than fifteen hours after the Council of State had handed down its decision, the Prime Minister issued the following communiqué:

> The Government takes as abnormal, to say the least, the jurisprudence such a decision would tend to establish, substituting the decision of the administrative judge in place of the rights of the constitutional authorities, created by universal suffrage, in a realm which engages their fundamental responsibility and even the very existence of the nation.
>
> The Government, responsible for public order, for the defense of republican institutions and the safety of the citizenry, considers that such decisions would necessarily constitute an encouragement to the forces of subversion and to further attempts.
>
> It goes without saying that the Government will continue to pursue and to strike down the authors of criminal plots directed against the State and against persons.

What then should have been the consequences of the Council of State's decision? For the legal profession the proper response of the Government should have been an appeal by the Public Prosecutor, acting on order of the Minister of Justice, to the Court of Cassation's criminal law section asking, in the interests of the law, for a decision annulling Canal's condemnation. Such an appeal could now be lodged by the defendant himself. Among informed legal opinion it was thought a matter of good taste as well as good politics for the public authorities to show respect for the

Council of State's decision. But President de Gaulle had other plans.

In legal theory the Council of State's decision in Canal's case was binding on all governmental authorities.[18] But Fouchet had announced that the Government considered the decision to be without value, implying that the Government did not expect to be bound by it in any way. The Government's counter-argument against the Council of State's position was based on three distinct propositions: (1) The Council of State has no jurisdiction over judicial matters, i.e., matters affecting the ordinary courts. The Court of Military Justice was an ordinary court, not an administrative body; hence the Council of State had no authority to intervene in Canal's condemnation. (2) The *ordonnance* which created the Court of Military Justice was an expression of what the French call in legal theory an *acte de gouvernement*. According to legal theory, acts of government are not subject to judicial review. (3) The *ordonnance* was an expression of popular sovereignty as shown through the April 8 referendum. Hence, the force behind it is the same force behind any legislative enactment, the popular will, except that in this case the people expressed their will directly in a referendum on the delegation of legislative power rather than indirectly by means of their representatives in Parliament.

Legal doctrine was sufficient to answer the first two contentions. The Council of State did not argue that de Gaulle had no right to establish a special court, or that such a court would have no right to render judgments. The formal right of delegation of power was not at stake, only its nature. By maintaining that this *ordonnance* was administrative and not legislative in character (i.e., it aimed at the execution of the Law of April 13, 1962) the Council of State clearly granted itself jurisdiction.

The Government's second contention was more easily disposed of. An *acte de gouvernement* had been defined for more than a century as a matter concerning either the relations between the executive and the legislative branches or the conduct of foreign policy. By no stretch of words could the question of the procedures used by the Court of Military Justice to condemn Canal fall within either of these categories.

The Government's last argument was more political than legal, and thus the most difficult to answer. The legal profession simply maintained that the very terms of the Article 2 of the Law of April 13, 1962, were not so broad as to give the Government authority to do anything at all. In support of this contention, the words of a previous Decree-Law passed by the National Assembly of the Fourth Republic were recalled. This law of "full powers" for Algeria, passed March 16, 1956, gave the then existing Government "the most extensive powers to take all exceptional measures dictated by the circumstances. . . ." In comparison, the wording of Article 2 of the Law of April 13, 1962, was restrictive.

Hence the basic question which the Council of State posed was: admitting that a special court could properly exist in the special circumstances of the time, could such a special court be authorized to follow procedures at variance with the "general principles" of the criminal law. Some derogation from these principles being admitted, how much was legal? What kind of proportion between the special difficulties of the period and the special executive acts designed to surmount them must be maintained? On this vital question, the Council of State answered in effect only that a proper proportion had not been maintained in Canal's case without giving any clue as to what a proper proportion might be.[19] Thus the Canal decision told the Government in effect that it had gone too far, but did not indicate what kind of court operating under which procedures would have been acceptable. In Canal's case, at any rate, the absence of procedures for appeal was clearly the major element in the decision, although the absence of civil magistrates on the Court of Military Justice added weight.

For Canal's lawyers, the immediate problem was to make sure that their client would not be executed before other agencies administering justice could become involved. For them, "it went without saying" that Canal's condemnation had been voided by the Council of State's decision, but to make sure, they had him sign an appeal to the Court of Cassation, asking it to annul the death sentence and release Canal from detention until a new arraignment before a legitimate court was effected. In French law an appeal to the Court of Cassation automatically suspends execution of the lower court's judgment. Canal's lawyers apparently suspected that the Council of State's decision alone was insufficient to protect their client, after the Government had announced that it regarded the matter as "abnormal" and "without value."

Their suspicion was based on more than the Government's expressed reservations, for the Canal decision by the Council of State was the second within the month unfavorable to a Government policy. In fact, October 1962 was a bad month for the regime.

Its difficulties began with the unfavorable advisory opinions of the Council of State and the Constitutional Council on the use of the referendum, under Article 11, for constitutional amendment, to provide for direct election of the President by the people. Then on October 2, Gaston Monnerville, longtime spokesman of the "former political parties" and articulate political foe of de Gaulle's regime, was re-elected unanimously to the presidency of the Senate. (The 29 UNR Senators abstained.) On October 5, the National Assembly voted censure of the Government, the first such vote successfully carried since the beginning of the regime. The debate before the vote was sharp. It recalled the almost forgotten fevers of the *Palais Bourbon* during a ministerial crisis under the Fourth Republic.

In spite of the passion in the National Assembly over the issues, the referendum campaign bored the country as a whole. The rather defensive position of the regime's spokesmen was hardly strengthened by the Council of State's Canal decision on October 19, or by a surprise strike of journalists working for the State radio and television services the day before. The strike was motivated by criticism of "the abusive use, for the purposes of political propaganda, of a film strip prepared by a colleague."

Nevertheless, despite the opposition of all the traditional parties, the entire press, and most other organized groups, de Gaulle won the referendum by issuing a threat to resign if he did not receive a solid majority. His majority of 62 percent of the ballots was the smallest in any referendum since his return to power, and for the first time he won the votes of fewer than half (46%) of the registered voters.[20]

The fortunes of the regime changed for the better in November. In that month's parliamentary elections the Gaullists, for the first time in the history of Republican France, won a one-party majority in the lower house. The Communists and others on the Left did fairly well too; the former increased their seats from 10 to 41, while the SFIO gained 24. But the election was an almost unmitigated disaster for the center parties. The MRP lost 20 seats, and the Independents fell from 106 to 28. The far Right simply ceased to exist in Parliament altogether, losing all of its 12 seats.

The Gaullist majority in the lower house meant that the President could use Parliament instead of the referendum to effect constitutional changes. The first fruit of the Government's realization of this new state of affairs was the bill for the Court for State Security. It was sent to Parliament, in special session, under the parliamentary rules governing emergency projects. The chamber's Committee on Constitutional Laws examined the bill in late December and it was placed on the agenda of the chamber for debate January 3 and 4, 1963.

Some thought they saw its purpose clearly enough: having diverted the armed forces through illusions of atomic grandeur and having gotten control of the legislature through an absolute majority, the President next wanted permanently to undermine the independence of the judiciary in political trials.

The approach to this judicial re-organization was not unlike that which he had already taken with respect to the legislature. The 1958 Constitution gave the Government complete control over the way the legislators spent their time and the subject matter of their debates. The November 1962 elections gave the Government a more or less permanent majority of the people's representatives. In this dual control over subject matter and personnel, the President saw the key to the successful execution of his policies. Perhaps not surprisingly, he attempted to assume the same kinds of control over the judicial system, at least in that restricted area of "political crimes" which he believed of vital importance to the Fifth Republic.

To this end the Government's project for the Court for State Security was contained in two bills. The first defined in general terms the extent of "political crimes" in a manner the regime thought desirable for its own defense, and the second put the trial of these political crimes in the hands of yet another special court, the procedures of which were set forth in the bill itself, but the personnel of which would be chosen by executive decree every year. Under the parliamentary rules governing bills submitted *en urgence,* debate on all other matters ceased immediately, in order that full attention of the legislature could be given during the two days which the Government was willing to allot to the subject in the lower house.

These bills revived in the opposition parties all the bitterness they had felt earlier about the means if not the ends of the Fifth Republic. And though there were now no representatives of *Algérie française* in the *Palais Bourbon,* the parties on the Left were there to raise the kind of legal issues which had previously been the main stock in trade of the Rightists. Even within the UNR-UDT majority itself there appeared doubts about the propriety of the Government's proposals.

But the legislature, with its assured Gaullist majority, could not now effectively block the President's plans. By means of this majority the Parliament was committed in advance to support whatever the Government wanted. It might express opposition in words, it might even make small amendments to executive plans, but ultimately it would vote for them, so that the executive's will could indeed become law. If effective opposition was to come at all, it would have to be the work of the courts themselves. But how could this possibly happen? The new proposals were made to destroy the effective opposition of the courts.

The Government did not present its plans to the Parliament in this light, of course. On the contrary, its *exposé de motifs* made the proposals for a new court sound eminently reasonable and even liberal, at least in comparison to previous proposals. The report of the chamber's Committee on Constitutional Laws retained this same favorable flavor.

According to the *rapporteur,* Monsieur de Grailly, France had never handled political crimes with either consistency or effectiveness.[21] Each succeeding regime had set up some special court for political purposes, but none had ever succeeded in creating a body of practice and jurisprudence useful to the succeeding regimes. So it was essential that the legislature now perform the fundamental duty of establishing a permanent definition of political crimes and a permanent agency for applying it. Only in this way could the State effectively protect itself and at the same time still give sufficient protection to the rights of the citizens, who were, above all, entitled to escape prosecution for crimes defined *ex post facto* by any Government in power for the sake of its own particular political interest or convenience.

Why were the ordinary courts, applying the ordinary Penal Code, not adequate to suppress political crimes? Because, the Government argued, modern subversion is far more extensive and subtle, far more like a foreign enemy prepared to wage total war, than was subversion in the past. Hence the essential element in suppressing modern subversion successfully is to attack it in its organizational or bureaucratic character. The ordinary courts may have been adequate to deal with bomb-throwing anarchists of the late 19th century. They had had no real organization nor institutional inertia. Their crimes were covered in the *droit commun* of the code under the headings of murder, destruction of property, incitement to riot, and so forth. But the code pertained only to overt acts traditionally defined as criminal, and not to nationwide preparations which could lead to the overthrow of a regime. To repress these activities successfully, it was argued, a single court of nationwide jurisdiction was needed, able to try anyone, anywhere, if his actions looked as if they were part of a conspiracy against the State. Only such a court could apply the law equally everywhere. To accomplish these purposes, the Government proposed several modifications to the Code of Penal Procedure and submitted a bill describing the "composition, the rules of operating, and the procedure of a Court of State Security." These proposals, according to the rapporteur of the bill, dealt with the legal problems of State security in their entirety for the first time in French history.

Then, to humor the deputies, they were told that they were at last going to have a chance to legislate on the subject of the rules of justice themselves, thus fulfilling their basic duties while taking the matter out of the hands of executive discretion, where it had been—how could they forget it?—for some time.

The opposition parties were not mollified by the apparent reasonableness of the Government's proposals. The most concentrated attack on them came from François Mitterrand, a former Minister of Justice under the Fourth Republic and deputy of the *Rassemblement démocratique*.

After reviewing briefly the various courts which the Fifth Republic had used to repress political crimes, he claimed that the present bills were only an attempt by the authorities to escape the embarrassing situation they had created. He quoted Maurice Garçon on the constant modifications which the regime had instituted in the code of penal procedure: "Ordinary criminal procedure is now used only in the case of theft of rabbits." [22]

Does the Court for State Security . . . fulfill the conditions one has a right to expect . . . ? I shall answer without qualification, no . . .

And why? Because, first of all it is an exceptional court, instituted under the pressure of events. It is nothing more than a supplementary agent in the hands of the executive. . . .

It is composed of professional magistrates, you say? Yes. But who appoints them and how are they appointed, if not by Governmental decree? . . .

The Court for State Security does away with military judges in peace time, you say? Then what does the presence of two military officers on the bench beside the two civilian judges mean? What does the clause which says that one of these civilian judges will be replaced by another military officer in cases involving military discipline, spying, and treason mean? What it means is that the military will have a majority on the Court.

Your bill permits two appeals in cassation? But you know as well as I do, *Monsieur le rapporteur,* that the envisaged procedure is very simple, that the Court of Cassation—forgive me for reminding you—is not a judge of facts but of law only. How often will appeals be made then?

If you vote for the Court for State Security, you must be aware that this court will be made up of judges chosen by the Power. . . .

M. Roger Dusseaulx (UNR). That's sophistry!

Mitterrand . . . that it will be organized under the pressure of circumstances, since more than 300 people caught in the collapse of the Court of Military Justice are now waiting to be sent before it; that they will be made subject to summary procedures, that they have been at least fifteen days in the hands of the police, held incommunicado from their families, their lawyers, even from the public prosecutor, . . . that they will have had but 48 hours after their being brought before the *juge d'instruction* to find a lawyer and that the letter they may write to one not having been delivered within that time will find themselves with a court-appointed lawyer . . .

You must further know that in the Court . . . no provision is made for seeking expert opinion, even though the essential point in certain cases will turn upon the analysis of documents, that it is the Government which will ultimately decide, after the arraignment, whether it is convenient to bring the defendant up for judgment, that in emergency all cases will be handled as though they were *in flagrante delicto,* and that the decision as to whether an emergency exists will be made by the President of the Republic. . . . so that none of the rules, these poor rules which continue to exist for the safeguard of the defendant, will any longer be applicable. . . .

What! It won't be an exceptional court . . . when the Minister of Justice . . . exercises the functions of the public prosecutor himself? It won't be an exceptional court . . . when it legitimizes fifteen days *garde à vue* even though M. Michel Debré himself thought four days a dreadful maximum in 1960. . . .

M. André Fanton (UNR). There wasn't any OAS then!

Mitterand. . . . and even though the same political figure declared in 1958: "It is an insult to justice not to bring the accused before the bar within 24 hours after his arrest. . . ."

It isn't an exceptional court . . . when the accused is sent before it by means of a decree from the Minister of Justice instead of the *juge d'instruction?*

Do you know what that means . . . to be sent for judgment by Government decree? Let me enlighten you: "The Council of Ministers can defer before the court the authors, co-authors or accomplices, of all acts, plots, or activities, however defined, the object of which has been of a nature to disturb order, internal peace, public tranquility, international relations or, in a general way, to harm the French people. The president, the vice-president, and twelve judges shall be designated by decree and divided into two sections. The president and the vice-president of the court are chosen among career magistrates on active duty or retired.

I have just read you the text of the Vichy law of September 7, 1941 which created the abdominable Tribunal of State. . . .

The Court of State Security is based on three fundamental innovations. If you don't make up your minds on these three innovations, ladies and gentlemen, you will not be able to vote on the bills submitted here in good conscience.

These three essential innovations, which I shall call fatal, are: article 16—the *garde à vue* and its concomitant strengthening of the police; article 47:—the crime *in flagrante delicto* and its summary procedures; article 49—retroactivity and its terrible fantasies. . . .

Ah! Ladies and gentlemen, to convince you must I trace the path of a suspect in the year of grace 1963?

This suspect—who will point him out? Who will arrest him? Who will interrogate him? Who will hold him incommunicado for two weeks? Who will decree his arraignment? Who will acquit or condemn him? Who will execute or pardon him? *Le Pouvoir,* the police and, I dare say it though I'm not attacking the judges but only defending justice—the Power, its police, and its judges. (Applause

on the *Rassemblement démocratique, Centre démocratique,* Socialist and Communist benches. Protests on the UNR-UDT benches.)

M. Roger Dusseaulx (UNR). They're in the Nation's service!

M. René Laurin (UNR). It's a former Minister of Justice talking
that way. It's a scandal!

Mitterrand. Under this system not only does the innocent person
risk being trapped by the infernal machine . . . but the guilty, instead of being punished as he should be . . . will likely appear as
a victim of arbitrariness . . . Soon we won't be able to distinguish
between the furies of vengeance and the rigors of justice. . . .

Perhaps this is what they call institutionalizing *raison d'Etat?*
But why institutionalize *raison d'Etat?* Hasn't *le Pouvoir* in France
got everything it could want under the Fifth Republic?

It has its Constitution, or rather its manner of interpreting its
Constitution!

M. Pierre Bas (UNR). No! It has the People with it! That's different.

Mitterrand. It has its Government. It has its majority. It has its
referendum.

M. Pierre Lemarchand (UNR). It has the French people with it.
That's what counts!

M. Henri Duvillard (UNR). It has public opinion behind it.

Mitterrand. It has its television! (Laughter and applause on the
Rass. dém. and Socialist benches.)

It has its nuclear striking force!

M. Roger Dusseaulx (UNR). It has its opposition!

Mitterrand. It would like to have its Senate.

M. André Fanton (UNR). You deserted the Senate! [23]

Mitterrand. It has its Europe. Perhaps now, quite simply, it also
wants its justice? After the executive power, the legislative; after the
legislative power, the judicial. I read this remark of a general who
knew whereof he spoke, I mean General Napoléon Bonaparte:
"Great powers die of indigestion." (Laughter and applause on the
same benches.)

Let our consuls look out! It is time the citizens became alarmed!

M. Roger Dusseaulx (UNR). But they're as calm as can be!

M. Pierre Bas (UNR). You are as expert on false alarms as you
are in false attacks! [24]

Mitterrand. "A society," says the Declaration of the Rights of
Man and Citizen, "a society in which the separation of powers is
not defined has no Constitution." Let me add that such a society is
not a Republic either.

The new UNR-UDT majority showed itself, on the whole, to
be unified and obedient. True, the Government did accept some

modifications of its bills and resorted to the *vote blocqué* to prevent others, but the Court for State Security project came out of the lower house much as it had gone in, within the two-day limit set by the executive. Those deputies with reservations about the new Court's procedures could at least console themselves that they were a considerable improvement over those used by the Court of Military Justice, and that at the very least, recourse was to be allowed to the Court of Cassation. Furthermore, had not the Minister of the Interior announced that the career of the OAS was finished, thus implying what nearly everyone wanted to believe —that the new Court for State Security would have virtually nothing to do after it had disposed of the cases pending? [25]

The Senate, however, was less easily mollified than the lower house. It demanded some important modifications of the bill. The most important of these changes consisted in reducing the *garde à vue* to the 48 hours permitted in the regular code of criminal procedures and the removal of all military judges from the bench. This action by the Senate required establishing a conference committee, representing both houses, to draw up a compromise text. For the first time under the rules of the Fifth Republic's Constitution, such a committee managed to reach a compromise on an important subject and the compromise bill was voted by both houses.

What was the final product of this unaccustomed participation between executive and legislature? Superficially, it appeared, that the new Court did go far toward putting the trial of political crimes on a regularized basis. True, the new Court had two military judges; these judges, civilian and military alike, sat for two years only; the role of the Minister of Justice in the prosecution was far more prominent than in the ordinary criminal procedure; and the *garde à vue* was maintained for ten days, and fifteen days under declaration of a "state of emergency" by the President of the Republic. But the civilian judges were at least to be professional magistrates of high rank, and the definition of the crimes for which a man could be sent before the Court were to be more precise than simply their connection with "the Algerian events." [26] In addition, defendants were given four days to get a lawyer instead of two, while any sanctions imposed by the Court on a defense lawyer were delayed until after the actual trial in which they were inflicted, so that no defendant would have to change lawyers in midstream. The Government was obliged to swallow these changes in its bills with more or less good grace.

But, perhaps to show that it had no ill feelings toward the Government, the Assembly also voted a change in Article 49 of the bill, the article which, as the Government had drafted it, gave retroactive legislative validation to the *ordonnance* of June 1, 1962, setting up the Court of Military Justice that had tried and condemned Canal.

The purpose of Article 49 was clear enough: since the Council of State's decision on October 19, the Court of Military Justice and all its works had been consigned to limbo; it was therefore essential, from the point of view of all the parties concerned, to get its status clarified. The whole Court for State Security project thus contained what seemed to many legislators a *quid pro quo* offered by the Government to the legislature: get us off the hook by validating Canal's trial and the Court of Military Justice, and we will reform our practices with respect to exceptional courts and offer you a chance to legislate once and for all on the basic question of political justice and due process.

Such an arrangement was no doubt pleasing even to the most ardent admirers of the Council of State's October decision. In a direct confrontation between the President, backed by an absolute legislative majority with great popular support, and a handful of civil servants in the Council of State, could anyone possibly suppose that victory lay with the latter? Yet, even as the Assembly was debating the Court bills, the occupant of the *Elysée* palace was advising the vice-president of the Council of State, Monsieur Parodi, of his intention to create a special committee of jurists to propose "reforms" in the Council of State.[27] The only apparent way to parry the manifest threat was to have the legislature put itself between the President and the Council of State by validating the former's June 1 *ordonnance* and thus render irrelevant the Council of State's temerity in pulling the rug out from under Canal's prosecution.

In its eagerness to make amends for this temerity the Assembly, upon the suggestion of Monsieur René Capitant, longtime admirer of both General de Gaulle and the law, amended the draft of Article 49, so that it validated all *ordonnances* taken on the basis of Article 2 of the Law of April 13, 1962, and not just the ones of June 1. Certain deputies were outraged by this amendment, seeing no reason why the Assembly should be more "royalist than the king." But the overwhelming majority saw it as a shrewd political move and it was voted 249 to 3. Canal's sentence had, in any case, already been commuted to life imprisonment by President de Gaulle, so few were as concerned about the purity of legal principle at that moment as they were about saving the Council of State from irreparable harm. And the fact that the new Court for State Security was to begin its functions according to law within 40 days of the bills's passage, gave assurance even to the skeptical that Article 49 really *was* retroactive, that validation of the June 1 *ordonnance* and the verdicts of the Court of Military Justice meant only giving a pseudo-official and hasty burial to the whole unsavory business.

Given these sentiments it is not hard to imagine what parliamentary feelings must have been on January 16 when, but a day after passage of Court for State Security bills, the Government made clear its intention to bring the conspirators of the Petit-Clamart attack on President de Gaulle before the Court of Military Justice rather than the Court for State Security. The Government's reasons were clear enough: threats to the President's life must be met by summary measures, if future attacks were to be deterred and public confidence maintained. Summary justice would hardly be possible if the Petit-Clamart group, whose crime had been committed back in August 1962, could now look forward to still another forty days' delay before their case would even be brought into court. Furthermore, in allowing a *recours en cassation,* the procedures of the new court were likely to provide skillful defense lawyers with still new occasions for dragging out their clients' cases.

Use of the Court of Military Justice seemed, to the Government, the obvious way of avoiding such difficulties. Could it not be claimed that such use had been validated by Article 49 of the Law of January 15? It apparently expected that the Petit-Clamart conspirators would be handily disposed of before the official birth of the Court for State Security on February 25, the date marking the final demise of the Court of Military Justice.

But any such expectation was soon dashed by the maneuvers of the defense lawyers before the temporarily resurrected Court of

Military Justice. They freely admitted that they hoped to slow down the trial of their clients long enough to necessitate removal to the unborn Court for State Security. Few doubted the accuseds' guilt; they themselves had already admitted it by trying to justify their attempt on the President's life. The question really involved whether they could benefit from a judicial finding of extenuating circumstances, as had General Salan nine months before. On the first day of the trial at Fort-Vincennes the issue was presented: could the Government have a verdict brought in before midnight on February 25, or would the defendants succeed in having the whole trial, with all the unheard of legal complications such a process would entail, transferred to the Court for State Security? The defense assumed that anything tending toward the latter result would not only gain the possibility of the *recours en cassation* but, just as important, a certain public receptivity to its political views and hence an atmosphere in which the judges would find it very difficult to find guilt without extenuating circumstances.

The first day of the trial, January 28, the defendants failed to appear at all, an absence at which the defense lawyers professed surprise and for which they profusely apologized. The bench was persuaded that an order would not be politically wise, and the lawyers in turn promised their clients' presence the next day. One day was thus lost. On the next, the principal spokesman among the defense lawyers, Maître Tixier-Vignancourt, raised the issue as to whether bringing his client before the Court of Military Justice was appropriate, despite passage of Article 49 in the Law of January 15. Inasmuch as the Government had decreed the appearance of the Petit-Clamart conspirators before the Court of Military Justice on January 16, it had, he argued, done so illegally. This was so, he said, because according to a traditional rule of French law, no new law could be acted upon or carried out until one full day— *un jour franc*—after its promulgation in the *Journal Officiel*. Had the Government respected this rule, it would have had to wait until January 18, before giving official notice of its plan under Article 49.[28]

Thus began the first two of seven distinct legal maneuvers aimed at holding up the trial as long as possible. Of these seven, the most dramatic occurred about a week later when one of the defense lawyers attacked one of the judges personally, by reading

a statement alleging that the judge was more interested in con-
victing than in the truth. The bench responded immediately by
ordering the lawyer's suspension for three years. But the bereft
client demanded the right to have a new lawyer and when this
request was granted, the new lawyer asked seven days suspension
of the trial in order to have the time to become familiar with his
new client's case.

By this time it was clear to all that the trial would hardly be
begun by February 25, to say nothing of terminated. The only
escape from the Government's embarrassment was to go back to
Parliament to ask for an amendment to the Law of January 15,
which would allow the Court of Military Justice to coexist with the
Court for State Security as long as would be necessary to convict
the organizers and participants of the Petit-Clamart attack. A bill
to this effect was introduced under the then customary emergency
procedures on February 7.

The opposition deputies took the occasion to renew their attack
on the Government's legal vagaries. If all agreed that it would be
unthinkable to have the Petit-Clamart defendants transferred to
another court before their trial was completed, they were nevertheless furious with the Government for having taken Article 49 as
a blank check for conducting another trial, rather than as a validation for Canal's verdict as they had intended. For once they
joined together to support an amendment to the Government's
new bill, which would open the *recours en cassation* to anyone convicted by the Court of Military Justice. To prevent such a recourse
was of course the major reason why the Government had revived
the Court of Military Justice on January 16.

Any pretense of good will between antagonists was dropped in
the ensuing debates. The Government flattered itself by saying
that its request to Parliament for a further extension of the Court
of Military Justice only showed how devoted it was to the principles
of democratic politics. And Prime Minister Pompidou pointedly
asked where the opposition's scruples had been when Article 49
had been voted in the first place. He brushed off all protests to the
effect that a majority had then thought of it only as validation of
past activities, not future ones.

Some UNR spokesmen were more direct than their nominal
leader in the Government. They accused the opposition of playing

the OAS' game and of condoning any methods for the overthrow of a regime. They thus re-emphasized the view, often previously urged by de Gaulle himself, that the legitimacy of the Fifth Republic was based wholly on its popular support. Possession of that support made superfluous and hampering any concessions to the more traditional institutions of government. Pompidou, on the other hand, perhaps because of his anomalous position as non-UNR messenger between the Presidential palace and the UNR majority in Parliament, was unwilling to use the plebiscitary theory undiluted. He seemed anxious to show rather that the Government's requested amendment represented a keeping of faith with the legislature. His dilemma was obvious to all, and the opposition groups had no intention of helping him out of it. If he was unwilling to offer any concessions to their demand for a *recours en cassation,* he could hardly expect to have their votes.

The Government was finally obliged to use the UNR majority in the lower house as its ultimate weapon, as the opposition groups, which refused passage of the amendment, concentrated their strength in the Senate. In the words of Senator Motais de Narbonne,

> You may kill an adversary . . . To judge him is something else, and in an old country with secular and traditional institutions like ours, a land of liberty and individual rights, I think it may be less serious in some circumstances to answer one crime with another— political assassination by summary execution—than to mutilate and degrade the judiciary.[29]

The lower house was called upon to vote on the issue again, as the Constitution permitted. By this means the life of that Court was continued until such time as it could hand down a verdict which, as the Government wanted, would be without appeal.

Not surprisingly, public opinion was much less finicky about the legal questions raised than the senators had been. No one doubted the guilt of the defendants.

As the trial in the Court of Military Justice continued, the ceremonial birth of the Court for State Security on February 25, lost much of the legal and political significance its midwives had hoped for. The newspapers devoted far more space to the provocative statements with which Bastien-Thiry assailed his judges at Fort-Vincennes than to the speech of the new court's presiding judge.

With its verdicts on March 4, the Court of Military Justice proved itself the most severe of all the special courts used for the repression of threats against the Fifth Republic. Six of the accused were condemned to death—three in absentia[30]—and eight others were sentenced to various prison terms. But of the three condemned men actually in the hands of the authorities, only one, Bastien-Thiry, was finally executed, thus bestowing upon him the dubious distinction of being the last of the six OAS terrorists actually executed in the whole of the regime's campaign against militant subversion.[31]

With the demise of the Court of Military Justice on March 4, one could say that the *l'affaire Canal* was essentially over but for one more sequence of events. Of course the consequences of such an affair can never be traced in all their ramifications. On the other hand, except for the yet to be revealed executive proposals for reform of the Council of State, which were presumably to make impossible a repetition of the kind of decision it had reached on October 19, the expression *affaire Canal* was about to be dropped from political discourse.

As for reform of the Council of State, we have already noted that President de Gaulle had suggested this on January 4 when the bills proposing establishment of the Court for State Security were being debated in the National Assembly. Perhaps in the President's mind, the idea of reform was set forth largely to induce the legislators to give favorable attention to those bills. In any case, when the committee he had appointed to propose specific changes in the structure of the Council of State made its report public in May, the outcry of those affected, however slight their popular base, was sufficient to prevent substantial ones.

The proposals had aimed at rendering the Council of State more "efficient" in a number of ways. They would have permitted the Government to transfer litigation involving "emergencies" from the regular *section du contentieux* to a group composed of the chairmen of the five branches of the Council. In addition, the reform proposed that upon reaching age sixty, each Councillor of State would have to petition the Government for continuation in his duties until the ordinary retirement age of 65. As it was clear that the vice-chairmen of the various sections were likely to be the oldest members of the Council—were, in fact, very likely to be near the age of sixty—the combined effect of these two proposals was seen as an attempt to get politically hot issues, such as the Canal matter had been, out of the hands of a group of Councillors made relatively independent by their traditional collegiality, and into the hands of another group whose careers could be threatened by the Government.[32] The failure of the Government to push these reforms against the opposition of the Council of State indicated how much the atmosphere of 1963 had moderated from that of 1962.[33] With some justice it could be claimed that by the summer of 1963 the President had gained all he needed, not the least of which was the effective repression of the OAS. Whatever the problems facing his regime from that time forward, and they were obviously many, the threat of military overthrow, of terrorist subversion, and even of political assassination, were largely passed.

The subsequent history of the Court for State Security indicated as much. With some 350 cases on its docket as leftovers from police actions against the OAS in 1962, few of its verdicts caused more than a ripple in public opinion, no doubt due to the fact that they condemned no one to death. The last important trial of an OAS figure before the Court for State Security came in December, 1963, and its importance was more diplomatic than legal so far as most Frenchmen were concerned. The accused was a former French officer, one Antoine Argoud, who had been previously condemned in absentia by a French court, but who had escaped arrest by exiling himself in Germany, there to practice his wiles on the more susceptible French officers stationed there with NATO forces. The means of his delivery into the hands of the French police in Paris remains a mystery to this day. All that is certainly known is that he was found, bound and gagged, in the back of a small truck abandoned in the capital, late in November. Shortly thereafter he was sent before the Court for State Security for his alleged role in the OAS.

The first issue to be settled at the trial was of course whether his departure from Germany was "legal." Clearly the Bonn Government had not authorized his extradition, so his defense lawyer decided to force the considerably embarrassed German Foreign Ministry to take a stand. In international law that stand had to be to ask for Argoud's return to Germany, there to await an official French request for his extradition and German consideration of such a request. Could the French Government, which had admittedly not asked for Argoud's extradition (officially, it had not even known where he was), proceed with his trial in the face of a point of international law and its own campaign to solidify good relations with the Bonn Republic? It could and it did, no doubt hoping to be finished with the OAS. Yet Argoud escaped the death penalty at the hands of the Court for State Security, as had all those previously brought before it. The OAS was at last nothing but a bad memory.

In retrospect one is inclined to think that the extraordinary efforts the Fifth Republic made to suppress the OAS were hardly reflected in the concrete results. Thousands had been arrested, it is true, and hundreds served prison terms. But only six men had been executed, for all the re-ordering of the judicial system. And of those six, not one could have laid claim to having been a political thinker or political leader of even unimportant stature. Their activities and fate once again suggested the "banality of evil" in modern times, the essential mediocrity of those who can be counted on to do the dirtiest work in politics.

CONCLUSIONS

L'affaire Canal exposes the major irony of Charles de Gaulle's rule and the major paradox of the Fifth Republic. The irony springs from the conflict between his wish to rescue the authority of the State from the disrepute into which he believes the parliamentary regime threw it and his attack on the basic institutions of political life with which modern Frenchmen had become most familiar. The paradox follows logically: a nation giving the most obvious external signs of renewed vitality nevertheless appears to be almost wholly dependent on an aged President. Is not an assessment de Gaulle made in his January 15, 1963, press conference, when the chances of assassination were high, still applicable today?

There are some nations, and especially France . . . which are at every moment in danger of sudden death.

Yet *l'affaire Canal* undoubtedly marked what President de Gaulle hoped would be a transitional stage in the life of the Fifth

Republic. The goal of this transitional stage was to have been the close association of the traditional, institutional view of constitutionalism with his own popular legitimacy. Personal power and institutional authority were to be united, each bringing its own unique contributions to the strengthening of the French government. Until the Court for State Security was proposed in January, 1963, with its implications of renewed legality in the handling of "political crimes," the judgment of the leftist newspaper *Libération* came as close as any to characterizing the Fifth Republic:

> This regime was born of a plot. Threatened from time to time by other plots, it draws from them the factors of its survival.

The question before us is whether with the disappearance of the OAS and the overt political crime, the Fifth Republic has modified its means of gathering and exercising power to make allowance for the moderating political atmosphere.

No attempt to answer this question can be made here. The decline in numbers and importance of the cases coming before the Court for State Security since 1964 can hardly be taken as indicating the restoration of authority to the customary judicial systems. It is rather simply a sign that there are no longer any nationwide plots being mounted against the Fifth Republic. Whatever the importance of the re-establishment of relative serenity in judicial proceedings, it is clear that this importance is subordinate to the re-establishment of order among the more characteristic political institutions such as parties, legislature, and executive. In these matters, it may be noted in passing, there is very little evidence of growth and development in institutional structures capable of maintaining the kind of unified authority provisionally established in the Fifth Republic. De Gaulle evidently regards the potential proliferation of centers of authority, which Americans are inclined to accept with some qualification as the characteristic feature of democracy, to be a sufficient threat to public order to warrant checking wherever he is able. This tendency of his hardly reflects an insatiable lust for personal power. It is more likely due to a feeling that the French have really not shown much capacity for governing themselves, nurtured in him, as in many other

Frenchmen, by an elitist tradition in education and in other facets of the social system.

Whatever his personal sentiments may be in this matter of power, there is a longstanding feature of French constitutional law which must also be taken into account. It has been a deep-rooted tradition in this branch of law to make a large place for what French jurists often call *circonstances exceptionnelles*. No doubt the theory and practice of "special circumstances" are a reflection of the relatively troubled political history of the nation. But whatever their origin, it is relatively easy for Frenchmen to look upon the whole of the current regime as a necessary concession to political expediency and therefore not as a model for future political practice.

In this respect the French remain very different from Americans, however little each nationality would give to the other in professing love of liberty. The theme of American constitutionalism was in one sense set forth perfectly by Chief Justice John Marshall in his famous opinion of *McCulloch v. Maryland,* in which he explained the meaning of the "necessary and proper" clause defining the powers of Congress.

> We must never forget [he wrote], that it is a *constitution* we are expounding . . . a constitution intended to endure for ages to come, and consequently, to be adapted to the various *crises* of human affairs.

From Marshall's time to our own, Americans have become fairly accustomed to the idea of constitutional development, of the adaptation of the institutions of government to the unending series of crises which appear to be the lot of contemporary mankind. Not so the French. For them, a constitution is a set of principles and as such must not, indeed cannot, be bent to suit the convenience of this or that ruling group in this or that time. There must admittedly be derogation of those principles for the sake of survival. But few Frenchmen would be inclined to believe political expediency equivalent to constitutional development. The very expression "constitutional development" would seem a contradiction in terms.

So in considering the future of the Fifth Republic, we should take into consideration an attitude on the part of the French that may incline them toward regarding the Fifth Republic, and its wholly remarkable President as necessary responses to a cruel circumstance of history, but not in any way essential to the idea of freedom.

NOTES

1. Francis A. Allen, *The Borderland of Criminal Justice: Essays in Law and Criminology* (University of Chicago Press, 1964), p. 128.

2. *Pied noir,* literally "black foot," a European born in Algeria, especially during the early period of French occupation when, supposedly, they plowed up virgin land in their bare feet.

3. The story is told in *Le Monde,* May 8, 1962.

4. OAS, the Secret Army Organization, terrorists opposing French withdrawal from Algeria.

5. See William G. Andrews, *French Politics and Algeria,* Appleton-Century-Crofts, New York, 1962, pp. 198-200. Also Dorothy Pickles, *Algeria and France,* Praeger, New York, 1963, pp. 32-38.

6. See *L'Année Politique,* 1961, Presses Universitaires de France, Paris, 1962, pp. 13-14, 24-27, 34-36.

7. *Ibid.,* pp. 51-52.

8. *Ibid.,* pp. 651-52.

9. *Ibid.,* pp. 49-60.

10. E.g. see P. Mendès-France, *Le Monde,* Oct. 27, 1962, p. 2.

11. *L'Année Politique,* 1961, pp. 62-69.

12. See "Special Courts in France," *Bull. of the Int. Comm. of Jurists,* The Hague, April 1963, pp. 16-26.

13. See Ord. no. 62-618 of June 1, 1962, *J.O., Administration: Lois, arrêts et décrets,* June 2, 1962, 5346.

14. See the resolutions taken by the French section of the International Commission of Jurists, meeting in Paris, February 10, 1962 in *Newsletter of the International Commission of Jurists,* Geneva, February 1962, p. 6.

15. "Garde à vue et l'inquisition," *Le Monde,* January 11, 1963.

16. See *Le Monde,* Sept. 15 and 16, 1962.

17. Although the Council of State has about 150 members, more than a quarter of these are generally employed in administrative agencies outside the Council for periods of one to two years at a time; and more than half of the remainder are not occupied with the judicial work of the Council. The Plenary Assembly in fact consists of 19 men: the vice-president of the Council, acting as chairman, the two deputy chairmen of the Council's *section du contentieux* (litigation section), the chairmen of the 11 subsections of the *section du contentieux,* and four Councillors representing the advisory branches of the Council. In addition, one other member of the Council takes part

in the hearings and arguments, but not in the formal decision. He is called the *Commissaire du Gouvernement,* but in fact he does not necessarily take the State's case in his argument, nor that of the plaintiff. His job is to state the law as he sees it and he is presumably free from any direct pressures to take one side or the other. The Government must state its case through its own spokesmen, who, of course, need be neither lawyers nor members of the Council of State, but are usually ministers or members of the Government or their agents.

18. The principle is called *autorité de la chose jugée* in French law.

19. In so doing, the administrative judges of the Council of State were adhering to their tradition of laying down only the minimum number of principles necessary to dispose of the present case, in order not to tie their hands in future cases.

20. For a more complete account of the 1962 referendum and elections see William G. Andrews, ed., *European Politics I: The Restless Search,* Van Nostrand, 1966, pp. 92-104.

21. See *Annexe No. 46,* "Exposé des motifs," *J.O., Documents de l'Assemblée Nationale,* 1962-63, pp. 97-98, and *Annexe No. 58, ibid.,* p. 110.

22. The debate is recorded in *J.O., Déb. de l'Assemblée Nationale, session extraordinaire,* séance du 3 janvier 1963: 212ff. Mitterrand's speech is at 219 ff.

23. Mitterrand was a Senator, 1959-62.

24. An allusion to an incident in which Mitterrand claimed he had been victim of an assassination attempt that his political enemies charged he had contrived.

25. *L'Année Politique, 1963,* pp. 10, 39.

26. The original Government bill had extended the proposed Court's jurisdiction to cover all crimes and delicts "of a nature to bring injury to the authority of the State." This wording had been modified in the Assembly's Committee to cover only crimes and delicts committed "in relation to an individual or collective undertaking consisting of, or tending toward, the substitution of an illegal authority for the authority of the State," thus making the question of intent the critical one.

27. *Le Monde,* January 4, 1963: p. 1.

28. *Le Monde,* January 29, 1963.

29. *J.O., Débats Sénat,* February 14, 1963, p. 833.

30. Death sentences passed in absentia (*par contumace*) have invariably been subject to review through re-trial when the accused has been caught. And re-trial has as invariably resulted in reduction of sentence in the case of OAS terrorists.

31. See "Special Courts in France," *Bulletin of the International Commission of Jurists,* The Hague, April 1963, 24-26, for professional comment on the misadventures of the Court of Military Justice in its final weeks.

32. *Le Monde,* May 19, 1963, pp. 1, 9.
33. *L'Année Politique, 1963,* pp. 67-68.

BIBLIOGRAPHY

Documents:
Journal Officiel de la République française, Débats de l'Assemblée.
————, *Documents de l'Assemblée.*
————, *Débats du Sénat.*
————, *Documents du Sénat.*
————, *Administration, Lois, Arrêts, Ordonnances.*

Books:
William G. Andrews, *French Politics and Algeria,* New York, 1962.
I. P. Callison, *Courts of Injustice,* New York, 1956.
La Déclaration du Colonel Bastien-Thiry, Paris, 1963.
Edgar S. Furniss, Jr., *De Gaulle and the French Army,* New York, 1964.
James Meisel, *Military Revolt in France,* Ann Arbor, 1962.
Le Procés de Raoul Salan, compte rendu sténographique, Paris, 1962.
Alexander Werth, *The Strange Case of Pierre Mendès France and the Great Conflict over French North Africa,* London, 1957.

Periodicals:
L'Année Politique, 1961, 1962, 1963, 1964, Paris.
Casamayor, "La Justice vivante," *Esprit,* October, 1962, Paris.
Paul-Marie de la Gorce, "Y a-t-il une justice française?" *France-Observateur,* October 25, 1962, Paris.
Jerome B. King, "Constitutionalism and the Judiciary in France," *Political Science Quarterly,* March 1965, New York.
Victor Silvera, "La réforme du Conseil d'Etat," *Recueil Sirey, 1963* (Chronique) : 51-60, Paris.
Paul Thibaud, "Les atteintes à la sûreté des Français," *Esprit,* 1961.
Georges Vedel, "L'inexpérience constitutionnelle de la France," *La Nef* (nouvelle série no. 6) April-June 1961, Paris.

Newspaper:
Le Monde.

West Germany: The *Spiegel* Affair

by Ronald F. Bunn

BETWEEN 8:30 AND 9:00 P.M., OCTOBER 26, 1962, INVESTIGATORS of the West German Federal Attorney's Office, assisted by *Land* criminal police and the Security Group of the Federal Criminal Office, raided the Hamburg and Bonn offices of the weekly news-magazine *Der Spiegel,* impounded the Hamburg office files and archives, and arrested three members of the staff. *Der Spiegel* publisher Rudolf Augstein, who could not be located that evening, turned himself in the following day. Conrad Ahlers, an associate editor, was vacationing with his wife in Torremolinos, Spain. At 3 A.M., October 27, he and his wife were awakened in their hotel room by Spanish police, provisionally taken into custody, and placed in jail for the rest of the night. The next day he was flown to West Germany and placed under arrest. In the weeks that followed additional arrests were made, including those of Colonel Adolf Wicht of the Federal Intelligence Agency and Colonel Alfred Martin of the Federal Defense Ministry. Altogether eleven suspects were seized and placed in temporary confinement. The Hamburg offices of *Der Spiegel* were placed under police surveillance and for some thirty days federal investigators searched its files and archives. On the morning following the raids, the Federal Attorney's Office announced that the action had been prompted by a strong suspicion that *Der Spiegel* had published state secrets in such a way as to "endanger the security of the Federal Republic as well as the safety and well-being of the German people," primarily in the feature article written by Ahlers for the October 10, 1962, issue of the magazine.

The *Spiegel* Affair was the most sensational political affair of postwar West Germany and one of the most consequential. Within a week following the October 26 raids, Wolfgang Stammberger, one of the five Free Democratic Party (FDP) members of the Adenauer coalition government, offered to resign as Minister of Justice. Shortly thereafter the FDP threatened to withdraw all its members from the cabinet, precipitating a government crisis. The three question periods (November 7 through 9, 1962) in the Bundestag concerning the *Spiegel* action were among the stormiest in the history of the Federal Republic. On the last day of the questioning Franz-Josef Strauss, Federal Defense Minister and chairman of the Bavarian Christian Social Union (CSU), admitted personal involvement in the action by having requested, through the West German military attaché in Madrid, the assistance of the Spanish police in arresting Ahlers. Strauss's admission, coupled with other events in the fast moving crisis, caused a second coalition break between the FDP and the Christian Democrats (CDU/CSU), as the FDP, which had agreed on November 5 to remain in the cabinet, withdrew all five of its members. Facing a rising tide of criticism for his role in the *Spiegel* action, Strauss fought back but eventually resigned his ministerial post and abandoned for the moment whatever aspirations he had to the federal chancellorship. Before the affair had run its course, Chancellor Adenauer fixed a specific time for his own retirement from public office.

This study examines the *Spiegel* Affair in terms of the functioning of the West German political system. The *Spiegel* Affair resulted in certain demands being imposed upon the Bonn system. What were they, why did they arise, and through what techniques were they processed? Attention is largely confined to the affair proper: from its inception on the night of October 26, 1962, to the announcement on December 7, 1962, of the formation of a new CDU/CSU-FDP coalition government. The analysis is premised on the belief that the *Spiegel* Affair, aside from its topical interest, exposed certain stylistic qualities and functional characteristics that are partially institutionalized and may persist for some time to come in the Bonn system.

No event of the magnitude and emotion of the *Spiegel* Affair occurs in a vacuum; it is rooted in the past. Although falling short of providing a neat causal explanation of the atmosphere that surrounded the affair, two factors of the immediate past require attention. One is the unique role which *Der Spiegel* has played in West German politics. The other is the sequence of skirmishes between *Der Spiegel* and Strauss prior to the *Spiegel* Affair.

"THE LOYAL OPPOSITION"

Der Spiegel began appearing regularly in 1947. From the outset the magazine adopted an aggressive style that was distinctive in postwar German journalism. *Der Spiegel*'s persistently critical treatment of policies and personalities of the successive Adenauer governments, its sensational exposés of the occasional Nazi past or corrupt practices of prominent West German officials, and the disappointment in various circles with both the party system and the press community as instruments of criticism, eventually earned it the title "the loyal opposition" in the eyes of its followers. Within five years its circulation grew to 118,000; by 1962, it exceeded a half million copies and its readership extended to five million persons.

Der Spiegel is frequently compared to the American news weekly *Time*. It borrowed from *Time* a format which, while permitting primary attention to political news, appeals to the varied interests of a reasonably sophisticated reader. In an average issue slightly more than half its space is devoted to political news and public affairs; the remaining space is distributed among such diverse categories as sports, business, culture, science, and medicine. Issues periodically contain, in addition, special features such as transcripts of interviews with prominent personalities, condensations of recent and controversial books (in several installments), or reports in depth on topics of particular interest for Germans. *Der Spiegel* stresses the "personal" flavor of the news, developing its reports around the personalities most directly involved in the subject being examined and interspersing its account with direct quotations. To give additional credence to its "inside dopester" approach, *Der Spiegel* takes pride in revealing intimate, and sometimes irrelevant, details about the personalities. Although lapsing into occasional tedium and long-windedness, the style of writing makes a valiant effort to emulate *Times*'s use of the provocative phrase and suggestive aside.

But too much stress on its formal similarities to *Time* blurs the distinctiveness of *Der Spiegel* and the iconoclastic nature of its publisher and staff. Augstein and his associates have sought to fashion the magazine into a type of press organ that they feel has been lacking in Germany in the past: one that can reach a wide audience, and at the same time assume the initiative in bringing to this audience information and views which cannot be found in the daily press. Rejecting the taboos and stuffiness of traditional German journalism, *Der Spiegel* does not simply condense and re-write news accounts which have already been published. Relying heavily on independent sources of information, the magazine has one of the largest dossier collections in Europe and probably the most resourceful staff of reporters in Germany. And success has bred success. Many Germans come to *Der Spiegel* on their own initiative with grievances, complaints, and tips, some of which have led to *Der Spiegel*'s most sensational revelations.

Der Spiegel's jaundiced editorial eye has been cast in many directions over the years, extending beyond the range of the Christian Democrats and fixed as much on certain aspects of the "new" culture in West Germany as on those strands of the past which are construed as factors conditioning the rise to power of the National Socialists. But in its avowed attempt to expose what it perceives to be the imperfections and hypocrisies of policies and personalities closely identified with the political system, *Der Spiegel* has more than once been accused of a reportorial myopia that distorts the facts and culminates in irresponsible attacks. In any event, this assumed function of protesting, of exposing, of acting as the keeper of the German conscience must be assigned considerable weight in any effort to understand the magazine's appeal.

One conclusion that can be drawn from the undoubted impact the magazine has made on the West German reading public is that, however far it may stray at times from acceptable standards of news gathering and reporting, *Der Spiegel* has struck a responsive chord among those West Germans who themselves have rejected certain traditions of the past but are not yet committed to satisfying alternatives. There is a type of political discontent within certain strata of the West German population who find *Der Spiegel* congenial with their desire to criticize and protest the allegedly aloof, interest-group oriented collectivity of personalities and institutions which they cynically refer to as the "Bonn system." [1] Disillusioned by the past, dissatisfied with the present, and uncertain of the future, the more extreme of these uncommitted West Germans find in nonconformity a kind of substitute for any positive political values.

It would be a mistake, however, to explain the magazine's following solely in terms of an ideological vacuum or lack of commitment to positive political values. Without condoning what they regard as *Der Spiegel*'s occasionally malicious and unprincipled methods, many reasonably "committed" and politically satisfied Germans have also given qualified support to the magazine for contributing to a more vigorous and informed political dialogue than may have existed in earlier periods of German history. Moreover, West Germany is not unique in experiencing the type of political dissent to which *Der Spiegel* seems to appeal. With the decline of the old ideological cleavages, premised on economic, class, and religious tensions that have been partially obliterated or blurred in many modernized societies, observers have noted a new wave of dissent, particularly among the intellectuals and younger age groups, against the stifling conformity of an over-consensualized and over-pragmatized political culture. Of special interest in West Germany is the fear of these observers that without adequate outlets for effective participation in the "Bonn system," these dissenting elements may be permanently, if passively, opposed not merely to the government of the day but to the state itself. Added justification for the focus of this study is derived from this line of speculation. During the *Spiegel* Affair did the elements of dissent find the Bonn system largely unresponsive to their complaints?

PRELUDE TO A CRISIS

Although the most spectacular, the *Spiegel* Affair was not the first encounter between *Der Spiegel* and the authorities. As early as 1950 the magazine created a major sensation by reporting that approximately one hundred Bundestag deputies had been bribed for voting to locate the provisional capital of the Federal Republic in Bonn. A special Bundestag committee of inquiry found no evidence to sustain specifically *Der Spiegel*'s accusations, but three members of the Bundestag were charged by the committee with having testified falsely and five deputies ultimately resigned their seats as a result of the committee's findings.

In the years that followed, *Der Spiegel* persisted in publishing news stories which, if sensationally presented, seemed basically well-informed and sparked the political interest of a relatively apathetic and economically preoccupied public. By the late 1950's, Franz-Josef Strauss had emerged as *Der Spiegel*'s prime target of criticism, prompted by both his policy views and his stylistic qualities. Skeptical of Adenauer's policy of armed strength and military alliance with the West as a means of inducing the Soviet government to negotiate the German reunification problem, Augstein and his colleagues became increasingly alarmed by the apparent commitment of Strauss (who became Defense Minister in 1956) to the view that the Bundeswehr must share in atomic weaponry systems. Equally important for an understanding of the anti-Strauss tendency of the magazine was its growing conviction that Strauss lacked personal qualities suitable for high public office in a democratic system. In 1961, as Strauss's remarkable rise to political influence was climaxed with his being selected chairman of the Bavarian CSU—a position which, when coupled with his position as Federal Defense Minister, made him a leading contender for the chancellorship—*Der Spiegel* mobilized its journalistic resources to alert West Germany to the impending danger. Beginning with its cover story of April 5, 1961, *Der Spiegel* ran a series of reports on Strauss, underscoring the magazine's concern.

The Fibag Affair

Der Spiegel's 1961 offensive against Strauss gathered momentum with the May 31 issue. In an article titled "Hans and Franz," the magazine accused Strauss of having recommended to the American authorities the "Fibag" firm (*Finanzbau-Aktiengesellschaft*) for the construction of a $75 million military housing project in West Germany, without properly examining the legal or technical competence of the firm and primarily upon the urging of Bavarian political supporter and personal friend, Dr. Hans E. Kapfinger, publisher of the Passau *Neue Presse*. According to the article, Kapfinger had been promised by the founders of Fibag, a one-fourth share ($30,000) of the original capital stock, simply for his "connections" and "promotional" talents.

For the *Spiegel* charges to produce a major controversy they had to be injected more directly into the mainstream of the political system. This was accomplished by the SPD Bundestag delegation when it submitted on June 15, 1961, a parliamentary question concerning *Der Spiegel*'s charges. Strauss's reply a month later denied any impropriety on his part in the handling of the Fibag matter. Specifically, he claimed that (1) one of the participants in the Fibag consortium, Lothar Schloss, was known to his ministry as one who in the past had done satisfactory construction work; (2) although the American military housing plan was of no immediate concern to the Defense Ministry, the housing facilities might be turned over to the Bundeswehr sometime in the future and for this reason it was his responsibility to ascertain whether the facilities would eventually be useful for German military housing; (3) agencies in his ministry had therefore scrutinized Schloss's plans and specifications and were satisfied that they met also the eventual needs of the Bundeswehr and that the anticipated American financing would be sufficient to implement the construction of the facilities at prevailing costs; (4) except for those presented by Schloss, no plans were submitted to the Defense Ministry for this particular project; and (5) the Defense Minister or his associates did not know of Kapfinger's economic interest, if there was one, in the Fibag firm. Communications between Strauss and Kapfinger concerning the Fibag plan had resulted simply from Kapfinger's inquiring about it.

The flurry of attacks by *Der Spiegel* against Strauss during the spring of 1961, culminating in the Fibag exposé, could only superficially be construed as an attempt by the magazine to harm Strauss's electoral prospects in the forthcoming (September 17, 1961) Bundestag election. Strauss's popularity in Bavaria and that of his party, the CSU, were too strongly grounded to permit *Der Spiegel*'s staff to imagine that the charges would seriously dilute his base of political support. The optimal expectation was that the charges would momentarily decelerate Strauss's advance within the ranks of the Bonn cabinet and surround him with sufficient controversy to make him unacceptable for the "next step," the Foreign Office, in his alleged drive toward the chancellorship.

The Fibag controversy occasionally entered the Bundestag election campaign, but both the FDP and the SPD hesitated to make the charges a central issue. The evidence was inadequately developed for either party to become too heavily committed to *Der Spiegel*'s version and soundings of public opinion did not reveal any substantial electoral mileage to be gained from stressing the matter. Considerations of campaign strategy also warned against focusing on the Fibag Affair. The FDP was particularly reluctant to alienate Strauss, not because it necessarily agreed with Strauss's political style or his policy views but because it needed Strauss in the months ahead. Seeking to pick up support in the elections from normally Christian Democratic and marginal voters who were disenchanted with Adenauer, the FDP campaigned strongly in 1961 on the promise of removing him from the chancellorship. This was to be effected by entering a coalition with the CDU/CSU, but only on the condition that the CDU/CSU propose someone (preferably Ludwig Erhard) other than Adenauer for the chancellorship. Although the FDP was unable to secure this concession from the CDU/CSU when the time came to negotiate on forming the new cabinet, the FDP leadership assumed prior to the election that Strauss might be persuaded to help the FDP dislodge Adenauer by throwing his CSU bloc of votes in favor of Erhard. To attack Strauss during the campaign might therefore jeopardize its strategy during the later coalition negotiations. The SPD was motivated by slightly different reasons. Many SPD members, followers, and Bundestag deputies shared *Der Spiegel*'s skepticism of Strauss's qualifications for public office, but the strategists of the SPD campaign reasoned that the "image" of the SPD as a responsible and constructive alternative to the CDU/CSU required it to emphasize the positive merits of its own program and leaders rather than the negative traits of its opponents. Superimposed upon all these considerations was the sudden shift in August, 1961, of West German public attention to the erection of the Berlin Wall.

Although the Fibag controversy was thus eclipsed by other events in the summer of 1961, *Der Spiegel* renewed and elaborated the Fibag charges in several issues after the Bundestag election. It published documents purporting to show that Strauss had tried to cover up his error and that Kapfinger had said in the presence of Schloss and Braun that he planned to share his profits from the project with Strauss. The magazine complained that the apparent inability to get the truth from the Minister had implications not merely for the personalities involved but for the Bonn system:

If in view of all this "carelessness" [by Strauss] the answer of the Minister to the modest question of the SPD is to be accepted as a full explanation, then there is no longer in this country any effective checks on the majority party, there is no effective public opinion and no system of control over the conduct of the members of the Government from the side of the opposition in parliament.

In keeping with its assumed role as the "real opposition" in West Germany, *Der Spiegel* formulated its own set of questions to which Strauss was asked to respond. Strauss responded on February 4, 1962, by filing a libel suit against the magazine. Undeterred by Strauss's court action, *Der Spiegel* re-asserted on February 21, 1962, its charge that the Minister had acted both improperly and impulsively in the Fibag matter.

The SPD *Fraktion** finally petitioned on March 13, 1962, for the creation of a special parliamentary committee of inquiry for the Fibag Affair. The committee held seven public and five executive meetings, heard thirty witnesses, examined documents from various federal ministries and agencies, and received sworn affidavits and records from the courts in which suits were pending or had been tried in connection with the Fibag charges. It decided that Strauss had committed several "administrative errors" in the handling of the Fibag matter, but that the evidence did not support a conclusion that he was improperly "motivated" or that he had committed an actual "service violation." The report also concluded that Strauss had had no knowledge of the alleged financial interest of Kapfinger in the Fibag matter and that he had answered truthfully the original parliamentary question submitted by the SPD.

The June 20, 1962, report of the Fibag committee was debated eight days later in the Bundestag on an order of business motion.[2] Gustav Heinemann, an SPD member of the committee, complained that contrary to the precedent fixed by eight earlier parliamentary committees of inquiry no written report of the committee had been circulated among the minority party members before being released to the public and that the witnesses before the committee had not been subjected to oaths during their oral testimony. Surprisingly, the FDP *Fraktion* supported an SPD proposal that the committee's life be extended and that it be charged with adhering to more acceptable procedural standards in developing its report. By the narrow margin of 226-224 a motion to that effect carried and the Fibag committee was instructed to re-submit its report

* Parliamentary caucus.

after obtaining relevant additional evidence and providing the
minority the opportunity to express more fully its estimate of the
findings. The vote on the recommittal motion was substantially a
straight party vote, with the FDP and SPD supporting it and the
CDU/CSU opposing it.

Although the second Fibag Committee report was entered in
the public record by August 30, 1962, the summer recess of the
Bundestag delayed a debate on the report. The findings may be
summarized as follows:

> 1. It was impossible to determine with precision whether Kapfinger
> in fact had alluded by name to Strauss when in a conversation on
> April 13, 1960, he mentioned to Schloss and Braun that he would
> have to share his anticipated profits from the American housing
> contract. The SPD joined the majority in voting that in the absence
> of firm evidence to the contrary Strauss could not be charged with
> having had a personal financial stake in the outcome of the Fibag
> deal.

> 2. The majority found that Strauss may have committed "indis-
> cretions" or "errors" in handling certain phases of the Fibag pro-
> posals, but he did not violate an official "service obligation." The
> SPD minority found that Strauss had, in fact, committed a *Dienst-
> pflict* by personally promoting the interests of a private group and
> without official jurisdiction or competence in the matter.

> 3. The majority found that Strauss had answered the SPD *Kleine
> Anfrage* to the "best of his knowledge." The SPD minority found
> that Strauss had lied to the Bundestag, particularly by asserting that
> his ministry had known, prior to the Fibag proposal, of Schloss's
> background as a satisfactory contractor with the Munich *Finanz-
> bauamt*. In fact, the SPD minority claimed Strauss's ministry had
> to phone the Munich office, after the Fibag proposal had been dis-
> cussed, to confirm that Schloss had performed work for it in the
> past.[3]

On October 25, 1962, after debate (one day prior to the *Spiegel*
raids and arrests) on the second Fibag Committee report the
Bundestag accepted the report and dissolved the committee, but
not without heated exchanges between the SPD and the government parties.

The Foertsch Article

In the midst of the Fibag Affair and numerous other 1962 skirmishes between Strauss and *Der Spiegel,* the magazine undertook

a second major inquiry concerning Strauss. This time it focused on his policy views. An article in the October 10, 1962, issue on the recently conducted NATO Fall Exercise (Fallex 62) analyzed the problems confronting NATO in devising an effective strategy in the event of a war initiated in Europe by the Soviet Union. But more than that, the author critically examined Strauss's alleged determination to increase the atomic and nuclear fire power of the Bundeswehr at the expense of conventional power.*

According to the 8,000 word article, Fallex 62 was the first NATO exercise based on the assumption that World War III would start with a major attack in Europe. NATO's units did not halt the advance of the Soviet forces. Most of northern Germany, including Schleswig-Holstein, was occupied within a few days by the enemy. Ten to fifteen million civilians in both the United Kingdom and West Germany were killed as a result of the combined ground and air attacks. "Chaos was indescribable" in West Germany in the forward zones of fighting. Facilities for the care of the retreating civilian population were "completely inadequate." West Germany's nine divisions which represented its contribution to NATO's exercise were ill-equipped, undermanned, and without sufficient numbers of non-commissioned officers. Weapons for the thousands of West German reservists were non-existent. The Bundeswehr received from the NATO inspectors the lowest possible rating on the basis of its performance and degree of readiness: "conditionally prepared for defense" (*Bedingt abwehrbereit*).

Against the backdrop of this rather dramatic and grim presentation, *Der Spiegel* then proceeded to unfold its analysis of the dispute that has prevailed, particularly in the West German Defense Ministry, between those who have stressed the necessity of responding to an attack from the East in such a way as to avoid the escalation of the conflict into a nuclear war and those who see no alternative for the West but to assume that it must respond at the outset with an immediate nuclear retaliation.

The article points out that in negotiating with NATO in 1952, Theodor Blank, who later became West Germany's first Defense Minister, sought to modify the NATO strategy that called for hold-

---

* The article is usually referred to as the Foertsch article because it was signalled by a portrait on that issue's cover of General Friedrich Foertsch, inspector general of the Bundeswehr.

ing a line along the Rhine River. The concession was made to Blank that when West Germany's anticipated contribution of twelve divisions had been realized, the "fall back" strategy would be replaced with a "forward defense" plan that would call for a concerted effort by the West to hold the line at the border separating East Germany from West Germany. In mid-1953, the timetable of West German re-armament scheduled the training and equipping of 500,000 soldiers within four years. West Germany promptly encountered serious shortages of officers, non-commissioned officers, weapons, camps, and training sites. Almost immediately the goals had to be modified: by 1956, 96,000 men; 1957, 270,000; 1959, 500,000.

At this point, according to the article, Franz-Josef Strauss entered the picture. While Minister for Atomic Affairs in the second Adenauer cabinet Strauss opposed Blank's acceptance of a purely conventional fire power for the Bundeswehr. When on October 16, 1956, Strauss became Minister of Defense, he immediately began to promote his concept of a "quality army," equipped with tactical atomic weapons. Strauss's views found support in Washington. The Eisenhower Administration had begun to question the feasibility of fighting a conventional war in Europe. On the other hand, the use of atomic weapons against the Soviet aggressors contained the danger of triggering a nuclear escalation. General Foertsch belonged to a group of high ranking officers who planned the 1959 war games and since January 1, of that year, he had been NATO's Deputy Chief of Staff. "I have warned my colleagues there not to start flinging nuclear weapons about immediately," he is quoted by the author of the Foertsch article, in an apparent suggestion that Foertsch, at that time, also had serious reservations about Strauss's concept of atomic and nuclear retaliation.

The Kennedy Administration initiated a reconsideration of existing NATO strategy. In the fall of 1961 the recommendations went out from Washington that European troop units should not only be brought to full strength but the number of units increased so that local boundary violations could be dealt with without having to resort to atomic or nuclear weapons. The Bonn Government authorized its NATO Ambassador von Walther in January, 1962, to accept this new plan as the "basis for planning," although he cautioned NATO that the particulars would have to be worked out through negotiations. Strauss opposed the Kennedy Administration's renewed emphasis on conventional force in NATO.

Crises over Berlin since 1958, it is argued, revealed the fallacy of Strauss's concept. There the danger of local fighting has been real. It has forced NATO to contemplate military operations which could effectively meet the local conflict without having to resort to nuclear weapons. One plan called for a blockade of the Baltic Sea as soon as the Soviets blockaded West Berlin. But a sanction of this type assumed sufficient conventional forces to enforce it in the event the Soviet Union tried to break out of the blockade. Strauss was not prepared to support militarily such a plan, and in the critical days after August 13, 1961, the day the Wall went up, he spoke in private against energetic action and accused West Berlin Mayor Willy Brandt of "playing with fire."

The Foertsch article contends that Strauss's highly skeptical view of the feasibility of any kind of conventional war in Europe led him to embrace the "pre-emptive attack" strategy, which calls for an immediate and massive nuclear attack on the Soviet Union, even before the Soviet Union resorts to tactical nuclear weapons in the combat areas. Air Force General Kammhuber, who at one time was the Inspector of the West German Air Force, is presented as having urged, with Strauss's endorsement, that the Bundeswehr be equipped with a weapons system that could strike as far east as the Ural Mountains. Strauss and Kammhuber began laying the foundations for their "pre-emptive striking force" through the Starfighter program. Fighter bombers would provide the initial delivery system for the atomic and nuclear bombs. Later the Starfighters would be phased out and replaced by missiles. The Strauss group continued its long-range planning on the basis of the massive retaliation concept, even though the United States government refused to endorse the "pre-emptive strike" plan because it violated the defensive character of the North Atlantic Treaty Organization. NATO, and particularly the United States, assume that the Soviet Union understands clearly that a nuclear war will not be initiated by the West. The battle plan of NATO air units calls for retaliation only after the West has been attacked. This retaliation would aim atomic and nuclear bombs at missile bases, airfields, and above all, at what are regarded as Russia's most vulnerable spots— the long supply routes. A series of responses would follow, each progressively more destructive and exacting increasingly higher tolls from the aggressors. Within these stages of responses, "pauses" would be injected, allowing an opportunity for the aggressor to calculate the alternatives and consider the consequences of continuous fighting. Under extreme conditions a "pause" would be introduced by a single nuclear strike carefully designed to correspond with the circumstances and the apparent earnestness of the aggressor's intent to continue the conflict. Only if this "selective strike" failed would the stage of rapid escalation arrive.

But the "forward defense" plan of NATO assumes that during the initial stages of a conflict with the Soviet Union a stand at the Elbe River requires a substantial contribution in ground forces by West Germany. This contribution is placed at 750,000 troops. To raise, train, equip, and maintain this force, armed with the atomic missiles desired by Strauss, would cost DM 30 billion—DM 10 billion in excess of the amount the Adenauer government had decided it could spend annually on military defense.

The Foertsch article revealed that, short of meeting those expectations, the Defense Ministry was considering three alternatives: (1) an armed force of 580,000 men, costing annually DM 20 billion; (2) 580,000 men with the atomic missiles desired by Strauss, costing annually DM 23 billion; and (3) 500,000 men, including the atomic missiles, at an annual cost of DM 20 billion. The first alternative was favored by one group of officers as being most congenial with NATO's plan. Strauss preferred the third alternative, the least compatible of the three with the views of NATO and the Kennedy Administration for reducing the threat of a nuclear war by re-emphasizing conventional power.

The Foertsch article was published on October 8, 1962, because the issue in which it appeared was placed in circulation two days prior to its cover date (October 10) in accordance with standard procedures. On either October 8 or 9 (the exact date is still unknown), an official of the Federal Attorney's Office in Karlsruhe expressed, in a phone conversation with the Defense Ministry official in Bonn, the suspicion that the Foertsch article contained state secrets. He requested the Defense Ministry to examine the article for security leaks and prepare a formal opinion specifying the items, if any, that seemed to be within the category of classified security information. On October 13 the Defense

Ministry informally confirmed to the Federal Attorney's Office that the article did, indeed, contain "military secrets." On October 19 the formal opinion was transmitted to the federal attorneys. At the request of the Federal Attorney's Office, the examining judge of the Federal High Court (which has original jurisdiction in treason cases) issued on October 23 warrants for the arrest of Ahlers and Augstein and search and seizure orders against the persons, residences, and offices of Ahlers and Augstein, and *Der Spiegel*'s offices, archives, and premises. The notation was added to the court orders that they could be implemented "at nighttime." Three days later the orders were executed.

THE "SPIEGEL" ACTION

In the early evening of October 26, 1962, Erich Fischer, an advertising salesman in Duesseldorf for *Der Spiegel,* had just finished some last minute grocery shopping for his wife when he was accosted by officials of the Security Group of the Federal Criminal Office. The car he was driving bore Hamburg identification letters on its license plates and was registered in the name of *Der Spiegel* publisher Rudolf Augstein. The officials asked Fischer for his driver's permit. Two additional Security Group officials then appeared. One of them showed Fischer a photograph, apparently of the person they were seeking. Unable to identify the person in the photograph, he was instructed to accompany the officials to the nearest police station. Shortly after arriving at the police station, Fischer asked that his wife be told of his whereabouts. When a police officer placed the call, Frau Fischer was requested to describe her husband in order to verify the identity of the man they had in custody. Two hours after his arrest, Fischer was advised that he was free to leave the police station without being told why he had been picked up. An hour after Fischer had been seized, the Security Group office in Bad Godesberg informed the Federal Attorney's Office in Karlsruhe of the Fischer incident and that an error had been committed. Erich Fischer had been mistaken for Rudolf Augstein. The Federal Attorney's Office ordered immediate execution of the "measures." The order went out at approximately 8 P.M.

Under West German law, the Federal Attorney's Office (*Bundesawaltschaft*) is responsible for investigating suspected acts of treason (*Landesverrat*) and, if the investigation warrants it, presenting the charges with supporting evidence to the Federal High Court (*Bundesgerichthof*) for possible adjudication. Federal criminal police may be used to assist federal attorneys in these investigations, but before any arrests or searches are made "proper" notice must be given to the government of the *Land* in which the action is contemplated. The Federal Interior Ministry supervises the Federal Criminal Office, to which the federal police are assigned, and thus has the responsibility for giving proper notice to *Land* governments. According to official sources, the notification prior to the *Spiegel* action was given at approximately 8:30 P.M., October 26, 1962. State Secretary Hölzl, of the Federal Interior Ministry, telephoned his counter-part, Ludwig Adenauer (a nephew of Konrad Adenauer), of the Northrhine-Westphalian *Land* Interior Ministry and told him that "police actions within Northrhine-Westphalia were imminent." Hölzl cautioned that particulars of the actions could not be divulged over the telephone, but that in the morning a full explanation would be transmitted to the Northrhine-Westphalian Interior Ministry via the wires of the police communications system. While Hölzl was phoning Ludwig Adenauer, Ministerial Director Toyka of the Federal Interior Ministry, who had been dispatched earlier to Hamburg, went to the residence of Hamburg Interior Minister (Senator) Helmut Schmidt and informed him of the measures which were about to begin within the jurisdiction of the *Land* of Hamburg. During their conversation, Toyka requested, on behalf of the Federal Prosecutor's Office, the assistance of the Hamburg criminal police in carrying out the raid on the central offices of *Der Spiegel*. Senator Schmidt agreed to issue the necessary instructions and immediately phoned the director of the Hamburg police. The director, however, already knew of the impending action, having been directly informed at 8:40 P.M. by an official of the Federal Criminal Office.

The Bonn Action

The staff of the Bonn bureau of *Der Spiegel* included, among others, Hans Dieter Jaene, an associate editor and director of the Bonn bureau; Hans-Roderich Schneider, a reporter; and Hans Schmelz, a specialist in military and national security policy. At about 8:30 P.M., a representative of the Federal Attorney's Office, accompanied by officials of the Security Group of the Federal Criminal Police, went to the Bonn bureau, which was found locked. Other officials of the Security Group were dispatched to pick up Schneider and Jaene. Schneider was found at his apartment and asked to come to the Bonn bureau. Apparently the bureau had already been under surveillance, for the officials instructed Schneider to bring the "papers" which he had been seen taking with him when he left his office earlier that evening. The "papers" turned out to be newspapers. Jaene was found at about 9 P.M. at his home and was simply advised that an investigator of the Federal Attorney's Office wished to speak to him at the Bonn bureau. At 9:45 P.M., Jaene arrived at the office, where he learned that a search had been authorized by an examining judge of the Federal High Court. The search began at 10 P.M. and "extended over several hours." Jaene was provisionally taken into custody.

Hans Schmelz was enroute to Budapest to interview Hungarian Deputy Premier Gyula Kallai when the October 26th raid was launched. On October 27 an order for his arrest was issued because of his suspected participation in the preparation of the Foertsch article. While he was still absent from West Germany on October 28, his apartment was searched, in the presence of his wife. According to *Der Spiegel*'s version, officials of the Security Group seized a "large number of writings," particularly those which "in any way concerned military matters," including materials about the Weimar Reichswehr and the Röhm putsch of 1934. A private telephone directory belonging to Frau Schmelz and Schmelz's bank records were also seized. On Tuesday evening, October 30, Schmelz phoned from Vienna the Security Group offices in Bad Godesberg for official confirmation that he was the subject of an arrest order. He promptly returned to West Germany and shortly before midnight, October 31, placed himself in custody of the Security Group officials in Bad Godesberg. He reportedly was offered, but declined, political asylum by the Hungarian government.

The Hamburg Action

Since 1951 the central office of *Der Spiegel* had been in the Pressehaus in downtown Hamburg. The Pressehaus housed not only the central office and archives of *Der Spiegel,* but also the editorial offices of the daily newspaper *Hamburger Echo,* the weekly newspaper *Die Zeit,* and the weekly magazine *Der Stern.* *Der Spiegel* leased about 100 rooms in the building, with additional facilities located in the nearby Miramar-Haus. Its Hamburg staff numbered more than 200 persons.

Shortly before the raid on the Hamburg offices, a task force (*Einsatzgruppe*) was organized by the Security Group of the Federal Criminal Office to assist the Federal Attorney's Office. Before proceeding to the Pressehaus, the members of the task force were briefed as to their duties and plan of operation. During the briefing session, according to the official account, particular emphasis was placed on the highly confidential nature of their mission, the rules of procedure which they must observe in carrying out the action, and the necessity of acting in an "absolutely correct" manner from the legal point of view. The plan of operation, devised by the Federal Attorney's Office, stipulated that:

> . . . for the purpose of later examination, everything in the offices of the accused Augstein should be secured in such a way as to prevent any possible obstruction of the investigation. First State Attorney Buback particularly stressed that the task force should immediately remove all persons who happened to be present in the offices to be searched and then place the offices under lock and seal.
>
> The offices of *Spiegel* in the Pressehaus and those also in the new building (Miramar-Haus) would have to be searched in the presence of officers of the publishing company. In doing this, care would have to be taken that none of them in leaving the offices took with him any materials or documents which might have a bearing on the case. After this had been accomplished, the doors of the offices would have to be locked and sealed.[4]

In the document later prepared by legal counsel for *Der Spiegel,* the following observation is made concerning the task force's plan of operation.

> Apparently the Federal Attorney's Office had planned simply to lock and seal the offices without an immediate searching of them. Failing to have anticipated that considerable activity would be going on [in *Spiegel*'s offices] at the time of the raid, they concluded that merely a few officers of the Security Group could do the locking and sealing, without any difficulty. In this matter, as in the case of the whereabouts of Augstein, Ahlers, and Jacobi, the Federal Attorney's Office was poorly informed. On the sixth and seventh floors of the Pressehaus, work was in progress on issue Number 44/

1962. . . . Altogether there were about 60 persons working that evening in the offices.[5]

The task force converged on the Pressehaus at 9 P.M. *Der Spiegel* co-editor Johannes K. Engel, who had just left the Pressehaus and was walking toward his car, was immediately taken into custody and held for 24 hours. On the fifth floor the task force discovered that Augstein had already left for the day. Locating co-editor Claus Jacobi in his office, the officials announced that he was to be placed under provisional arrest. Jacobi was shown the search order issued against the business and editorial offices of *Der Spiegel* and advised to instruct all employees to evacuate immediately. Jacobi demurred on the ground that he was not authorized to make such a decision. Two members of the task force were then assigned to keep Jacobi under surveillance in his office.

Commissioner Schütz, the Security Group official in charge of the task force, instructed two of his men to locate the other entrances to the *Pressehaus* which were not yet guarded, while he and the remaining officers under his command attempted to get the employees to evacuate. Through radio communications, three members of the "flying squad" (*Ueberfallkommando*) of the Hamburg criminal police were asked to assist in clearing the premises. By this time, many of the employees had assembled in one of the main corridors. In the words of the official account, "excited groups gathered together and, using unfortunate expressions, claimed that they were not going to leave the premises. . . . The task force leader urged them to use prudence and reason." When the protestations of the employees continued and grew "threatening," Commissioner Schütz warned them that by their conduct they could incur criminal liability for obstructing the law. "In this manner a type of sit-down strike occurred." [6]

At this point Commissioner Schütz's problem was compounded by the hesitancy of the three "flying squad" Hamburg policemen to cooperate in clearing the premises of all employees. Schütz had informed the gathered employees that, if they continued to refuse to leave voluntarily, he would have them forcibly ejected. He called upon the three Hamburg policemen to help him carry out this threat. The leader of the "flying squad" questioned whether his instructions authorized this type of *Amtshilfe,* or official assistance. A brief conference was held between the Security Group

officials and the "flying squad." Schütz "most emphatically" repeated his request for assistance from the "flying squad" policemen and argued that it was essential to have the premises cleared
of all employees in order to prevent the danger of evidence being
stolen or destroyed. The leader of the "flying squad" policemen
finally agreed to permit his group to render this type of help. By
this time Director Dr. Land of the Hamburg Criminal Police had
arrived with twenty Hamburg criminal police officers, who were
immediately posted throughout the *Spiegel* complex of offices. A
houseplan of the Pressehaus was obtained from one of the house-
masters, and a systematic effort was begun to clear all offices of
employees and to place the offices under lock and seal. By midnight of October 26, most of the *Spiegel* offices in the Pressehaus
and those on the second floor of a neighboring building had been
cleared of employees and sealed. Keys to these offices were placed
in envelopes and deposited with a representative of the Security
Group who was stationed in the porter's room.

Commissioner Schütz and his task force experienced additional
complications in attempting to carry out their plan of operation.
About 9:45 P.M., Jacobi requested that a small staff of employees
be allowed to continue the final phase of work on the next issue of
the magazine; otherwise its scheduled appearance would be jeop-
ardized. Schütz assured Jacobi that it was not their intention to
prevent the publication of future issues of *Der Spiegel*. He tenta-
tively agreed to an arrangement by which a small staff of ten employees, headed by "Chief of Service" Johannes Matthiesen, would
remain in the Pressehaus until the proofs of the next issue were
ready for the press. State Attorney Buback, representing the Federal Attorney's Office in the operation, approved this decision at
10:10 P.M. Final approval came from his superiors in the Federal
Attorney's Office at 2:45 A.M., October 27, but one condition was
attached: Buback was instructed to secure the proofs of the next
issue. The justification for this procedure was officially explained
later in the following terms: "Since the proofs could have a bearing
on the case, it had to be determined whether they contained information related to the Foertsch article and which might be
regarded as evidence for purposes of the investigation."

After some negotiation, Matthiesen permitted the officials to
place the proofs "in his presence, in an envelope which would

be turned over to the examining judge of the Federal High Court for an authoritative decision." The issue was subsequently permitted to go to press and be distributed.

The final work on the issue was completed around 5 A.M., October 27. The premises were evacuated by the remaining employees and placed under lock and seal. In Hamburg, the total office space which was sealed exceeded 30,000 square feet. On October 31, some ninety-two percent of this space was still under police control. By November 12, some twenty-five percent of this space was still sealed off by the authorities.

The search for evidence among the archives, containing one of the most extensive dossier collections in West Germany and consisting of several million separate items, seemed a task much beyond the capacity of the relatively small staff of investigators. A system was improvised by which employees of *Der Spiegel* were allowed to go into certain areas under police control, to use, temporarily, materials for forthcoming issues, although this arrangement was far from satisfactory in the view of *Der Spiegel's* editors. Under this system, some fifty-six specific and written requests, involving some 325 separate items or documents, were approved by the Federal Attorney's Office while the search was in progress.[7] Each temporarily released item was scrutinized by an investigator before it was turned over to *Der Spiegel's* staff and had to be returned promptly after the staff was finished with it. At 8:45 P.M., of November 25, 1962, thirty days after the initiation of the action against *Der Spiegel,* the publishing company finally had free access to all the space originally sealed by the authorities.

Number 44 of *Der Spiegel,* dated October 31, 1962, appeared as scheduled. Virtually completed by the time the October 26 raids occurred, except for editing and proof-reading, it contained no reference to the affair. *Der Spiegel's* staff then went to work, no doubt wholeheartedly, on the story of the *Spiegel* action. Number 45, dated November 7, 1962, featured Rudolf Augstein on the cover and a lead story titled "They Came by Night." Approximately two-thirds of its contents dealt with the raids and initial arrests. In spite of a greatly increased press run, issue Number 45 was quickly sold out. Whatever the ultimate consequences of the action for *Der Spiegel* and its publishers, one result was immediately evident: *Der Spiegel's* weekly circulation made a dramatic jump.

The Arrests

Much of the criticism against the October 26 action centered around certain procedures and the timing of the searches of the Hamburg and Bonn offices. But equally interesting to many of the critics and observers was the scope and circumstances of the arrests which were made during the first few weeks after the raids. In the initial stages of the search and seizure actions, October 26-31, the round-up of persons was confined to those directly concerned with the publishing and editing of the magazine: Rudolf Augstein; co-editors Jacobi and Engel; Conrad Ahlers, author of the Foertsch article and one of the associate editors; Bonn Bureau Director Jaene; and Schmelz of the Bonn Bureau.

Augstein was neither at home nor at his office in the Pressehaus when the investigators launched their raids. The West German press gave extensive treatment to almost all conceivable aspects of the investigation, but in a rather curious oversight failed to account for Augstein's activities immediately prior to and during the Hamburg raid. Augstein had been in the Pressehaus earlier that day. Speculation later suggested that he had been warned in advance that a raid was imminent and fled the Pressehaus shortly before the raid, to put his personal affairs in order before his anticipated arrest. Although it is now known that Augstein and his associates had been secretly informed by Colonel Wicht, of the Federal Intelligence Agency, that an inquiry was under way in the Federal Attorney's Office concerning the Foertsch article, they were not aware of the specific plan to raid the Hamburg and Bonn offices.

Augstein's home was searched in the presence of both his wife and Jahr, a friend and former co-owner of *Der Spiegel*. The search began about 9:30 P.M., October 26. A large number of private papers were taken, including letters written during the war by Augstein and a notebook containing his school themes. Augstein, who was not at home, turned himself in the next day and was kept in continuous police confinement until February 7, 1963.

Co-editor Claus Jacobi, who was placed under arrest on the evening of October 26, accompanied members of the Security Group that night to his home in Kuckels (Holstein), just outside Hamburg. According to *Der Spiegel*:

Around midnight Anneliese Jacobi was awakened by the noise of a passing car. Through the bedroom window she saw several men coming through the garden with a flashlight. Reassured by a familiar whistle signal from her husband, she came to the door. Her husband was accompanied by three criminal investigators. . . . With a glance at the men with her husband, Anneliese Jacobi: "Do you really want me to open the door?" Claus Jacobi: "Don't look so upset, these men can't help it."

The search began upstairs, in the bedroom, guestroom and children's room of the Jacobi house. Frau Jacobi asked her husband: "What is that all about?" Immediately an investigator warned Jacobi: "I must point out to you that nothing is to be said about this."

They raised the mattresses and looked under the beds. They opened the writing desk of Anneliese Jacobi and assembled part of her private mail, they shook books, carefully pulled underwear out of the dresser and just as carefully put it back, even glanced at the toys of the Jacobi children. The children, who were asleep, were transferred by their parents to another room, so that all beds, including the children's, could be searched.

Basement, garage, and the pony stall, even the pony's straw became the object of a police search—nothing was omitted. The search lasted about two hours. By two o'clock [A.M., October 27], a pile of papers had been collected and seemed to be of interest to the investigators—personal letters, old manuscripts, memoranda—and each item was listed on a receipt.

The next time Anneliese Jacobi heard her husband's voice was Sunday morning. He called from a jail in Hamburg and told her he was under arrest.[8]

But of all the arrests arising out of the action against *Der Spiegel,* that of Conrad Ahlers aroused the greatest criticism. The circumstances surrounding his seizure and the procedures employed in bringing him within the jurisdiction of the West German authorities played a decisive role in converting the events of October 26-27, 1962, into a political crisis. An associate editor of *Spiegel* and author of the Foertsch article, Ahlers served from 1952 to 1954 as press officer in the "Blank Office," created in 1952 by the Adenauer Government to conduct studies and negotiations anticipating the re-arming of West Germany. When the Blank Office was superseded in 1955 by the newly formed Federal Defense Ministry, Theodor Blank became West Germany's first defense minister, a post he held until October 1956, when Franz-Josef Strauss assumed the position. After leaving his job as press officer in the Blank Office, Ahlers was briefly associated with the

Frankfurter Rundschau, one of West Germany's largest dailies, generally sympathetic with the views of the Social Democratic Party. From the *Frankfurter Rundschau* he went to *Der Spiegel.* His earlier service in the Blank Office and his professional interest in and writing on national defense matters made him one of West Germany's better informed journalists, with extensive contacts in agencies responsible for security and military policies.

Ahlers began working on the Foertsch article in the late summer of 1962. It was originally scheduled to appear in the issue of September 26, but was postponed until the October 10 issue, to permit a partial revision in light of the results of Fallex 62, which did not take place until September 21.

On October 26, 1962, around 10 P.M., two officials of the Security Group went to Ahlers's Hamburg apartment in order to take him into custody and to search his apartment. At the apartment they found Frau Ahlers's aunt, Fräulein Wildhagen, who was baby-sitter for the Ahlers children while their parents were on vacation in Spain. Fräulein Wildhagen explained to the Security Group officials that Ahlers and his wife had been in Spain since October 20, and were due to return to Hamburg on November 8. She also informed the officials that earlier that day, October 26, Frau Ahlers had phoned from Torremolinos, Spain, to say that she and her husband would probably go to Tangiers on October 27 to visit a former school friend, return to Torremolinos in about three days, and spend the rest of their vacation there before returning to Hamburg.

Whatever the reason for the failure of the authorities to know of Ahlers's departure on October 20 for Spain, this lack of accurate intelligence and planning on the part of the investigators resulted, during the night of October 26, in a series of hasty improvisations that had profound consequences for Franz-Josef Strauss. The Spanish authorities were contacted during the night of October 26 and were requested to take Ahlers into custody, although the extradition agreement between West Germany and Spain did not authorize rendition of persons accused of political crimes, including *Landesverrat.* At approximately 3 A.M., October 27, Ahlers and his wife were awakened in their hotel room in Torremolinos by Spanish police and requested to accompany them to police headquarters in nearby Malaga. Ahlers was kept in confinement until he and his wife were returned to West Germany on a non-stop Lufthansa flight from Madrid to Frankfurt, arriving at the Frankfurt airport on Sunday, October 28. Ahlers was immediately arrested by West German investigators and kept in jail until December 22, 1962. His wife was permitted to proceed to their home on the outskirts of Hamburg.

In the weeks following the October 26 raids, additional arrests were made. Hans Detlev Becker, publication director of *Der Spiegel,* was appointed temporary editor-in-chief shortly after the arrests of the two co-editors. On November 2, 1962, he was taken into provisional custody, along with Colonel Adolf Wicht, a Bundeswehr official on duty with the Federal Intelligence Agency. On November 29, 1962, Colonel Alfred Martin of the Federal Defense Ministry, and Paul Conrad, a West German lobbyist in the Bonn and Consul for the Republic of Tunisia, were seized. Dr. Josef Augstein, brother of *Der Spiegel*'s publisher, was arrested on December 4, 1962.[9] By the end of December, 1962, these four individuals had been released. Eventually statements from the Federal Attorney's Office indicated that the strongest suspicions of treason centered on Rudolf Augstein and Conrad Ahlers for publishing state secrets in the Foertsch article, and on Colonel Martin for having passed classified information to them.

On the morning following the October 26 raids and initial arrests, a spokesman in Karlsruhe, for the Federal Attorney's Office, issued a cryptic statement that the actions and arrests stemmed from "strong suspicion" of "betrayal of country (*Landesverrat*), treasonable falsification, and bribery" on the part of *Der Spiegel*'s publisher and certain of its staff through the publication, particularly in the Foertsch article, of "state secrets in such a manner as to endanger the welfare of the German people and the security of the Federal Republic." [10]

FRAMING THE ISSUES

Complex events defy neat demarcations in time, but we can distinguish roughly two stages, in both time and function, of the *Spiegel* Affair. The *formative* stage lasted approximately two weeks, extending perhaps to November 9, 1962, when the Bundestag ended its three days of debate on the affair. During this stage, the organized "publics" within the West German community framed their responses, projected them into the political arena, and shaped the tone and configurations of the controversy during its later stage. The primary group actors in this stage were elements of the press and the party system, although the role of the intellectual elites and academicians should not be discounted. The *bargaining* stage began shortly after Stammberger offered on November 1 to resign as Minister of Justice, and subsided on November 6 when the Free Democratic Party agreed to remain in the coalition government, and then erupted again in mid-November when the FDP renounced its earlier commitment and withdrew from the cabinet. This stage of the affair was formally closed on December 7 with the formation of a new coalition cabinet. We shall deal with these stages in sequence, first presenting the formative stage and in the subsequent section, the bargaining stage.

Initial Public Reactions, October 27-31, 1962

Not surprisingly, West German press reaction was immediate, massive, and largely critical. *Der Spiegel* was no ordinary publication. Any attempt by the authorities, however discreet and "proper," to restrain the magazine would have immediately captured the public spotlight. By Monday, October 29, the *Spiegel* action was already rivaling the Cuban missile crisis for front page attention in all major West German newspapers. It continued to be the center of press attention for the next few weeks. Probably no single episode in postwar Germany has had so much written about it in so short a span of time in so many newspapers.[11]

But the news-worthiness of the October 26 police action does not explain the significantly hostile editorial reaction of the West German press. In examining this aspect of the press response, we have tried elsewhere to measure through a content analysis the scope and nature of these responses.[12] Based upon a sample of thirty-four of West Germany's best-known and most widely-circulated daily newspapers, our findings showed that by October 31 a clear majority (62%) of them had formulated a "critical" view of the action; only six (18%) of them were editorially "sympathetic" with the authorities; and the remainder (20%) took no definable position.

Specifically, to what did the critical segment of the sample object? Nine elements of the action aroused the most criticism. Taken as a whole, these nine elements suggest that the critical editorial writers were motivated by two primary concerns: (1) procedures in the *Spiegel* action might set precedents jeopardizing the appropriate rights and functions of a free press, and (2) acceptable norms for the investigation of suspected violations of law appeared to have been sacrificed in favor of a discriminatory and "politically inspired" investigation of a magazine that had long been a persistent and enterprising critic of the government.

The rights of a free press were clearly uppermost in the thoughts of many editorial writers in the first few days following the *Spiegel* raids. The staging of the raids and the interrogation of suspects in the dead of night suggested a type of insensitivity, on the part of the public authorities, to the importance of the press in a participatory political system, an insensitivity which certain newspapers argued had broader implications involving the parallel between the timing of the raids and the "midnight" arrests of the Nazi era. The complaint of precensorship, specifically forbidden in Article 5 of the Basic Law, stemmed from reports that the investigators had seized for examination the master proofs of the forthcoming issue of *Der Spiegel*. The impounding and searching of the archival material in the Hamburg central office seemed to challenge the presumed privileged source of information of a free press. The interruptions of future publication schedules, caused by the temporary police occupation of the Hamburg offices and the provisional police monitoring of the internal and external communications systems of the Hamburg offices, were interpreted as a type of economic harassment, intentional or not, that would be financially disastrous for many press media.

But the critical segment of the sample also responded out of an apparent fear that "political" or "personal" considerations conditioned both the substance and the procedure of the investigation. This tendency was apparent by October 31, as the government seemed unable to supply the information needed to allay these fears. The complaint voiced by the greatest percentage of the critical newspapers—that too much time had elapsed between the appearance of the article and the October 26 action—implied the possibility that the investigation may have been partially intended as a retaliation for the magazine's role in the Fibag Affair. Why, the press complained, had there been a delay both in securing the search and seizure warrants (fifteen days from the time the Foertsch article was published) and in executing the warrants (a delay of three days from the time they were issued). Were the raids timed to coincide with the "acquittal" of Strauss by the Bundestag (on October 25) for his role in the Fibag incident? The seizure in Spain of Ahlers suggested collusion by the Spanish and West German authorities, with little regard for the niceties of legal or international practices, particularly when viewed in the context of the extradition agreement between West Germany and Spain, which precluded the rendition of persons accused of political crimes and treason. And, aside from the strictly legal question in the Ahlers incident, there was additional basis for suspecting that officials in Bonn had intervened in such a manner as to call into question the essential motivation of the *Spiegel* investigation. Both the West German Foreign Office and the Federal Attorney's Office denied responsibility for the intervention of the Spanish police in securing Ahlers. By October 31, when it was known that the West German military attaché in Madrid had requested Spanish assistance in locating Ahlers, the critical newspapers no longer discounted the possibility of Strauss's personal involvement in the Ahlers incident.

Aggravating the critical mood of the newspapers were two additional circumstances. The failure of the federal attorneys to bring charges promptly against those within the federal government who may have leaked "military secrets" to *Der Spiegel* strengthened the belief, as time went on, that the investigation was primarily designed to intimidate *Der Spiegel*. Moreover, the confused and contradictory account the press was receiving from the authorities about the various aspects of the investigation compounded the suspicious nature of the whole affair. At best, the official news releases and the statements reflected a poorly coordinated and hastily conceived investigation that bordered on gross incompetence; an even harsher interpretation concluded that the contradictions and omissions in the official news releases hinted at a deliberate attempt to avoid answers to some embarrassing questions. Toward the end of the formative stage, the conviction grew that one person, Franz-Josef Strauss, could solve the riddle posed by these questions and ambiguities. As one writer expressed it, he "smelled a large Bavarian rat."

Only in a qualified sense was there a correlation between the editorial response and political orientation of the newspaper. The "leftist" papers, as contrasted with the "rightist" papers, were more likely to be critical. Thus all of the pro-SPD newspapers in the sample mentioned above were classifiable as critical; the one obviously nationalistic newspaper was sympathetic. Yet between these two poles in the "left-right" continuum, the correlation was less defined. For example, the two pro-business newspapers in the sample were both critical and over one-half of the pro-CDU/CSU newspapers, if not critical, at least refused to defend the *Spiegel* action. And a number of these pro-CDU/CSU newspapers became noticeably critical of the government as the affair progressed. Most significantly, 79 percent of the non-partisan or avowedly independent newspapers took a critical attitude toward the authorities, including such prestigious newspapers as the *Frankfurter Allgemeine Zeitung,* which had generally supported the policies of the Adenauer government.

What a quantitative analysis of the press reactions does not indicate is the tone of the editorial criticisms. A few excerpts will perhaps illustrate the bitterness and intensity that characterized the editorials of many major newspapers.

Frankfurter Rundschau: If now . . . someone knocks on the door at midnight we no longer know whether, at worst, it is only a telegram or a drunk who, staggering home, has come to the wrong door. We must now consider the possibility of its being the political police who under cover of darkness are looking for traitors. If we hear children whimpering because late at night they are disturbed by someone searching their beds for material to be used in prosecuting their parents, if we hear that someone's writings and drafts of articles have been confiscated and taken to the censor, if we hear that the offices of *Der Spiegel* in Hamburg and Bonn have been suddenly invaded by armed police commandos and that colleagues in adjoining offices cannot be reached by phone—if we hear all this we cannot be certain any longer that these are simply reports coming out of Moscow, Prague, Leipzig, or from Berlin in 1944. . . .

Frankfurter Allgemeine Zeitung: The excesses which agitate in this matter and produce distrust . . . are due partially to a plain stupidity, to a clumsiness and coarseness, which a young and still untried democracy as ours ought not to have to bear. . . . What stinks here concerns not only *Der Spiegel,* not only the entire press, but it concerns the whole democratic system in our country, which, without a free press, without universal press freedom, cannot endure.

Hamburger Echo: One may think what he will about *Der Spiegel.* But at the same time the *"Nacht und Nebel"* action has shown to even those reluctant to admit it that laws are needed not only to prevent precensorship but also to protect newspapers, periodicals, radio, and the like against wholesale seizures of their sources of information.

Die Welt: It is of utmost importance to know how the Federal Attorney's Office could effect in Spain the arrest of a German citizen, without apparently a formal request from the federal government. Through the assistance of the Secret Service? Through the Falange, through the Abendländische Academie [a nationalist-conservative organization]? We are being grotesque, but only because the incident is grotesque.

Various press associations and professional journalist groups soon voiced their protests against the *Spiegel* action. As early as October 28, the Hamburg Journalists Association, the Federal Press Conference, the Bonn Correspondents Association, and the Bavarian Journalists Association, either announced their opposition to the methods employed or requested explanations. The German Journalists Association, the Association of German Periodical Publishers, and the International Press Institute in Zurich followed suit, with various expressions of concern.

Other manifestations of public protest were mounting. *Der Spiegel* announced it was receiving wires and letters of sympathy at the rate of 2,000 a day. Student demonstrations, initiated at Hamburg University, quickly spread to Frankfurt, Bonn, West Berlin, Munich, and Freiburg. Academicians wired or wrote various state officials, asking for clarification or repudiation of the methods used in the investigation. More than forty of West Germany's most distinguished writers and artists, in a public statement, deplored the action against *Der Spiegel* and gave additional impetus to the controversy by declaring that "in a time when warfare is outmoded and inconceivable, it is not only the right, it is a moral responsibility, to reveal so-called state secrets."

Initial Response of the SPD

Although the Social Democratic Party had not yet joined a national government in postwar West Germany, it had frequently carried responsibility for governing at the *Land* levels and had steadily improved its national popular vote and its proportion of seats in the Bundestag. In the most recent election (1961) prior to the *Spiegel* Affair, the SPD for the first time in the postwar period broke through the "35% barrier" by polling slightly more than thirty-six percent of the popular vote and securing 190 of the 499 voting seats in the Bundestag.

If the *Spiegel* Affair had erupted just prior to a Bundestag election, the electoral mileage to be gained by the party from exploiting the Government's embarrassment as a result of the controversy might have been maximized. However, the *Spiegel* Affair was not entirely timed to the advantage of the SPD. The next Bundestag election required by the four year limitation fixed in the Basic Law would not occur before 1965. But two important *Landtag* elections were in the offing shortly after the outbreak of the *Spiegel* Affair: in Hesse on November 10, 1962, and in Bavaria on November 25, 1962. Riding a crest of rising electoral support since 1961 in all *Landtag* elections, the SPD leaders could not ignore the implications of the *Spiegel* controversy for these two elections. And, whether the initial response of the SPD was viewed in terms of partisan motives or principled indignation at apparent violations of democratic and constitutional norms, there was never any doubt that the SPD leadership understood that it would have to engage itself in the *Spiegel* Affair.

If the SPD leaders initially reacted indecisively, it was due largely to the complexity of formulating a policy. Aside from the bureaucratic or procedural problem that arises when a major political party must activate quickly its decision processes to formulate a position on a major and unexpected crisis, a number of factors cautioned against too hasty a response. First, the significant press hostility to the *Spiegel* action did not necessarily reflect a correspondingly high degree of public hostility toward the action. Systematic opinion polls had not yet been taken and could not be expected for several weeks, nor could the various student demonstrations and protests from other groups—which were now beginning to occur—be accepted as firm evidence of an overwhelming popular repudiation of the *Spiegel* action. Second, the objective facts about the action were still surrounded with ambiguity. The SPD leadership could not be certain, in spite of extensive newspaper coverage, just what had happened that might properly be exposed to criticism. The SPD had devoted too much attention to cultivating an image of "responsibility" and "moderation" to embrace uncritically the charges being levied against the Government and Strauss by the newspapers. It was especially important, or so the SPD leadership reasoned, that the party not rush headlong into a defense of *Der Spiegel* at the risk of appearing to condone treasonable publication of state secrets. The SPD, in short, did not wish to adopt a course of action that might later be turned against it and give credence to the long-standing accusation by the rightists that the Socialists were insensitive to German national interests. Finally, the well-established *"Legalitätprinzip,"* the principle that criminal investigations are non-political and non-discretionary responsibilities of juridical authorities (examining judges and state attorneys), implied considerable immunity for the investigators from attacks or criticisms by political parties. This principle suggested therefore to the SPD leaders that they (1) clearly distinguish between the "political" and "non-political" agencies involved in the *Spiegel* action and (2) withhold any criticism of the "non-political" agencies and officials until—and only then—the latter were definitely shown to have violated their trust.

The first reactions to the *Spiegel* action were expressed not by the party leadership collectively, but individually by SPD Bundestag deputies. On Saturday, October 27, Fritz Sänger, a leading SPD Bundestag spokesman for the press, lodged a protest by phone with the Federal Attorney's Office that the criminal police and investigators were illegally restricting the freedom of the press by interfering in Hamburg with the efforts of private citizens to contact the *Spiegel* offices. The same day, Herbert Wehner, the controversial deputy chairman of the SPD Bundestag *Fraktion* and former (1927-42) member of the German Communist Party, issued a statement in which he complained of the methods being used in the action and chided the authorities by suggesting that if, as alleged, *Der Spiegel* was guilty of so grave a crime as treason, they should move with equal vigor against the informants within the government. The protests from Sänger and Wehner were immediately taken by a third SPD Bundestag deputy, Ulrich Lohmar, who had served since 1954 as the chief editor of the SPD journal,

Die Neue Gesellschaft. Lohmar called for a prompt meeting of the Bundestag standing committee on cultural policy and journalism, of which he was deputy chairman. Lohmar's suggestion was rejected by the CDU committee chairman, Berthold Martin, on the ground that under the Bundestag rules of procedure such a special meeting could not be called without the initiative of the presiding officer of the Bundestag.

The first official response of the SPD indicated its difficulty in determining specifically the focus of its attack. Four points were stressed in the party statement: (1) The case obviously had implications for freedom of the press and was not simply, as CDU executive secretary Dufhues argued, a matter concerning one organ of the press; (2) All available evidence indicated that the authorities had failed to give proper advance notice to the appropriate *Land* agencies of the use of federal police within their jurisdiction; (3) The extensive search of *Der Spiegel*'s archives appeared to be an illegal search and seizure of material irrelevant to the specific cause of the accusation; and (4) The arrest in Spain of Ahlers required clarification.[13]

The SPD *Land* organizations seized upon the developing dispute between the Hamburg and Northrhine-Westphalia *Land* governments, on the one hand, and the federal government, on the other, with regard to the alleged violation of inter-jurisdictional notice procedures. On October 29, for example, the SPD delegation in the Northrhine-Westphalia *Landtag* moved that the *Land* Interior Minister (Weyer, FDP) report within two days to the *Landtag* Committee for Internal Administration on the background of the police raids conducted on October 26 against the Bonn office of *Der Spiegel.* The issue concerned the presumption expressed in federal legislation that, as a rule, criminal investigations arising under either *Land* or federal law were under the jurisdiction of *Land* authorities. The Federal Criminal Police can only be employed in criminal investigations within a *Land* if the *Land* Interior Minister so requests or if the Federal Interior Minister, for "overriding considerations," so orders. If the Federal Interior Minister, on his own initiative, orders such an investigation, he is obligated to inform the *Land* Interior Minister "without delay." [26] In Hamburg, the appropriate authority, Interior Minister (Senator) Schmidt, was informed about thirty minutes before the police raids on the Hamburg offices of *Der Spiegel*. The Northrhine-Westphalia *Land* Interior Minister was not personally contacted before the Bonn raid. The State Secretary of the Ministry, his subordinate, was contacted a few minutes before the raid began. The procedure used by the Federal Interior Ministry *vis-à-vis* the Northrhine-Westphalia Interior Ministry looked particularly suspicious and politically inspired, since the State Secretary, Ludwig Adenauer, was a member of the CDU while his uninformed superior, Weyer, was an FDP member. It is still unexplained why State Secretary Adenauer failed to get in touch with Weyer immediately.

The difficulties confronting the national SPD in devising the most effective strategy for exploring the many questions about the *Spiegel* Affair were apparent by October 29. On that day, the SPD Presidium announced that the SPD would request an immediate parliamentary investigation focusing on the legality of the methods used in the actions against *Der Spiegel*. This technique raises certain problems, however, several of which had been revealed during the Fibag Affair. A parliamentary inquiry is slow; more decisive than that, it is controlled by the majority coalition. If the FDP and the CDU/CSU remained united, as they had during the production of the first and second reports of the Fibag Committee, an exhaustive inquiry into the *Spiegel* Affair was unlikely. At this point the FDP was expected to act as it had during the Fibag investigation. A parliamentary inquiry presented another problem. Hints were circulating in Bonn that *Der Spiegel*'s informants included members of the SPD Bundestag *Fraktion*. However valid these rumors—and at this point the SPD leadership did not know —the SPD wished to avoid giving the Government the opportunity of diverting attention from its own embarrassment to the possible involvement of SPD deputies in the preparation of the Foertsch article. In any event, the SPD decision to ask for a parliamentary inquiry, using either a special committee or an appropriate standing committee, was soon reversed. Instead, the SPD Bundestag *Fraktion,* upon the urging of *Fraktion* chairman Fritz Erler, announced on November 4 that it would use the question hour technique and hold in abeyance the inquiry committee technique.

Challenge and Response: The FDP

In 1949 the CDU/CSU and the SPD together received 60 percent of the total vote cast in the Bundestag election; by 1957 their combined share of the electorate had grown to 82 percent. Because of this bipolarization tendency, speculation persists that the days of the FDP in the Bundestag are numbered. But the FDP has managed to survive, thanks to the principle of proportionality in the electoral system. Recent polls, supported by the 1965 Bundestag election results, suggest that the FDP's strength may have stabilized at around eight to ten percent of the national electorate. Although in 1961 the party did "abnormally" well, receiving thirteen percent of the votes and 67 seats in the Bundestag, the aggregative character of the CDU/CSU and the efforts of the SPD to develop a broad electoral appeal constantly threaten to submerge the programmatic identity of the FDP. As a result, the Free Democrats have stressed in recent years the *functional* contribution which the party can make as the "third force" in West German politics. It argues that the inner checks and conventional restraints which constitutionalize and limit the power of the majority party in Britain or the United States are not securely anchored in the West German environment. Only through an arrangement in which the FDP can serve as the "balance wheel," as a coalition partner, can restraints and moderation be imposed upon the dominant party and the Government.

For the FDP to implement the third force idea, it must overcome a number of formidable problems. The starting point is to preserve the existing electoral system of proportional representation. Secondly, the FDP must win at least five percent of the popular vote in the Bundestag election to qualify for its proportionate share of the seats. Third, the FDP must frame an electoral appeal that will cut into the votes of the two major parties sufficiently to prevent either party from obtaining an effective majority in the Bundestag. Finally, to strengthen its bargaining power in forming the coalition, the FDP must be sensitive to the electoral appeal of other minor parties and in its electoral strategy attempt to prevent a rival minor party, as an alternative coalition partner, from winning seats in the Bundestag.

The area of maneuverability open to the FDP, in negotiating

the terms of a coalition, is restricted by the probability that in choosing between the two major parties the FDP will have to opt for the Christian Democrats. Although the SPD has, from time to time, formed various *Land* governments with the FDP, the SPD has so far been reluctant to make the kind of concessions to the FDP that would permit an SPD-FDP coalition at the national level. In addition, the dominance of the economic conservatives within the FDP, and the financial dependency of the FDP upon business contributions, make it difficult for the FDP to assist the Socialists toward being the dominant partner in a national government.

The probability that the FDP will have to opt for the CDU/CSU has certain implications for the FDP's electoral and coalition strategy. Why vote for the FDP if, in fact, it merely supplies the additional margin of votes necessary to ratify CDU/CSU proposals? To avoid this "deadly embrace," the FDP must insist upon genuine concessions in both ministerial assignments and policy questions. This paradoxical position, that of maintaining a separate identity within a framework of dependency on the larger coalition party, has more than once erupted into open warfare between the CDU/CSU and the FDP.

The most dramatic example of the uneasy alliance between the FDP and the CDU/CSU, prior to the *Spiegel* Affair, was the "Duesseldorf Revolt" of early 1956 in which the FDP withdrew from the *Land* coalition government in Northrhine-Westphalia and forced the CDU into the opposition by aligning with the SPD in a new government. Although the incident occurred at the *Land* level, the split developed out of dissatisfaction among FDP elements with Adenauer's refusal to relax trade restrictions with Eastern Europe and his decision—which he later reversed—to support the French plan to place the Saar under international control. The breach was widened by Adenauer's endorsement in December, 1955, of an electoral reform which, if effected, would have eliminated the FDP from representation in the Bundestag.

Out of the 1956 Duesseldorf Revolt emerged a new leadership cadre which directed the FDP campaign in the 1957 Bundestag election. These "Young Turks" included Wolfgang Döring, who played a key role in devising the FDP strategy during the *Spiegel* Affair. But as a result of the 1957 election, the FDP was temporarily isolated from the national government, formed out of a coalition of the CDU/CSU, which had for the first time won an absolute majority of the seats, and the relatively insignificant German Party. In formal opposition to the government between 1957 and 1961, the FDP Bundestag *Fraktion* enjoyed greater freedom in criticizing Adenauer's policies, but its third force role was nullified.

During the 1961 Bundestag election campaign, the FDP returned to a third force strategy. Under the chairmanship of Erich Mende, the FDP promised to enter a national coalition with the CDU/CSU, if "appropriate" concessions were made in negotiating the terms of the coalition. One concession was that Konrad Adenauer retire from the chancellorship. The *"ohne Adenauer"* strategy was motivated by a prevailing mood within the FDP that he was too inflexible in his policies toward the East and that, in general, he could not be trusted to abide by any agreement which the CDU/CSU made with the FDP in forming a coalition government. But such a move was also premised on the hope that the FDP could capitalize upon the declining prestige of Adenauer by attracting votes from former CDU/CSU supporters, who, while agreeing with the government's economic policies, were dissatisfied with Adenauer's leadership, particularly in foreign policy. To some extent the FDP campaign strategy succeeded, with an unexpected assist from Adenauer's hesitant reaction to the Berlin Wall crisis of August 1961. Its 1961 resurgence of strength in the Bundestag, plus the elimination both of all other minor parties and of the absolute majority of the CDU/CSU, seemed to have vindicated the FDP's emphasis on the third force notion.

During the protracted negotiations in the fall of 1961 over the formation of a new government, however, Adenauer outmaneuvered the FDP. He quickly isolated the opposition to him within his own party and won the support of the overwhelming majority of his party's *Fraktion* for the chancellorship. After complex negotiations, during which both parties made half-hearted overtures to the SPD, the FDP capitulated by accepting Adenauer as his own successor. Adenauer promised, without fixing a precise date, to retire sometime prior to the next (1965) Bundestag election. The CDU/CSU assured the FDP that it would make no effort during the life of the coalition government to modify the principle of proportionality in the system for electing Bundestag deputies.

One must consider the role of the FDP during both the formative and bargaining stages of the *Spiegel* Affair against the background of these events. Although several FDP *Land* organizations immediately complained of the apparently improper administrative procedures in alerting the Hamburg and Northrhine-Westphalia governments of the impending use of federal police to carry out the raids, the national leadership seemed uncertain at the outset about the response it should make to the *Spiegel* investigation. They were not insensitive to the complaints, but they also recognized that as coalition partners in the national government they were not entirely free to criticize the action. The Cuban missile crisis, still potentially dangerous, warned against any unnecessary disruption in the national coalition, and the various doctrinal strands represented within the FDP's leadership group also caused initial disunity in formulating a position. The libertarians were disturbed by apparent violations of individual and press freedoms, but the more conservative elements within the FDP were concerned by possible leaks in the government's security system and did not wish to be cast in the role of defending traitors. Finally, the FDP's leaders, particularly national chairman Erich Mende, were sensitive to criticism that the party was opportunistic and unprincipled. An ill-considered and hasty condemnation of the handling of the investigation might easily be interpreted as irresponsible, designed more to stabilize the FDP's position within the coalition government than to clarify the controversy. The key to the FDP response to the *Spiegel* investigation was provided by Federal Minister of Justice, Wolfgang Stammberger, one of five FDP members of the coalition cabinet.

The relationship between the Federal Attorney's Office and the Federal Ministry of Justice is governed by the general premise that the investigation of suspected violations of federal law is non-discretionary and non-political, immune from binding instructions from the "political" executive, the Government. Thus the Minister of Justice is not responsible for initiating criminal investigations. This role is assigned to the state's attorneys within each *Land,* and to the Federal Attorney's Office in cases of such suspected federal crimes as treason. The public attorneys, in turn, work closely with the examining judges of the appropriate courts to secure the warrants necessary to implement an investigation.

Nevertheless, the Justice Ministry has a quasi-supervisory relationship with the Federal Attorney's Office. The director of the Federal Attorney's Office is appointed by the President of the Federal Republic upon the recommendation of the chancellor, who is advised by the Minister of Justice. The chief federal attorney (*Generalbundesanwalt*) may also be dismissed for legal cause by the President of the Federal Republic, upon the recommendation of the Chancellor and Justice Minister. The Ministry of Justice is authorized to "recommend" to the Federal Attorney's Office the need for a particular investigation, although the final decision to initiate the investigation remains with the attorneys. Finally, the relevant statute explicitly obligates the federal attorneys to inform the Federal Ministry of Justice of investigations that have "a particular public importance."

Minister of Justice Stammberger had gone to Munich on October 26 to address a group of Bavarian lawyers on the need to reform the German criminal code. Saturday morning, while eating breakfast in a Munich hotel, he learned from the newspapers of the police actions against *Der Spiegel* the previous evening. In interviews that day with newspaper reporters, he stressed that he had not been informed in advance of the raids and initial arrests. He added, however, that the investigations were under the sole jurisdiction of the Federal Attorney's Office. Instead of returning promptly to Bonn, he proceeded to Stuttgart. As originally planned, he returned to Bonn on Sunday. The following day he was interviewed by a reporter of the Hesse Broadcasting Network. His responses to the questions confirm the impression that Stammberger still assumed that neither he nor the FDP had any reason to question the procedures used in the investigation:

> *Question:* Has the Federal Attorney's Office received any instructions from you?
> *Stammberger:* No! The Federal Attorney's Office is in no way affected by instructions from me, but rather it has the independent responsibility of determining violations of this type. In this particular case, then, I gave no instructions . . .
> *Question:* There is mention also of active bribery in the charges against *Der Spiegel's* staff. . . . However, one has not heard of any actions yet against officials in the Defense Ministry.

Stammberger: [Because the case is a pending juridical matter] . . .
I am not free to give you any details. But I may say that in any event
all those responsible and guilty will be brought to justice, quite irre-
spective of where or who they are.

Question: . . . In the public media there has been conveyed the
unfortunate impression that this action might be a retaliation by the
Defense Minister against *Der Spiegel*. Could you comment . . .

Stammberger: . . . I believe such an impression is unfounded.
There is . . . a coincidental conjunction between the action, which
was initiated on the authority of juridical decisions, and the termination of the so-called Fibag Affair. But both matters undoubtedly
stand separate from each other.[14]

However, by Tuesday, October 30, both the FDP and Stammberger were beginning to feel the heat generated by the *Spiegel*
action. Press criticism was circulating widely in both West Germany and abroad. Complaints were flowing into Stammberger's
office, including those of his party colleagues in the various *Länder*.

The FDP was clearly faced with a dilemma. How, and to what
extent, could it disassociate itself from the *Spiegel* investigation?
An unexpected answer was provided by Stammberger. From both
his state secretary, Dr. Walter Strauss (unrelated to Franz-Josef
Strauss), and officials in the Federal Attorney's Office, he learned,
on October 30 of several curious circumstances surrounding the
investigation. Walter Strauss had been taken into full confidence
by the planners of the police actions; yet he had not passed on
this information to Stammberger. Stammberger had simply learned
from a letter, dated October 18, that an investigation had been
initiated in the Federal Attorney's Office. The letter, for still unexplained reasons, did not reach Stammberger's desk until October 24. It did not mention the course of action the attorneys
were planning against *Der Spiegel*. Stammberger learned, also on
October 30 that Walter Strauss had been advised by his counter-
part in the Defense Ministry, State Secretary Wolfgang Hopf, to
keep the planned police actions in "strictest confidence." Why had
Stammberger been uninformed about the planned police raids?
Who had authorized State Secretary Hopf to advise State Secretary Strauss? Had Hopf specifically warned Walter Strauss against
informing Minister Stammberger of the planned action? Was
Franz-Josef Strauss the central figure in this "conspiracy of si-

lence?" Of what significance was it that Walter Strauss belonged
to the CDU?

On October 31 Stammberger was prepared to act, with or without support of his party's colleagues. He announced that he would
ask to be released from his ministerial post, unless the Chancellor
supported an effort by him to explore fully the responsibility for
this affront to the authority of the Minister of Justice. Whatever
the legal obligations of the Federal Attorney's Office *vis-à-vis* the
Minister of Justice concerning impending investigations, Stammberger reasoned, a serious transgression had been committed against
him, as minister, by the failure of his state secretary to keep him
informed. With Wolfgang Döring taking the lead in discussions
of the FDP *Fraktion,* Erich Mende and others, who had cautioned
against disrupting the coalition, were finally persuaded that the
party could not ignore the implications of the Stammberger episode
for the coalition relationship. They thus decided not only to support Stammberger in his demands but also to extend them: (1)
Stammberger must remain Minister of Justice; (2) Stammberger
must be permitted to conduct an inquiry into the planning of the
Spiegel action and locate the responsibility for Stammberger's being circumvented by his own state secretary; (3) those "directly
responsible" for circumventing Stammberger must be brought to
"account"; and (4) the chancellor must provide assurances that
in the future the coalition party would be more "fully integrated"
in the governmental decision process.

Following the FDP conference, Mende contacted Adenauer, advised him of the FDP position, and requested an immediate meeting between the Chancellor and the FDP leaders. During the meeting, later that day, Stammberger repeated his intention to the
Chancellor to resign, unless he was supported in an attempt to
explore the handling of the *Spiegel* investigation. Mende reminded
the Chancellor of the need for mutual confidence between the
coalition parties. Adenauer asked for time to consider the FDP
demands. The FDP leaders decided that until Adenauer made his
decision no FDP minister should attend the cabinet meeting,
which, having recessed earlier that day, reconvened at 7 P.M.

At the evening session of the cabinet, Adenauer, who had made
no public statement on the *Spiegel* controversy, committed what

must be regarded as a serious tactical error. After indicating to his Christian Democratic colleagues that he anticipated no disruption in the coalition government, he permitted a consideration of the two policy items in which his unrepresented coalition partners were vitally interested: the social welfare proposals (*Sozialpaket*) and the 1963 budget recommendations. Upon hearing of this brazen affront to the FDP, Mende alerted all members of the FDP national committee and FDP Bundestag deputies that a caucus would be held November 2, to decide future FDP strategy in the *Spiegel* Affair.

POLITICAL BARGAINING

By November 2, 1962, Adenauer was faced with a cabinet crisis. The FDP ministers were instructed by the party's leadership to withdraw from the cabinet if its conditions were not met. The collapse of the CDU/CSU-FDP coalition, assuming the FDP did not coalesce with the SPD to replace Adenauer, would deny in the months ahead the certainty of the 67 FDP Bundestag votes, badly needed by Adenauer for majority approval of his government's proposals. After five days of hectic, and sometimes confused political bargaining, a solution seemed to have been found.

An Irrelevant Solution

During the first cabinet crisis a central question of the *Spiegel* Affair was skirted by both the FDP and the CDU/CSU. It concerned, only indirectly, the circumventing of Stammberger and focused on the possibly improper intervention by Franz-Josef Strauss in implementing the raids and arrests, especially of Ahlers in Spain. If, as Adenauer and his advisers argued in their talks with the FDP leaders, the principle of *Legalität* had governed the *Spiegel* investigation, then Strauss had no greater claim than did Stammberger to an independent role in the investigation.

What, so far, had Defense Minister Strauss admitted about his role in the *Spiegel* action? Strauss's first public statement was contained in an interview published in the October 30 edition of the *Abendpost* (Frankfurt). To the question, "Did you or did you not cause this [investigation]?", Strauss replied:

I have other interests than—let me use the vulgar expression—to dirty my own nest, and I can say neither I personally nor my office had absolutely anything to do with the instigation of this action.

The qualifying word, "instigation," should be noted, since the suspicion against Strauss by this time was not so much that he had instigated the investigation, but that he improperly and independently *intervened after* the investigation was under way. Thus Strauss's October 30 statement was not addressed precisely to the central issue. On November 1, Strauss refused to elaborate for reporters on his role in the action, saying that any statement by him might be "construed as a deliberate attempt to influence the course of a juridical matter." However, on November 3, he departed from the no-comment policy by submitting to an interview with the *8-Uhr-Blatt* (Nürnberg). The relevant segment of the interview reads:

8-Uhr-Blatt: It is not important what we do or do not believe. It is a matter of simply getting an answer to the question whether the action against *Der Spiegel* was an act of revenge on your part.

Strauss: It was no revenge on my part. I have had nothing to do with the matter. In the truest sense of these words, nothing to do!

8-Uhr-Blatt: Did you know of it, that this action was planned?

Strauss: When I came back from vacation [on October 16], the Federal Attorney's Office had already requested an opinion from the Defense Ministry whether certain published material in *Der Spiegel* satisfied the condition of treasonable publication. I approved, of course, the complete cooperation of my office, but at the same time decided that two particular experts should be appointed, rather than my ministry generally, to prepare the opinion.

8-Uhr-Blatt: The mere promise of official cooperation, however, might be attributed to you as an act of retaliation against Augstein?

Strauss: I proceeded with this in mind. For this reason I asked State Secretary Hopf to come to me—he is not a party colleague of mine but subscribes to the tenets of another party—and laid the matter before him. I brought to Herr Hopf's attention our precarious situation with these words: If we do nothing, the Ministry will be placed in the position of contributing to the act of treason. If we do something, it will be said that Strauss wanted revenge against Augstein. State Secretary Hopf took the position that regardless of the consequences we could not refuse our official cooperation with the Federal Attorney's Office. We both agreed and decided that the entire *Spiegel* matter would be handled [insofar as the Defense Ministry was involved] by State Secretary Hopf. In this case I therefore assigned to the State Secretary the full powers of the Minister and authorized him to deal in complete freedom with the matter and in making the decisions. If you will, in this instance Herr Hopf was for the moment the head of the ministry.

On November 5, the chancellor's office announced that the FDP-CDU/CSU dispute had been resolved without the need for any changes in cabinet posts. The official communiqué read:

Under the chairmanship of the Federal Chancellor, representatives of the CDU/CSU *Fraktion* and the FDP *Fraktion* met today. They have asked the Federal Minister of Justice to withdraw his resignation offer. The Federal Minister of Justice agreed to this request.

Moreover, the consensus concluded that State Secretary Strauss would be relieved of his duties as State Secretary of the Ministry of Justice. State Secretary Hopf has proposed that he go on an indefinite leave of absence. The Federal Defense Minister has granted this request. The participants were unanimously agreed that particularly because of the present political situation [the Cuban missile crisis] the existing coalition should continue without any changes.

The FDP's conditions for remaining in the cabinet had been partially, but not entirely, fulfilled. One was obviously met: Stammberger would be retained as Justice Minister. The second was implicitly accepted: Stammberger would undertake an inquiry into the conduct of the *Spiegel* investigation. How far he might go, in uncovering the particulars, was left in doubt. Nothing was said about a third condition—that the FDP be more fully integrated in the governmental decision process. Presumably, the FDP felt it had demonstrated over the past few days that it would no longer tolerate the kind of treatment it had received in the *Spiegel* case.

The fourth condition, that "all persons directly responsible" for the circumvention of Stammberger be brought "to account," presented the greatest difficulty. Here the "solution" left unanswered as many questions as it resolved. The release of state secretaries Hopf and Walter Strauss could only be a creditable solution, if, in fact, these two civil servants had acted during the *Spiegel* controversy upon their own initiative in circumventing Stammberger. To many critics this conclusion seemed incredible. Ignoring for the moment the reputation of both Hopf and Walter Strauss as discreet and experienced civil servants, what possible motive could they have had in presuming on their own authority to carry out this intrigue against Stammberger?

The Hopf-Strauss formula was also irrelevant in explaining Ahlers's arrest in Spain. The West German public still did not know who had authoritatively requested the Spanish authorities to arrest Ahlers. Rumors persisted that Franz-Josef Strauss must have initiated the request, since it was reasonably well established that the West German military attaché, upon the instructions of someone, had requested on the night of October 26, that the Spanish police in Madrid assist in locating and returning Ahlers to West Germany. The Ahlers episode was also causing some embarrassment to the Spanish Government. Its version pointed to the Security Group of the West German Federal Criminal Office. In Bonn, spokesmen for the West German government promptly denied that the Federal Criminal Office had initiated the request.

The Options

Why had the FDP accepted the dubious Hopf-Walter Strauss formula in fixing responsibility for the circumvention of Stammberger? The FDP could hardly have wanted to shield Franz-Josef Strauss, at all costs, from further embarrassment. To the contrary, relations between the Defense Minister and the FDP had been strained during the past few days, particularly as a result of the criticisms Strauss was making of the FDP in the Bavarian *Landtag* campaign, which was in progress. The position Hopf had taken provides a partial answer. In meetings with the FDP, he assumed responsibility for short-circuiting Stammberger by acknowledging that he had instructed State Secretary Walter Strauss to keep in "strictest confidence" the impending police raids. Hopf added, however, that it was a misunderstanding if Walter Strauss concluded that Stammberger was also to be excluded from the group entitled to know of the plans. Hopf refused to implicate his own minister, Franz-Josef Strauss. More importantly, the FDP may have reasoned that if the Defense Minister had played an improper role it would be uncovered by Stammberger's inquiry. The tension created by the Cuban crisis and Adenauer's impending trip to Washington, coupled with the lack of firm evidence that Defense Minister Strauss was at fault, possibly persuaded the cautious Erich Mende to urge a quick termination to the cabinet dispute. There still remained, however, the question of the Ahlers arrest. The FDP seemed content to ignore this issue, at least for the moment.

But what if the FDP had rejected the CDU/CSU terms for settling the dispute? What options were available to the FDP? The FDP could have simply withdrawn from the cabinet and, without joining the SPD in an effort to unseat Adenauer, reverted to its 1957-61 role as an independent *Fraktion* in the Bundestag. However, Mende had consistently warned his colleagues of the futility of the FDP's isolating itself in the Bundestag. Excluded from the formulation of cabinet decisions and hopelessly overshadowed in the Bundestag by the SPD as an opposition party, the FDP would jeopardize whatever remaining electoral appeal it had and invalidate its functional importance as a third force in the bipolarizing party system.

Alternatively, the FDP could withdraw from the Adenauer cabinet and then regain its position as a third force by entering a coalition with the SPD. Even if the FDP could overcome the formidable opposition within its own circles to a Socialist dominated coalition, the SPD cancelled this option by deciding on November 5 to refuse to discuss an FDP-SPD coalition and, instead, to utilize parliamentary queries to explore the unanswered questions surrounding the *Spiegel* Affair.

A final option, that of remaining in coalition with the CDU/CSU without Adenauer as chancellor, who seemed to be obstructing any greater concessions to the FDP during this stage, did not present itself. No CDU/CSU faction construed the dispute as essentially involving Adenauer's leadership and none was willing to collaborate with the FDP to displace Adenauer as chancellor.

Questions and Answers: The Bundestag Debate

By November 5 the tentative strategy of the SPD Bundestag *Fraktion* had been decided. It could not accept the CDU/CSU argument that the central issues of the *Spiegel* controversy were juridical, best left to the appropriate courts for eventual determination. Questions concerning precensorship, the prolonged search of *Der Spiegel*'s archives, and the guilt of Augstein and his associates of treasonable publication, the SPD acknowledged, required judicial processing. But the clarification and locating of the responsibility for violations of political norms did not lend themselves to adjudication. Had the *Spiegel* investigation been politically inspired? If so, by whom? Had the seizure of Ahlers, in Spain, been initiated improperly by political, not legal, officers of the West German government? If so, by whom? Had state secretaries Hopf and Walter Strauss deliberately circumvented Justice Minister Stammberger on instructions from a politically accountable official? If so, upon whose instructions? Of the various techniques available to the opposition party in the Bundestag—committee of inquiry, written questions, oral questions, and the question hour—the question hour had the advantage of quickly compelling the Government to answer these questions. Thus on November 5, Dr. Karl Mommer, executive secretary of the SPD Bundestag *Fraktion,* submitted eighteen questions to Bundestag President, Eugen Gerstenmaier, with the request that the Bundestag be convened at the earliest moment to receive them in formal Question Hour. Anticipating that the FDP and the CDU/CSU were about to resolve their coalition dispute, Mommer added that the questions would be pursued regardless of the decision of the FDP about remaining in the cabinet.

The November 7 Question Hour produced little new information that could clarify the major areas of dispute.[15] Why did the Federal Interior Ministry immediately prior to the raids fail to contact the *Land* Interior Minister in Northrhine-Westphalia? Why did it, instead, contact Ludwig Adenauer, state secretary of the *Land* Ministry? Federal Interior Minister Höcherl had no explanation. He simply declared that his ministry "assumed" that State Secretary Adenauer would notify his ministerial superior. Why did State Secretary Walter Strauss fail to inform his superior, Stammberger, of the impending action? Höcherl, reading the answers supplied to him by Stammberger (who had excused himself because of sickness), "did not know." Who had initially placed the phone call to Madrid that led Military Attaché Oster to ask the Spanish police to take Ahlers and his wife into custody? Höcherl ruled out the Justice Ministry, the Federal Attorney's Office, and Interpol. He alluded weakly to an official of the Security Group of the Federal Criminal Office, out of the country at the moment, who "might" supply the information needed for this answer.

If the first day's question period failed to supply answers to key questions, it was nevertheless one of the stormiest sessions in the history of the Bonn Republic. The sensation occurred technically after the Question Hour had ended. From the Question Hour, the agenda moved to a 90 minute reading by Finance Minister Starke of the 1963 budget proposals. Following Starke's report, SPD Deputy Ritzel read a statement clarifying the motives of the SPD in initiating the *Spiegel* debate. He disavowed any lack of interest by his party in uncovering treason where it existed, but, he added, the SPD also insisted that the authorities, including the public attorneys, use procedures consistent with constitutional and legal norms. Following Ritzel's statement, Chancellor Adenauer took the floor and admonished the chamber:

> Ladies and gentlemen, from my knowledge of the matter I extend to all officials . . . my thanks and my respect. (*Applause from the CDU/CSU.—Protests from the SPD.*)
>
> I would like here to direct to all parties and to the German people a request. (*Incessant, lively protests from the SPD.*)
>
> Treason has been committed—that is very probable—(*Prolonged protests from the SPD.*)—by a man who had in his hands a power, a journalistic power. I take the position: the more power, including journalistic power, anyone has in his hands . . . the more he is obligated . . . to remain true to the limits, which the love of the people—(*Lively protests from the SPD. Calls returned by the CDU/ CSU.* Deputy Dr. Schmidt (Wuppertal): Spiegel-Party!)
>
> *Bundestag President Dr. Gerstenmaier:* Please allow the Herr Chancellor to continue. (Deputy Wehner: But any pimp may slander the SPD!—*Further protests from the SPD.*)—Permit the Chancellor to continue! (*Calls of "Oho" from the SPD.*)—The President of this House also must protect the freedom of speech of the Chancellor. (*Applause from the CDU/CSU.*)
>
> *Federal Chancellor Dr. Adenauer:* Ladies and gentlemen, is it therefore not disturbing, (*Very true! and applause from the SPD.*)
>
> is it therefore not disturbing, (*Calls from the SPD: Yes!*)
>
> when a colonel of the Bundeswehr, after he hears that an investigation might be initiated against Augstein and the editors of *Spiegel*, goes out and tells them that, enabling them to cover up the evidence? (*Calls from the center: Scandalous!—Deputy Seuffert [SPD]: Has anyone said anything here about that?*)
>
> Yes, just read through what you have said, (*Deputy Seuffert: About entirely different things!*)
>
> and then wait for the results of further revelations! Then you will

regret that you have even placed these questions. (*Applause from the CDU/CSU.*)

I declare again, ladies and gentlemen: I think as chancellor I am obligated to do it, (*Calls from the SPD:—to investigate!*)

to thank the Federal High Court and the officials of the Federal Attorney's Office and of the Federal Criminal Office for having pursued this case with such intensity. (*Applause from the CDU/CSU and the FDP.—Protests from the SPD.*)

SPD *Fraktion* chairman, Fritz Erler, moved quickly to respond to Adenauer's remarks:

Herr President! My very respected ladies and gentlemen! The intervention of the Herr Chancellor makes me extraordinarily unhappy. It makes me unhappy because with it unfortunately—unfortunately! —while one questions with concern the constitutional conduct of our authorities he adds to that concern by creating an environment which arouses further doubt about the strength of constitutional-legal principles in this country. (*Applause from the SPD. "Pfui" calls, protests, and great commotion from the CDU/CSU. . . .*)

Where treason is committed, it must be uncovered. (*Prolonged and lively commotion and catcalls from the CDU/CSU.*)

But at the same time an investigation of suspected treason does not suspend the constitutional-legal norms of the Basic Law. . . . A parliament which did not respond to the obligation to see that in an investigation of treason, which has been initiated, the residual constitutional and legal norms do not get trampled would not fulfill its controlling function. This is today what is involved and nothing else. (*Applause from the SPD.—Commotion from the Government parties.*)

Adenauer took up the argument again by repeating certain phrases in Ritzel's original statement and added:

Ladies and gentlemen, in the declaration which Herr Ritzel read, (*Sustained protests from the SPD*) or in those which he added, stands the following: on one side treason, but on the other side the protection of citizens before the abuses of ministers, state secretaries and—(*Approval from the CDU/CSU.—Lively protests from the SPD.*)

And then, ladies and gentlemen, he declared: The concern about the methods which have been used—(*Lively calls from the SPD: Very true!—Deputy Seuffert: Have you no concern? Has the Justice Minister no concern?—Calls from the SPD: Why did the Justice Minister want to resign?—Deputy Hermsdorf: He doesn't understand, he no longer understands!*)

Now, ladies and gentlemen, (*Sustained protests from the SPD*)
we have (*Continuous protests from the SPD*)
an abyss of treason in the land. (*Deputy Seuffert: Who says so?*)
—I say so. (*Loud calls from the SPD: "Aha!" "So?"—Deputy
Seuffert: Is this a pending juridical matter or not?*)

For, ladies and gentlemen, . . . when a sheet which has a circulation of 500,000 copies systematically commits treason for money
—(*Excited calls from the SPD: Pfui! Huh!—Whistling and sustained
protests from the SPD, among them Deputies Seuffert and Hermsdorf*).

Bundestag President Dr. Gerstenmaier: Ladies and gentlemen, I beg
you to maintain order, which is necessary to permit the discussion
to continue. There is no purpose—Herr Deputy Hermsdorf!—Herr
Deputy Hermsdorf, be quiet! (*Prolonged, continuous loud calls
from the SPD.*)

Federal Chancellor Dr. Adenauer: I am quite surprised. You don't
want to look at *Der Spiegel.* (*Applause from the CDU/CSU.—Prolonged, lively calls from the SPD.*)

You merely want to look at the methods with which a case of treason
has been exposed,—they do not please you. That you have just said.
(*Continuous commotion.*)

Ladies and gentlemen, I repeat: I am bound by my conscience to
say that the officials of the Federal High Court, the Federal Attorney's Office, the Criminal Office, and the cabinet deserve our fullest
support and the thanks of the German people. (*Applause from the
CDU/CSU.—Deputy Seuffert: Why did you dismiss the state secretaries?—Additional, excited calls from the SPD.*)

For the first time during the debate, Erich Mende of the FDP
took the floor. Obviously disturbed by the tone of the proceedings,
Mende cautioned the chamber that it was in danger of interfering
with a pending juridical matter. Mende explained briefly that the
dismissal of Hopf and Walter Strauss had been prompted by their
failure to inform a superior properly and had thus "called into
question the political bases of confidence between the competent
minister and his state secretary." Mende, in short, was clinging to
the myth that the state secretaries were entirely responsible for the
circumvention of Stammberger. He moved that the *Spiegel* debate
be ended immediately and that other techniques be used to inquire into the various aspects of the case.

After the defeat of Mende's motion, in which both the SPD
and the CDU/CSU voted in the negative, the debate continued.

At one point SPD Deputy Herbert Wehner was called to order for unparliamentary language. Adenauer, refusing to remain silent, again took the floor:

> . . . in the person of Augstein we have two complexes . . . On the one side he makes money from treason; and that I find vulgar, pure and simple. (*Call from the SPD: Is that proved?—Deputy Wehner: Hear! Hear!—Further calls from the SPD: Unbelievable!*)
>
> and second, ladies and gentlemen, he makes money from attacks generally on the coalition parties; and that pleases you, which you cannot deny. (*Commotion and applause from the CDU/CSU. Call from the SPD: Infamous!*) . . . I never read *Der Spiegel*, I would like to add here. (*Approval from the CDU/CSU.*)
>
> I have better things to do.—(*Approval and applause from the CDU/ CSU.*) . . . God, what is Augstein to me! The man has made money with his methods.
>
> There are those who have helped him in this by subscribing to *Der Spiegel* and placing advertisements in it. These persons are not very high in my esteem, those who have given so many advertisements. (*Applause from the CDU/CSU.*) But he has made much money, he has made a great deal of money. In my view that is no measure of his moral worth; I can not help myself. (*Jeers from the SPD.*)

Adenauer's remarkable and reckless performance was too much for FDP *Fraktion* deputy chairman Döring, who was reported to have been disappointed that his party had capitulated so easily on November 5 to Adenauer and the Christian Democrats. Döring took the floor and lectured the chancellor:

> . . . Herr Chancellor, it is very difficult for me to say what I believe I am now obligated to say. I think I need say to no one in this House that for years I have been a friend of Herr Augstein. I think I need tell no one in this House that no one would be more upset than I if, according to law and justice, the objective fact of treason is established in this case.
>
> But, Herr Chancellor, I am obligated not only to my friends but also to citizen Augstein and all others to protest what you have said here: Herr Augstein makes money from treason. For then you have already rendered a judgment which falls only to the competence of the court. (*Stormy applause from the FDP and the SPD.*)
>
> Herr Chancellor, I know what I am talking about. I am not prepared—and it is not a problem of coalition politics here—to accept without protest . . . that persons can be convicted before they have even seen a courtroom. (*Applause from FDP and SPD deputies.*)

Press reaction to the first day of the *Spiegel* debate was critical. The respected *Süddeutsche Zeitung* wondered whether the Federal Republic was still "a constitutional state." The cautious *Frankfurter Allegmeine Zeitung,* long a supporter of Adenauer's policies, called his action "reckless." Less restrained was the *Neue Rhein Zeitung:*

> This is a black day, if not the blackest day, in parliament of the young German Federal Republic . . . This must be unique in the history of our young parliament; no, in the history of parliamentarianism anywhere: from the speaker's podium of the revered house the head of the Government intervenes in a judicial proceeding!

The *Westdeutsche Rundschau* called for Adenauer's resignation and the SPD-oriented *Frankfurter Rundschau* called him "temperamentally a Fascist." *Der Spiegel* announced it was filing a complaint with the courts requesting an injunction restraining the Chancellor from publicly repeating his charges of treason against Augstein and his associates.

On November 8, Defense Minister Strauss finally took the floor to respond to questions concerning the arrest of Ahlers in Spain. Following a circuitous route of questions and answers, Strauss officially confirmed what the press had reported for several days: West German Military Attaché Oschim Oster, on the night of October 26, was asked through a phone call from the West German Defense Ministry to request the Spanish police to take Ahlers into custody. Who placed the call? Strauss evaded the question by repeating his original response, that his Ministry had placed the call, since it believed that Military Attaché Oster knew of Ahlers whereabouts and thus ought to help locate Ahlers. As Strauss explained it, the Defense Ministry was informed of:

> the Ahlers case, . . . because as a result of the unsuccessful attempt to have this arrest carried out the Security Group of the Federal Criminal Police learned . . . that Ahlers was in Spain . . . and the German Military Attaché knew about it. The Security Group of the Federal Criminal Office did not communicate [with the Defense Ministry] merely out of . . . technical requirements in this instance, but because the Security Group wanted to know . . . What is going on here? We have an arrest warrant issued by the highest court and the author of the incriminating article involved centrally in the investigation is, if you will, with the knowledge of

the Defense Ministry in another country . . . The German Military Attaché, who knows Herr Ahlers since they both worked with the Blank Office—one of them was a press aide; this is generally known of course and there is nothing new in revealing it; the other had been an intelligence officer—was contacted in the night [of October 26, 1962] and asked whether he knew anything about the trip. For if Herr Ahlers . . . were to travel on to Morocco, a vacation destination which he had given, and not return . . . the shadow of suspicion would be cast that with the assistance of an agency or of a person in the service of the Defense Ministry a man had been permitted to escape having to testify, one who according to our best information was best informed about the security leaks [in the Ministry and through which the Foertsch article was developed]. . . .

In light of Strauss's admission that his ministry had contacted Oster and asked him to have Ahlers arrested, SPD deputy Metzger inquired, in a supplementary question, whether the Government was still of the opinion that in all instances the law had been observed:

Interior Minister Höcherl: Herr Metzger, have you put the question to me?

Metzger: To the Federal Government! (*Deputy Wehner: How can anyone know who is responsible? Calls of Huh! from the CDU/CSU.*)

Höcherl: . . . Morally seen, everyone has cooperated in bringing back a traitor and placing him before the prosecutor . . . The Federal Government naturally takes the position that the regulations should be respected. But in such a situation one should not apply too trivial a standard.

The second day of the debate ended with Strauss trying to justify his ministry's involvement in assisting with the investigation. In alluding to the expert opinion which his ministry prepared and completed on October 19 for the Federal Attorney's Office, Strauss was interrupted by FDP deputy Dr. Kohut, the only member of the FDP *Fraktion* who participated in the questioning:

Herr Minister, are you prepared and in a position to repudiate the rumor that the person who drafted the expert opinion in your office earlier held a high rank in the [Nazi] SS? (*Call from the center: Ah, now it gets primitive!*)

Strauss: I certainly do not want to dodge any questions, but please understand that I can not answer such a question. . . .

Kohut: Herr Minister, do I understand then that questions concerning earlier activities in the SS may no longer be asked in the

German Federal Republic under the Adenauer government? (*Applause from the SPD.—Vigorous jeering from the CDU/CSU: Scandalous! Unheard of! Persistent commotion from the center.*) . . .

Strauss: Herr Colleague Kohut, (*Prolonged disturbances and commotion*) I am being courteous to you and also candid and I ask you to refrain from playing the role of the prosecutor with me (*Laughter and jeers from the SPD*) . . . I do not know the background of those, (*Jeers*) who have prepared the expert opinion and I have not troubled to find out. At the moment someone is admitted as a civil servant or as an officer, I cease looking into his past and conducting a second or third denazification. (*Bravo-calls from the center and applause from the center.—Deputy Dr. Kohut: I then conclude that SS people now write expert opinions concerning democrats!*) . . .

Dr. Kohut's line of questioning must have disturbed his FDP colleagues who were still seeking to maintain a semblance of harmony with the CDU/CSU and ride out the *Spiegel* controversy with the coalition intact. At the request of the FDP leaders, Kohut read into the record of the day's proceedings a statement toning down considerably his insinuation and denying that he intended to impute "collective guilt."

One thing was clear from the second day's questioning. Strauss was adept at evading the central issues around which the controversy had clustered: who, and by what authority, placed the phone call to Spain asking for the police arrest of Ahlers, and who had instructed state secretaries Hopf and Walter Strauss to ignore Stammberger in assisting with the investigation against *Der Spiegel?*

After several diversionary questions and answers, SPD *Fraktion* Chairman Fritz Erler returned the third day's questioning to a key issue by asking Strauss pointedly whether he personally talked with Military Attaché Oster and asked Oster to bring in the Spanish police for the arrest of Ahlers. Strauss finally admitted that he did:

. . . Since the military attaché . . . did not want to know the circumstances but said: "I recognize only the voice of the Minister," I was connected with him and I repeated to him the nature of the situation: (*Calls from the SPD: Aha!*) The Security Group of the Federal Criminal Office has called and maintains that Colonel Oster knows of this trip, Herr Ahlers is being sought because of the suspicion of treason, a court warrant for his arrest has been issued, it is based on the danger of his fleeing and obstructing justice, what goes on here?

Strauss was then asked, after several supplementary questions, whether he or his ministry had also asked the Security Group, of the Federal Criminal Office, to send a teletype copy of the arrest warrant to the Spanish police. The question was important in establishing whether the initiative for the seizure of Ahlers really came from the Federal Attorney's Office or some other appropriate agency, or inappropriately from the Defense Ministry. Strauss evaded the question. When pinned down, he said "Nothing is known to me of this."

Erler then returned the questioning to a second crucial area of controversy by asking Strauss whether he had taken part in any discussions between October 16 (when Strauss returned from vacation) and October 26 with state secretaries Hopf and Walter Strauss about any aspect of the *Spiegel* investigation. Strauss first equivocated, then concluded with this statement:

> . . . I was informed on October 16 because a few persons in my ministry, including State Secretary Hopf, came to me and gave me information about the events of October 9 to October 16. From October 16 to October 26 . . . I took part in no conference. However, obviously I was told by the appropriate personnel in my office that this matter was in progress. More I did not know. I did not know what was coming; I did not know when it was coming; I did not know against whom it was coming, etc.

The closing words of this statement should be noted in any final assessment of the accusation that Strauss lied to the Bundestag.

Strauss ended the third day's discussion by reading into the record a formal denial that the expert opinion prepared in his ministry had been written by anyone formerly in the SS. Mende, apparently angered that his colleague Kohut had circulated the charge, acknowledged that the story had originated with the East German and Moscow radio networks and announced that the "*Fraktion* has made sure that Kohut would not let such rumors fall in the future."

If the Government had a strong defense against the criticisms which had been aroused against it by the *Spiegel* Affair, it seemed peculiarly inept in presenting it. The contradictions uttered by various governmental press aides during the preceding ten days had been fully exposed by the press. During the *Spiegel* debates the Government once again seemed to have done its position more harm than good. An opinion survey, conducted shortly afterward, revealed that out of a representative population sample (16 years of age and over) 59 percent had "followed" the debates. Of those who had followed the debates, only 16 percent felt that "Adenauer and the Government" had made "a good impression." A clear majority (54 percent) felt that Adenauer and the Government had "*not* made a good impression" and the remaining 30 percent were "undecided." [16]

The "Truce"

In a November 9 meeting, Chancellor Adenauer secured an agreement with the leaders of the CDU/CSU, the SPD, and the FDP for a truce during the next seven days, permitting Adenauer and his advisers to prepare for their trip to the United States, where he would discuss the Cuban missile crisis and its implications for West Germany with President Kennedy. Already postponed once because of the *Spiegel* Affair, the trip would take Adenauer to Washington on November 14 for several days. During the truce, the SPD withheld additional parliamentary questions concerning the *Spiegel* controversy.

Although spokesmen for the FDP voiced concern about the general tone of the *Spiegel* debates, the FDP's basic response offered no immediate threat to the November 5 coalition agreement. From the beginning, the FDP had maintained that procedural errors in the *Spiegel* investigation could be ferreted out and corrected, if necessary, without disrupting the coalition. The deliberate denial to Stammberger of prior knowledge of the police actions had implications for the coalition. When on November 5 it was decided to relieve state secretaries Hopf and Walter Strauss of their duties, the responsibility for this apparent violation of the spirit of the coalition had been fixed and the punishment exacted. Thus, even though Franz-Josef Strauss seemed to have admitted, in the debates, a role in the affair greater than he had previously acknowledged, the FDP refused to regard this new information as requiring a reconsideration of the November 5 settlement.

The FDP position had two weaknesses. It assumed that the

state secretaries were entirely responsible for the circumvention of Stammberger and it failed to satisfy the public's curiosity about Strauss's conduct in the arrest of Ahlers. FDP leaders were aware of these weaknesses in their position, but found no strategy to overcome them. Siegfried Zoglmann, executive secretary of the FDP Bundestag *Fraktion,* suggested on November 9 that, whatever the remaining questions presented by the *Spiegel* controversy, the "legitimate" freedom of the press clearly had not been endangered by the *Spiegel* case. His party colleague, Hermann Busse, a former judge with the Constitutional Court of Northrhine-Westphalia, agreed with him and added that perhaps a parliamentary committee of inquiry should now be constituted to explore "calmly" the remaining issues in the affair. Even Justice Minister Stammberger refused to say, in an interview on November 11, whether Strauss had acted improperly and warned that, however defective the procedures, no reasonable analogy could be drawn between the *Spiegel* action and "Gestapo techniques."

The most reliable index of the FDP's position during the "truce" is found in Mende's extended comments of November 11. He announced that his *Fraktion* believed that the Bundestag standing committee on law should now inquire into possible legal errors in the *Spiegel* investigation and the standing committee on defense should inquire into questions with "military implications" arising out of the *Spiegel* Affair. Mende chided the SPD for having unnecessarily diverted the *Spiegel* controversy and asserted that the SPD must assume responsibility for delaying the procedures for discovering the truth. In Mende's opinion, if the SPD had refrained from invoking the Question Hour technique, a special committee of inquiry could have already begun receiving testimony that would "clarify" the Ahlers episode. Mende admitted that in light of Strauss's statements before the Bundestag, it would have been "better" if Strauss had rendered appropriate assistance in the Ahlers case three days prior to the actual arrest, thus avoiding the hasty improvisations on the night of October 26. Mende concluded, most significantly, with the warning that, whatever the merits of the continuing criticisms against Strauss and the authorities, the Defense Ministry could not recall State Secretary Hopf to active duty without prior approval of the FDP Bundestag *Fraktion*. Defense Minister Strauss was apparently unimpressed with Mende's warning. Later that day on a radio interview, Strauss explained that Hopf was simply on sick leave and implied that he would soon return to his duties.

The position of the SPD after the Bundestag debates differed markedly from that of the FDP. According to its spokesmen, the answers given by the Government left the basic issues unresolved. Responsibility for Ahlers's arrest had not been fixed. Strauss had lied concerning his role in the *Spiegel* case. As to the FDP suggestion that parliamentary committees be utilized to explore the remaining issues, the SPD discounted their usefulness, both because of the time-consuming nature of their processes and the control of the committees by the Government's majority coalition.

Publicly the CDU/CSU spokesmen continued a show of unity, insisting that the charges against the authorities had not been proved. Alluding to the rumor that *Der Spiegel* had obtained security information from SPD deputies, they suggested that a more fruitful line of inquiry, for those interested in the truth, would be to take up the question of security leaks. Behind the scene, however, there was growing uneasiness about the vulnerability of Franz-Joseph Strauss and its implications for the Christian Democrats. At a November 12 meeting of the executive committee of the CDU/CSU Bundestag *Fraktion,* Foreign Minister Schröder revealed a memorandum from the German Ambassador in Madrid, showing that Strauss phoned not once but twice on the night of October 26. This bit of information contradicted Strauss's account before the Bundestag and suggested that, contrary to the accepted procedures, Strauss had taken the initiative in involving the Spanish police in arresting a German citizen.

It is also possible that the electoral significance of the *Spiegel* Affair was beginning to assert itself and to cause the Christian Democrats to reconsider their position. On November 11, in the Hesse *Landtag* election in which the *Spiegel* Affair became one of several major issues, both the FDP and the SPD increased their popular vote and representation in the assembly. In the 1958 *Landtag* election, the SPD received 46.9 percent of the valid votes; in the 1962 election, it received 50.9 percent. The FDP had received 9.5 percent of the votes in the earlier election; now it received 11.4 percent. The CDU slipped from 32 percent to 28.8 percent. Whether the *Spiegel* Affair had any substantial effect on the results is uncertain; a number of major newspapers concluded that it had been significant and CDU/CSU Bundestag *Fraktion* chairman von Brentano, in the November 12 meeting of the CDU/CSU leaders, warned that the electoral significance of the *Spiegel* Affair could no longer be ignored.

At this point Chancellor Adenauer publicly confirmed Strauss's view that Hopf would soon return to the Defense Ministry. In an interview with a group of American journalists on the evening of November 13, Adenauer remarked that had he been "Herr Strauss . . . I would have promptly revealed that I had personally intervened in the Ahlers case." Then he added: "Herr Hopf will return to his duties as soon as his health permits. And I am myself pleased that Herr Hopf will be returning." In one sentence the Chancellor had exploded the myth of the Hopf-Walter Strauss formula on which the FDP had staked its reputation as the third force in the Bonn system. And he had done it without giving the FDP advance warning. Completely taken by surprise, Mende, the same night, hurriedly called a meeting of his FDP *Fraktion* colleagues.

Mende's cautious approach during the *Spiegel* Affair, contrary to that preferred by Döring, was now discredited. He had apparently already lost significant support within his own *Fraktion*. During a routine re-election of the FDP *Fraktion*'s executive committee members, just after the *Spiegel* debates, Mende had received fewer votes (44 of 62) than had Döring (51 of 59) for the chairmanship and vice chairmanship respectively. Mende now accepted the "hard" line. After a nine hour session, the FDP *Fraktion* leaders agreed that, with the recall of Hopf, the settlement of November 5 was untenable. Franz-Josef Strauss would have to go. The FDP ultimatum was transmitted on November 15 to Minister of Special Affairs Heinrich Krone, who had been left in charge of the *Spiegel* problem while Adenauer was in Washington. Krone phoned Adenauer and urged the chancellor to return as quickly as possible. Adenauer re-scheduled his flight twenty-four hours earlier than originally planned.

But once again the SPD had taken the initiative from the FDP. The previous day, the SPD *Fraktion* announced that it was preparing a resolution for immediate introduction in the Bundestag, that would call upon Chancellor Adenauer to recommend the dismissal of Strauss from the cabinet to Federal President Lübke. For both the FDP and the SPD the "truce" had ended.

Judgment at Nürnberg

The Bavarian *Landtag* election was entering its final phase when the FDP demanded Strauss's dismissal. At the Bavarian rallies Strauss vigorously defended his conduct and warned his audiences that those who wanted to remove him from the Defense Ministry were following the line of the East German Communists. Strauss stressed that no less a crime than treason was involved in this dispute. Writing in the November 23 issue of the *Münchener Merkur,* Strauss argued his case:

> I have fulfilled my duty and in full approval of the Federal Chancellor. Where the betrayal of military secrets is concerned, the Defense Minister is involved and responsible. I did not set the investigation in motion. The Federal Attorney's Office decided the facts were sufficient for it on its own authority and without drawing in anyone else to initiate the measures. It is the obligation and responsibility of all governmental agencies to lend official assistance insofar as feasible. Nothing other than this was done by my ministry. Those who try to ensnarl me in the matter should first reveal frankly their motives and the background . . . In this hour the people want no government crisis and certainly not a state crisis induced by partisan politics and electoral tactics. For six years the Moscow propagandists have worked for the downfall of the Adenauer government. In recent weeks they have intensified their propaganda.

On November 14, the Bavarian leadership of the CSU rallied to Strauss's support. They urged the national CDU leadership not to abandon Strauss. The Bavarian FDP leadership issued a statement that it stood united behind its national leadership in the *Spiegel* controversy, although it carefully added that it was not renouncing in advance the possibility of entering a coalition in Bavaria with the CSU after the November 25 election. As late as November 16, Mende emphasized that while the FDP could no longer work with Strauss, he hoped an "appropriate" solution could be found without forcing the FDP to withdraw formally from the Government.

The personal rivalry between Adenauer and Minister of Economics, Ludwig Erhard, intensified since 1959 by the succession question, precluded Erhard from attempting to arbitrate the CDU/CSU-FDP dispute. Had he been chancellor, Erhard might have reacted differently than Adenauer to the controversy. He had been one of the few Christian Democratic leaders to voice an early concern about Strauss's role in the *Spiegel* action. Urging repeatedly in public that "all the cards be laid on the table," Erhard resisted the temptation to construe the affair as simply a matter of partisan and petty politics. At a CSU voting rally in Hof, Bavaria, on November 18, he counseled the Germans:

> It is necessary that we not only re-examine our political style, but that we modify it. Only in this way will we avoid the confusion of ideals in which it is possible to mix together the highest and lowest values into a kind of potpourri and convey to the citizen the impression that the "government" and the "opposition" are merely matters of tactics and pacts.

Adenauer still rejected a quick surrender to the FDP. Although Adenauer and his advisers finally recognized that Strauss would have to resign his ministerial post, this would now happen whatever the strategy of the CDU/CSU. Since Strauss would have to be jettisoned, Adenauer wanted concessions in return from the FDP. Primary among these was Adenauer's being allowed to retain his own position, which seemed increasingly in jeopardy as the FDP began hinting that the unresolved question of the succession was an unsettling and intolerable obstacle to continued cooperation between the coalition parties. Strauss compounded Adenauer's difficulty by hinting in the Bavarian campaign that he had acted with the approval of the chancellor. On November 19, Adenauer's office denied that the Chancellor had expressly approved any of the questionable circumstances surrounding the *Spiegel* investigation, including the circumvention of Stammberger. In any event, on November 19, the FDP Bundestag *Fraktion,* called a special caucus in Nürnberg, and, with Mende's urging, finally carried out its threat to withdraw from the Government. As the *Kölner Stadt-Anzeiger* dramatically described the event:

> The . . . doors of the Marmorsaal open. . . . "It is decided," says Erich Mende. "My recommendation has been accepted. I shall now notify Adenauer . . ." Outside, the banners have been lowered. One remains: "Out with Strauss."

Restoring the Coalition

Somewhat belatedly, the Chancellor turned his full attention to the *Spiegel* Affair. At a cabinet meeting on November 20, he discussed with his CDU/CSU colleagues, the possibility of reconstructing the FDP-CDU/CSU cabinet, excluding Strauss and Stammberger, with a minimal number of changes in the other ministries. The CDU executive secretary, Hermann Dufhues, persuaded Adenauer to overhaul the cabinet drastically in order to restore "public confidence" in the coalition government and to remove personal "tensions" left in the wake of the controversy. To facilitate the plan, the CDU/CSU ministers had already agreed to offer their resignations, permitting the Chancellor a free hand. On November 22, Adenauer met with the executive committee of the CDU, in a special meeting in Berlin, to map the strategy for coalition negotiations.

On November 25, the Bavarians elected a new *Landtag*. Strauss's supporters had been calling for a massive vote of confidence for the battle-scarred, but still popular (in Bavaria) Defense Minister. But with the decision already made to remove Strauss, the Bavarian election, whatever the results, could not save Strauss's position. The CSU showed a slight increase in its popular vote (47.5 percent), as compared with its 1958 vote (45.6 percent). The SPD increase was larger, with its vote moving from 30.8 percent in 1958 to 35.3 percent. The FDP's share remained about the same, 5.6 percent in 1958 and 5.9 percent in 1962. On November 30, Strauss announced that he would "resign" his ministerial post.

Twice during the *Spiegel* Affair, Adenauer had tactlessly aggravated the dispute between the FDP and the CDU/CSU. On October 31, the Chancellor had allowed his cabinet to discuss the *Sozialpaket* and the 1963 budget proposals in the absence of the FDP ministers. In both of these policy areas the FDP had staked a particular claim to influence. On November 13, Adenauer had brazenly challenged the FDP's claim to importance by publicly revealing that Hopf would be returned to active service. In the negotiations with the FDP during the remaining days of November, the Chancellor and his advisers discovered that the FDP, reacting to these repeated rebuffs, had raised the price for returning to a coalition: Adenauer would have to resign, if not immediately, at least at some specific time in the near future. The FDP had finally returned to its 1961 pre-coalition strategy of *"ohne Adenauer."*

In an effort to soften the demands of the FDP, Adenauer resorted to a tactic he had employed in the fall of 1961, when the FDP was insisting on Adenauer's retirement. After securing the approval of a bare majority of the CDU/CSU Bundestag *Fraktion,* he instructed his negotiators to explore the possibility of a "grand coalition" with the SPD. On December 4, the SPD executive committee agreed, by a vote of 26 to 13, to discuss the basis for such an arrangement with the Christian Democrats. Formal negotiations began that day, even while negotiations with the FDP were being continued. Adenauer wanted the SPD to agree to two major conditions in exchange for the privilege of entering the cabinet. No insistence would be made by the SPD on a specific date for Adenauer's retirement from the chancellorship, and the SPD would support a move in the Bundestag to convert the Bundestag electoral law into an exclusively single-member constituency system. The FDP complained at these obvious pressure tactics of Adenauer, but did not call off its negotiations with the CDU/CSU.

On December 5, the SPD negotiating team reported the terms of the Adenauer proposal to its Bundestag *Fraktion.* Without specifically accepting either of them, the SPD deputies authorized a continuation of the talks with Adenauer's group. However, the report carried by the German news agency, *dpa,* of the SPD meeting announced that the SPD *Fraktion* had decided it could accept Adenauer as chancellor only upon the condition that he fix a time for retirement in the near future. Six months was rumored to be the maximum time the SPD was willing to serve in a coalition under Adenauer's leadership.

Upon hearing of the *dpa* account of the SPD decision, Adenauer cancelled his scheduled talk with SPD *Fraktion* chairman Ollenhauer, who insisted that the position of the SPD had been misunderstood. But it was clear that the Chancellor no longer saw any advantage to an SPD-CDU/CSU coalition. He confidentially informed his advisers that he was prepared to retire prior to the opening of the fall session (October, 1963) of the Bundestag. The way was open for the return of the FDP to the coalition. On December 7, the cabinet crisis ended.

The new CDU/CSU-FDP cabinet with seven changes, including the ministers of justice and defense, was announced on December 11. Kai-Uwe von Hassel, minister-president of Schleswig-Holstein and one of four deputy national chairmen of the CDU, was appointed as Strauss's replacement, to be effective January 15, 1963. Stammberger was replaced by his FDP colleague, Ewald Bucher. The new coalition rested on agreements that the Christian Democrats would not pursue, during the life of the coalition, any plan to modify the electoral system; that "cooperation" between the coalition parties would be "bettered"; that no new policies were anticipated in the fields of finance, agriculture, and social welfare; and that all financial, social, and economic questions should be "discussed between the coalition partners for the purposes of finding mutually acceptable answers."

PUBLIC REACTIONS

During the formative and bargaining stages of the *Spiegel* Affair, did the press reactions correlate with the reactions of the broader public? Did the responses of the parties correlate with the responses of their supporters? Upon whom did the "public" fix responsibility for the *Spiegel* Affair? What in the public mind was the most objectionable feature of the *Spiegel* case? Was the forced resignation of Strauss consistent with the desires of the "public"? Surveys conducted in November and December, 1962, by the *Institut für Demoskopie* suggest partial answers.

The *Spiegel* Affair was probably the most publicized political controversy in the history of the West German Republic. By November 22, 1962, 91 percent of the representative population sample (sixteen years of age and over) "knew" of the *Spiegel* Affair.[17] A second survey, conducted between November 28 and December 6, shows that a remarkable 96 percent of the sample had "heard" of the Affair.[18] This degree of awareness was uniformly high among all sex, age, and political-orientation categories. How well the public was informed about the complex controversy is not revealed in the survey, but the communications system had undoubtedly secured a large "attentive" audience during the *Spiegel* Affair.

As noted in an earlier section of this study, a sampling of press reaction immediately after the *Spiegel* raids revealed two primary causes of criticism against the authorities: (1) the methods used in the action, with particular implications for freedom of the press; and (2) the motives for the investigation, especially in light of *Der Spiegel*'s earlier encounters with Strauss. A public opinion survey conducted between November 10 and 22 reveals 31 percent objecting to the actions because of the methods used and 16 percent objecting because of questionable motives.[19] Combining these two responses, a majority (57 percent) of the men and a plurality of the entire sample (47 percent) were critical of the *Spiegel* action. In our earlier section we had noted that 62 percent of the press sample was critical, either for motivational or procedural reasons.

In a separate survey the SPD followers were most (56 percent) inclined to question the motives behind the *Spiegel* raids, although a significantly high proportion (47 percent) of the FDP followers had the same concern. Only in the case of the Christian Democratic followers was the sample predominantly sympathetic with the authorities' undertaking the action.[20] Thus the roles the three parties played in the formative phase seem to correlate reasonably highly with the attitudes of their respective followers. These surveys neither confirm nor deny, of course, a causal relationship between party roles and followers' attitudes.

How did the public view Strauss's role in the *Spiegel* Affair? And should he have resigned? Surveys taken between November 28 and December 6 suggest that *Der Spiegel*'s exposés, prior to the *Spiegel* Affair, had already harmed Strauss's public image. Thus 35 percent of those who responded that he should resign mentioned the Fibag Affair and "other unclarified matters" as the reason for their attitude. More than a third of the sample believed that Strauss was responsible for the arrest of the *Spiegel* publisher and editors.[21]

End of an Affair

Adenauer's pledge to resign cleared the way in the spring of 1963 for the selection of Ludwig Erhard as chancellor. Until the final vote in the CDU/CSU caucus, Adenauer persisted in opposing Erhard, maintaining that he lacked the decisiveness essential for an effective chancellor.

Erhard succeeded Adenauer as party chief in 1966, but was forced from office in the Autumn of that year when the FDP withdrew from his coalition.

After resigning his ministerial post, Franz-Josef Strauss assumed the leadership in the Bundestag of the CSU, whose support is vital to the larger CDU. The FDP, taking credit for forcing Strauss's resignation, campaigned in the 1965 Bundestag election with the promise to continue to Strauss's isolation from ministerial power. Ironically, by defecting from the Erhard government, it opened the way for his return (as Finance Minister) in the CDU/CSU-SPD coalition under Kiesinger. His critics detect no substantial change in his brusque and aggressive political style, while his supporters continue to discount the fear that he is temperamentally unsuited for the give and take of a parliamentary system. He seems even more committed now to the concept of a "quality" Bundeswehr and the uncreditability of a defense policy premised on a conventional response to Soviet aggression.

Strauss is a major political "problem" in West Germany. Around his personality are clustered and symbolized strongly felt attitudes, reflecting the tensions between the anti-Strauss "intellectuals" and in 1966 the Straussian devotees of personal leadership and hard-headed "realism." Many see in the Strauss issue the persistent problem of the undigested past, erupting from time to time in charges and counter-charges of Nazism, arrogance, and demagoguery. His pivotal position as leader of the CSU, and the dependency of the CDU upon it for the votes that continue to make it the largest party in parliament, make it unwise to predict his political future.

Ousted from his ministerial post by the "Solomon's decision" of the Adenauer group during the *Spiegel* Affair, Stammberger bitterly denounced the FDP in 1964 and switched his party affiliation to the SPD, reasoning (incorrectly in light of developments in 1966) that only the SPD could be trusted to resist Strauss's return to power.

What about the accusations against Strauss during the *Spiegel* Affair? Were they valid? Did Augstein and Ahlers treasonably publish state secrets? What about Adenauer's role in the *Spiegel* Affair? Does the Affair permit any generalizations about dissent in the Bonn system? In concluding this study, brief attention must be given to these questions.

Who Did What to Whom?

Using the Government's version of the *Spiegel* investigation that was finally released to the public on February 4, 1963, we can conclude that Strauss was substantially guilty of two major accusations.[22] On his own initiative, he personally telephoned Military Attaché Oster on the night of October 26, and ordered him to request the Spanish police to take Ahlers into custody. He resorted to this procedure after learning, through State Secretary Hopf, that both the Federal Criminal Office and the Federal Attorney's Office refused, for lack of legal competence, to secure the arrest of Ahlers. Also, two days prior to the *Spiegel* action in a conference with Hopf and State Secretary Walter Strauss of the Justice Ministry, Franz-Josef Strauss ordered the circumvention of Stammberger, invoking the Chancellor's authority. To the extent that Strauss denied his roles in the Ahlers and Stammberger incidents, Strauss knowingly misrepresented the facts to the public and the Bundestag. A third accusation, that he *originated* the investigation against *Der Spiegel,* appears unfounded.

The evidence in the *Spiegel* Report raises doubt about Adenauer's role in the controversy. In the Bundestag debates, he implied that he learned of the *Spiegel* investigation from the federal attorneys "at the last possible moment." He actually learned of the investigation from Strauss at least eight days prior to October 26. The evidence is inconclusive concerning Strauss's later contention that in circumventing Stammberger he acted with express permission of the Chancellor. Apparently this was Strauss's interpretation of the blanket endorsement given him by Adenauer to cooperate fully with the Federal Attorney's Office for the purpose of bringing to justice "all persons regardless of rank or position" who had trafficked in state secrets. In any event, Adenauer's reluctance during the bargaining stage to take a stronger position against Strauss may, in retrospect, have been prompted partially by the Chancellor's insecurity in his own mind as to whether Strauss had acted with proper authority. Probably the most serious indictment that might be lodged against Adenauer, however, is his general carelessness in failing to perceive at the outset the potentially explosive nature of the *Spiegel* investigation. Had the Chancellor acted promptly during the week prior to the *Spiegel* raids to insure that neither Strauss nor any other official under his direct authority misunderstood the delicacy of the investigation, much embarrassment would have been spared him and his Government. Without discounting his substantial accomplishments during his fifteen years as chancellor, Adenauer's conduct during the *Spiegel* Affair reveals a significant insight into his political blindspots.

The *Spiegel* Report supports the conclusion that the Federal Attorney's Office was extraordinarily casual in discharging its administrative obligations to the Justice Ministry. The statutory relationship between the Federal Attorney's Office and the Justice Ministry imposed three specific obligations upon the federal attorneys in charge of the *Spiegel* investigation: (1) To inform the Justice Ministry as soon as the investigation assumed the characteristics of one that required court orders and police action; (2) To inform it specifically of planned police actions; and (3) To report directly to the Minister of Justice. The first obligation was technically met through the letter of October 18, reaching Stammberger's desk on October 24. Neither of the other two obligations was satisfied and there appears to have been no attempt by the attorneys to fulfill them.

Walter Strauss's conduct during the *Spiegel* investigation is difficult to justify. Within the West German ministries, the state secretaries occupy an ill-defined position. They enjoy certain civil service prerogatives; at the same time they are quasi-political officials, subject to transfer for partisan reasons, entitled to and expected many times to have active party connections, and competent to represent their ministerial superiors in policy matters. But the ambiguity of their accountability does not really explain the role of Walter Strauss, who, following his "leave" from the Justice Ministry, was appointed by the Government to a seat on the European High Court. Surely he violated the presumed relationship of confidence between a minister and his state secretary, when he accepted the instruction of Defense Minister Strauss to keep Stammberger uninformed of the impending police action. The Walter Strauss incident gives credence to the suspicion in Bonn that the major party will wish to "encircle" the ministers of the minor party with politically reliable state secretaries. In any event the "personnel" problem over which coalition parties haggle includes, for good reason, not only the ministerial posts but also the state secretary positions.

The Court Decision

In 1963, the federal attorneys completed the preparation of their case against Augstein, Ahlers, and Colonel Martin. The Federal High Court, on May 13, 1965, dismissed the charges of treasonable publication against Augstein and Ahlers, and held open the charge against Martin of passing state secrets to *Der Spiegel*.[23] Although admitting the possibility that the Foertsch article may have contained "state secrets," it concluded that the evidence was insufficient to the major holding that state secrets had been treasonably published, i.e., "so as to endanger the security and well-being of the Federal Republic." The court took into account the apparently untreasonable intent of the publisher and author, the effort by Ahlers, prior to publication of the article, to check out the state secrets problem with Colonel Wicht of the Federal Intelligence Agency, and the improbability that the material endangered the Republic, because of the difficulty any hostile power would have in establishing the accuracy of the material. The cautious and delimiting wording of the opinion, and the controversy which surrounded the case, warned against easy generalizations. The West German press generally welcomed the decision, but renewed its plea for a uniform federal press law clarifying the boundaries between press freedom and treasonable publication.

Functioning of Dissent

If a sizable number of participants in a political system are suddenly antagonized by, and wish therefore to protest, a specific act of the authorities, how do they translate their attitudes into demands upon the political processes? The *Spiegel* Affair points to the key role which the press can play, within the West German system, in articulating the attitudes and circulating them broadly in the political community. At the same time, the atypicality of the *Spiegel* Affair should be stressed before drawing any hasty conclusions. Performing a significant role in framing the issues, the press also identified with the object of the controversial act of the authorities. If the procedures employed in the investigation had been similar, but the object of the investigation had been a person or organization without a press function, would the response of the press community have been as vigorous and hostile? Probably not. This conclusion need not detract from the contributions which the press made to the clarification of the issues. It does suggest that *Der Spiegel* had the good fortune to have for its ally the press, an institution peculiarly equipped in a pluralistic and competitive power system to mobilize criticism of authority quickly.

If the articulation mechanism during the *Spiegel* Affair performed impressively, the same can not be said for the "output" apparatus in the system of dissent. By this we mean that both the press and the party systems, when confronted with the sluggishness of the Adenauer government in responding to the criticism, seemed temporarily stymied in extracting acceptable explanations and concessions. It was at this point that the FDP played its unique role in the *Spiegel* controversy. Only when the Adenauer Government seemed threatened with the loss of its controlling majority in the Bundestag did it begin to respond promptly to the flow of dissent. Perhaps this does not validate the FDP's claim to the third force function as much as the FDP would have us believe. The apparent ease with which the CDU/CSU diverted the FDP from the major areas of controversy, by offering the Hopf-Walter Strauss formula, weakens the FDP claim to an exclusive role in exposing the Government's, and Strauss's, position. Inadvertently, Adenauer returned the FDP to a more relevant course when he announced that Hopf would be returned to duty in the Defense Ministry.

From the outset, in fact, the SPD focused more consistently than did the FDP on the major areas of the controversy. Although it could not dislodge Strauss, or exact tangible concessions from the Adenauer government, it did force the Bundestag debates, during which Strauss's position, if not fully exposed, was weakened to the point of encouraging the dissenters to cling to their original demands. Both the SPD and the FDP, in short, translated the criticisms into demands upon the political process. Neither alone achieved the final result.

The Primacy of Politics

Before it began and during its unfolding, the *Spiegel* Affair called for the exercise of judgment. The *Legalitätsprinzip* did not and could not make the discretionary decisions for the principals in the investigation. At the outset certain of the principals, particularly Adenauer, did not recognize the need for political judgment; in the course of the investigation and the ensuing controversy when certain principals, particularly Franz-Josef Strauss, did make discretionary decisions, they were incorrect. The lesson of the *Spiegel* Affair is ancient: personal commitments, not codes of law, are the surest foundation of a constitutional system.

NOTES

1. Two excellent sources of data on public opinion and political attitudes of the West Germans are Elisabeth Noelle and Erich Peter Neumann, *Jahrbuch der öffentlichen Meinung, 1958-1964* (Allensbach and Bonn, 1965) and Gabriel Almond and Sidney Verba, *The Civic Culture,* (Boston, 1965).

2. *Verhandlungen des Deutschen Bundestages, Stenographischer Berichte, 37. Sitzung,* pp. 1581 ff.

3. The full report is titled *2. Schriftlicher Bericht des 1. Untersuchungsausschusses gemäss Antrag der Fraktion SPD, Deutscher Bundestag, 4. Wahlperiode, Drucksache IV/639.*

4. *Der "Spiegel"-Bericht,* p. 202.

5. *Verfassungsbeschwerde der Spiegel-Verlag,* p. 37.

6. *Der "Spiegel"-Bericht,* p. 202.

7. *Ibid.,* p. 204.

8. No. 45 (November 7, 1962), p. 59.

9. Colonel Wicht was provisionally arrested for advising Ahlers and Becker, prior to publication, whether state secrets were contained in the Foertsch article. Colonel Martin was revealed, belatedly to the federal attorneys through material seized in *Der Spiegel's* offices, as the informant from the Defense Ministry. Martin had first approached Paul Conrad in the spring of 1962 with his information about Strauss's views. Conrad, in turn, placed Martin in touch with his lawyer, Dr. Josef Augstein.

10. *Bulletin des Presse- und Informationamtes der Bundesregierung,* Bonn, October 31, 1962, p. 1716.

11. During a six-week period, the Press Evaluation Section of the Bundestag Library clipped and filed, from some 40 German newspapers, more than 2,000 articles and commentaries on the Spiegel Affair.

12. Ronald F. Bunn, "The Spiegel Affair and The West German Press: The Initial Phase," *The Public Opinion Quarterly,* Spring, 1966, pp. 54-68. This article contains tables summarizing the results described here.

13. *SPD Pressedienst,* October 29, 1962, P/XVII/219.

14. *BPA Abt. Nachrichten, Rundfunkaufnahme, Deutsche Gruppe West, Hessischer RF, 29.10.62/1905 Anhang I.*

15. The record of the three day's question hours is found in the *Verhandlungen des Deutschen Bundestages, Stenographischer Bericht, 4. Wahlperiode* (Sittings 45, 46, and 47), pp. 1949 ff., 2013 ff., 2075 ff.

16. Erich Peter Neumann, "Die Spiegel-Affäre in der Öffentlichen Meinung," Allensbach am Bodensee, June 19, 1963, offset print, p. 18.

17. *Ibid.*, p. 7.

18. *Ibid.*, p. 8.

19. *Ibid.*, p. 16.

20. *Ibid.*, p. 14.

21. *Ibid.*, pp. 28-30.

22. *Der "Spiegel"-Bericht,* as cited in the bibliography.

23. *Bundesgerichtshof-Beschluss vom 13. Mai 1965, 6 StE 4/64.*

SELECTED BIBLIOGRAPHY

The full citation of the Government's version of the *Spiegel* investigation is *Der "Spiegel"-Bericht, Darstellung der Vorgänge beim Ermittlungsverfahren gegen Verleger, Redakteure und Informanten des Nachrichtenmagazins "Der Spiegel"-Bericht der Bundesministerien des Auswärtigen, des Innern, der Verteidigung und der Justiz,* published in the *Bulletin des Presse und Informationsamtes der Bundesregierung,* No. 23 (February 5, 1963), pp. 195-204. The legal brief prepared by *Der Spiegel's* counsel for presentation to the Federal Constitutional Court in support of its constitutional objections to certain aspects of the investigation was published for private circulation as *Verfassungsbeschwerde der "Spiegel"-Verlag Rudolf Augstein GmbH & Co. KG, Hamburg—1BvR 586/62—Schriftsatz der Beschwerdeführerin vom 1. Mai 1963.* An appendix to this document seeks to show the extent to which the most revealing information in the Foertsch article had been substantially published prior to the appearance of the Foertsch Article: *Belege zur Titelgeschichte Foertsch, Eine Dokumentation von Heinz Höhne und Robert Spiering.* Following the publication by the Government of its Spiegel Report, the SPD Bundestag Fraktion published its own findings and conclusions in *Bericht der Sozialdemokraten über die Behandlung der "Spiegel" Affäre durch die Bundesregierung* (Neue Vorwärts Verlag, Bonn, 1963). Other relevant public documents, including the Fibag Committee Reports, the Bundestag debates, and the Federal High Court's decision are cited in the footnotes.

Commentaries on the *Spiegel* Affair are extensive, particularly in German newspapers during and immediately after the Affair. The best collection of such articles is contained in the *Spiegel* Affair files in the Press Evaluation Section (*Pressauswertungabteilung*) of the Bundestag Library in Bonn. A few of the more elaborate commentaries and interpretations include: Jürgen Seifert, "Die Spiegel Affäre," in *Erich et al, Franz-Josef Strauss, Ein Typus Unserer Zeit* (Verlag Kurt Desch, Munchen, Wien, Basel, 1963), pp. 233-314; Theodor Eschenburg,

Die Affäre, Eine Analyse (published by *Die Zeit,* Hamburg, 1962); Otto Kirchheimer and Constantine Menges, "A Free Press in a Democratic State?" in Gwendolen M. Carter and Alan F. Westin, eds., *Politics in Europe* (Harcourt, Brace & World Inc., New York, Chicago, Burlingame, 1965), pp. 87-138; George Bailey, "The 'Spiegel' Affair: A Distorting Mirror," *Reporter* (December 6, 1962), pp. 29-32; Sebastian Haffner, "The End of the Affair," *Encounter,* Vol. 20 (March, 1963), pp. 62-67; and John Gimbel, "The 'Spiegel Affair' in Perspective," *Midwest Journal of Political Science,* Vol. 9 (August 1965), pp. 282-297. The implications of the *Spiegel* Affair for the "constitutional" function of the press are examined in Martin Löffler, *Der Verfassungsauftrag der Presse, Modellfall Spiegel* (Verlag C. F. Müller, Karlsruhe, 1963). A projected three volume collection of commentaries and documents, under the general editorship of Jürgen Seifert, will in the future be an indispensable source of information on the *Spiegel* Affair. The first two volumes, now in print but appearing after the completion of the present study, are titled: *Die Spiegel-Affäre: Die Staatsmacht und ihre Kontrolle;* and *Die Spiegel-Affäre: Die Reaktion der Offentlichenkeit* (Walter-Verlag, Olton and Freiburg im Breisgau, 1966).

For the relevant laws in judging the legality of the investigatory procedures, see Otto Schwarz and Theodor Kleinknecht, *Strafprozessordnung, Gerichtsverfassungsgesetz, Nebengesetze und ergänzende Bestimmungen* (C. H. Beck'sche Verlagsbuchhandlung, München and Berlin, 1963, 24th edition). A convenient collection of Rudolf Augstein's articles, published originally in *Der Spiegel,* is found in Rudolf Augstein, *Spiegelungen* (List Verlag, München, 1964). The Fibag Affair is examined in Erich Kuby, *Im Fibag-Wahn* (Rowohlt Taschenbuch Verlag GmbH, Reinbek bei Hamburg, 1962).

Among the flood of articles on treasonable publication which appeared in the wake of the *Spiegel* Affair, the following might be mentioned: Adolf Arndt, "Das Staatsgeheimnis als Rechtsbegriff und als Beweisfrage," *Neue Juristische Wochenschrift,* Vol. 16 (May 14, 1963), pp. 465-469; Gustav Heinemann, "Der publizistische Landesverrat," *Neue Juristische Wochenschrift,* Vol. 16 (January 10, 1963), pp. 4-8; Heinrich Jagusch, "Pressefreiheit, Redaktionsgeheimnis, Bekanntmachung von Staatsgeheimnissen," *Neue Juristische Wochenschrift,* Vol. 16 (January 31, 1963), pp. 177-183; and Erich Kuechenhoff, "Landesverrat, Oppositionsfreiheit und Verfassungsverrat," *Die Neue Gesellschaft,* 1963, pp. 124-127.

A pre-*Spiegel* Affair critique of the style and function of *Der Spiegel* is Paul Sackarndt, *Der Spiegel-Entzaubert, Analyse eines Deutschen Nachrichtenmagazins* (Essen, 1961). A useful collection of essays on the development and characteristics of the West German press is contained in Harry Pross, *Deutsche Presse seit 1945* (Scherz Verlag, Bern, München, Wien, 1965).

ACKNOWLEDGMENT

While in West Germany in 1963, on a Fulbright Senior Research Grant, I was able to initiate my research on the *Spiegel* Affair. Later I was able to continue the field research through a grant (1965) from the Louisiana State University Research Council. To those who made these grants possible, I am grateful. To the directors of various research institutions, and to civil servants, political party leaders, and Bundestag deputies who assisted me, I must also acknowledge a very great debt of appreciation.

The Soviet Union: Literary Conflict and the Sinyavsky-Daniel Affair

by Michael P. Gehlen

It isn't necessary to lie to young people.
It isn't necessary to convince them of things that are false.
It isn't necessary to persuade them that God's in his heaven and all's
    right with the world.
They understand.
    They are also people.
Let them know
    that there are uncounted troubles.
And let them see
    clearly see
        that which is.
Obstacles will often confront them.
Sorrow and misfortune really happen.
But what of it!
    Whoever doesn't know the price of happiness
        will never be happy anyway.
Those who recognize mistakes—
    don't forgive them,
Or else they'll be repeated
    all the more strongly.
The faults we forgave our elders
    our children may not so easily forgive us.[1]
          —YEVGENII YEVTUSHENKO

THIS POEM WAS WRITTEN BY THE POPULAR YOUNG SOVIET POET, Yevgenii Yevtushenko, shortly after the Twentieth Congress of the Communist Party of the Soviet Union (CPSU) in 1956. Khrushchev's speech attacking Stalin at the conclusion of the Congress had become common knowledge. Pointed criticism of the former dictator repeatedly appeared in the Soviet press. Denunciation of the "cult of personality" became synonymous with denunciation

167

of Stalin's heavy-handed methods of rule and the adulation that he had demanded for himself. For two decades prior to his death every speech by Soviet officials and the whole of the mass communications media had portrayed Stalin as the man of steel which his name denoted—strong, wise, benevolent, infallible. Now the very same men who had surrounded him during his rule had deliberately set out to destroy the image that they had helped to create. It was the deception, pawned off on the Soviet people during the Stalin period, that inspired Yevtushenko's poem, "It Isn't Necessary to Lie to Young People." It was an open and moving appeal to the new leadership for candor and honesty.

Yevtushenko is but one of many writers who have generated a renaissance in Soviet literature in the post-Stalin period. The result of this rebirth of literature has been sharp divisions among the members of the Union of Soviet Writers and periodic conflicts between writers and their professional organizations, between writers and official censors, and between writers and literary organizations on the one hand and the Party leadership on the other. Perhaps the most important political implication of these literary controversies is that they have been conducted in relatively open debate. For this reason, they represent the most public discussion of official policy that has taken place in the Soviet Union since the street debates between Stalinists and Trotskyites in the mid-1920's.

The history of rigorous state control of literature in the Soviet Union had begun with the implementation of the first Five-Year Plan from 1928 to 1933. In 1932 the Central Committee of the Party ordered the abolition of all writers' organizations. In 1934 the new Union of Soviet Writers convened the First Writers' Congress. The meeting was a hallmark in the development of Soviet literature, for it set forth the basic guidelines which all writers were expected to follow. These guidelines were given the name of *socialist realism*. The Congress defined the newly articulated doctrine in a resolution: "Socialist realism, being the basic method of Soviet literature and literary criticism, requires from the artist a truthful, historically concrete representation of reality in its revolutionary development. Moreover, truth and historical completeness of artistic representation must be combined with the task of ideological transformation and education of the working man

in the spirit of Socialism." The Congress went on to set forth the
objective of the members of the Writers' Union as "the creation
of works of high artistic significance, saturated with the heroic
struggle of the international proletariat, the glory of the victory
of Socialism, and reflecting the great wisdom and heroism of the
Communist Party."

As it developed over the succeeding two decades, the doctrine
of socialist realism came to signify the glorification of labor, the
ability of Soviet man to overcome all obstacles and enemies
through the leadership of the "positive hero," and the ultimately
happy resolution of all conflicts. The doctrine further required
emphasis on contemporary and future life, containing implicit
disapproval of excessive pre-occupation with the past. In support
of the concept, the chairman and board of the Writers' Union were
given the authority to see that literary works not meeting the
standards of socialist realism remained unpublished by requiring
everyone who wrote for publication to be a member of the union.
Armed with this weapon as well as with general control over
editorial boards, the Union was placed in a position of supreme
censor over all Soviet men of letters. By expelling an author from
the union, the censors could prevent even the possibility of publication.

Perhaps the harshest period of control began in 1946 with a
campaign directed by Andrei Zhdanov, one of Stalin's chief lieutenants. Strict guidelines were introduced that were designed to
govern the style as well as the substantive content of literature,
painting, sculpture, and music. Despite the fact that its principal
architect died in 1948, "Zhdanovism" continued as the basic official policy toward the creative arts during the remainder of Stalin's
dictatorship. Defenders of socialist realism used the forum of the
executive meetings of the Union of Soviet Writers and the editorial
pages of political and literary newspapers and journals to condemn
"formalism" and Western influence. At best, they demanded public confessions and recantations of authors judged guilty of literary
"errors." At worst, exile to concentration camps or in extreme
cases outright death penalties were imposed upon the greatest offenders. The nascent anti-intellectualism of the dogmatic supporters of socialist realism also took the form of anti-semitism,
for some campaigns against literary and theater figures clearly fell

most heavily upon persons of Jewish extraction. After the death of Stalin, official statistics were released that claimed that 617 writers had been sent to camps for political reasons and 305 of these had died in Siberian concentration centers.[2]

The central purpose of this case study is to examine and analyze the relationship between literature and politics between 1953 and 1966. The climax of the conflict in Soviet literary development in this period came with the trial of Sinyavsky and Daniel in February 1966. The trial itself, however, cannot be properly appreciated without an understanding of previous events and the setting within which it took place.

LITERARY CONFLICT IN THE POST-STALIN PERIOD: 1953-1956

In many respects Soviet creative artists were the first to give public expression to dissatisfaction with some of the basic tenets of Stalinism, especially as they applied to their domain. Only a few months passed after Stalin's death before critical evaluations of the state of Soviet literature began to appear. A series of publications in 1953 set forth the principal criticism of moderate and liberal writers of official policy and particularly of the colorless works that they considered to be the inevitable product of that policy.

The first critical evaluation to attract widespread attention was Olga Bergholts's essay, "Words About Lyricism," which appeared in *The Literary Gazette* on April 16, 1953. Good poetry, she contended, could only be found in works where the author permitted himself the liberty of genuine self-expression. The implication was that writers who indulged themselves by filling official orders for prose and poetry on subjects with which they had no familiarity and for which they had no real feelings of their own could not possibly create a sense of lyricism in their works.

Discontent with restrictions imposed on the arts and letters by administrators became a principal topic of discussion among creative artists in the summer of 1953. Abram Khachaturian, the prominent Soviet composer, noted that "creative problems cannot be solved by bureaucratic methods." This feeling was articulated most clearly in two essays as well as in a column in *Pravda* that appeared later in the year. The first essay was by the venerable figure of Soviet journalism and literature, Ilya Ehrenburg. The periodical *Znamya* (*The Banner*) published his comments entitled "The Writer's Work" in the October issue. Ehrenburg contended that writers should be free to choose the topics of their works as they pleased and should be able to write them spontaneously, without having official deadlines and subject matter regularly presented to them. "A writer is not an apparatus mechanically recording events," he told his readers. He writes not in order to meet deadlines, but "because he is compelled to tell the people something he personally feels, because he has begun to ache from his book. . . ." Ehrenburg pointedly remarked that in creative endeavors "statistics do not play the same role as they do in industry."

Pravda, the official newspaper of the CPSU, contained a surprisingly liberal column by N. K. Cherkasov on October 9, 1953. The author wrote, "There is nothing more harmful to art than attempts to . . . limit artistic individuality. Those artists who confuse unity with conformity do not have enough breadth of scope." Cherkasov proceeded to attack bureaucratic controls in literature. "Why is it that some official in the apparatus . . . thinks he knows better than the theater group itself whether a work that has been chosen conforms to the potentials of a given theater or not?"

Perhaps the sharpest criticism of the state of Soviet literature appeared in the literary journal, *Novy mir,* in December. It was then edited by the politically astute liberal, Alexander Tvardovsky. This critical analysis was contained in an article by Vladimir Pomerantsev under the name "On Sincerity in Literature." Provoking the greatest controversy over literary criticism in the early post-Stalin period, the author asserted quite bluntly that there had been very little good literature published in recent years. Pomerantsev contended that the chief reason for this unhappy state of affairs was the lack of honesty among writers. Sincerity in self-expression was a prerequisite of good literature, he claimed, and there was little evidence of it in most contemporary works.

Pomerantsev's charges could not be expected to go unanswered. *The Literary Gazette,* on January 30, 1954, published an article by Vitaly Vasilevsky entitled "From Wrong Positions." The author sharply rebuked Pomerantsev by name for his "wrong" assertions.

From this point on, the conflict and accompanying debate between the liberals and conservatives of Soviet literature became increasingly manifest. In general, the liberals demanded either the removal or at least the reduction of restrictions on their choices of subjects and on the styles in which they chose to write. The conservatives wanted state enforcement of a more dogmatic interpretation of socialist realism, some of them fully embracing Zhdanovism and others settling simply for their continuing influence on the executive committee of the Writers' Union and for strong representation on the editorial boards. The role of the Party and of state organs in the conflict remained the big question.

In addition to the critical essays of Bergholts, Ehrenburg, and Pomerantsev, the liberals challenged the conservative position most vigorously and effectively in poetry, prose, and drama. Fyodor Panfyorov's novel, *Mother River Volga,* contained an unadorned attack on bureaucracy. The protagonist proclaims, "Forget about planning and think of the needs of the people." Valentin Ovechkin's novel, *Workaday Life in a Rural District,* contained explicit descriptions of the poverty of contemporary village life instead of sugar-coated accounts of the glories of peasant life and labor. The once half-filled theaters of Moscow and Leningrad had sold-out performances for a series of new plays. Drama, however, was more easily censored by officials, for plays could be suspended, whereas once a poem or novel had been published, the damage to conservative policy had already been done. Thus, Leonid Zorin's play, *The Guests,* which suggested the moral decay of bureaucrats who had become too comfortable in their positions, ran for only two performances (both of them to packed houses).

One of the most controversial literary publications of the 1953-1956 period was Ilya Ehrenburg's novel, *The Thaw*. The first part appeared in *Znamya* in May 1954. When it was published in book form in September of that year, all copies were sold out in Moscow by the time the shops closed on the day of its release. While the novel is far from a literary masterpiece, it was received with such enthusiasm that the book gave its name to the lessening of controls over art forms. Ehrenburg makes no overt reference to politics, but the symbolism he employs leaves no doubt concerning the intentions of the inferences. A "thaw" in human relations accompanies the spring thaw in 1953. His characters become less restrained, more given to self-examination and to a new awareness of the importance of human relationships. About the same time that *The Thaw* was released, another indication that Ehrenbrug's assessment was valid came with the publication of several of Boris Pasternak's poems that belonged to his novel *Doctor Zhivago*.

The conservatives wasted no time in launching a counter-attack that carried the official support of a major portion of the Party elite. In May, *Pravda* printed a column by Alexei Surkov, a poet and a faithful party representative in the Union of Soviet Writers. Surkov attacked "new trends" in literature and defended the policy lines enunciated in 1946-1948 by Zhdanov. By August the campaign against the liberals attained new momentum, as the conservatives demonstrated their continued dominance in the writers's organization. Four liberal writers were expelled from the Union of Soviet Writers and others, including Ehrenburg and Pomerantsev, were given public reprimands. A meeting of the executive committee of the Union approved a resolution condemning the "errors" of the journal *Novy mir*. The resolution dealt a serious blow to the opportunity of the liberals to publish their work by removing Alexander Tvardovsky from his post as editor-in-chief and replacing him with Konstantin Simyonov, a trusted member of the conservative camp.

The actions of the executive committee were designed as a prelude to the convocation of the Second Congress of the Union of Soviet Writers, the first time the whole membership had been called into session since 1934. The Congress met in December 1954, with conservatives clearly holding the upper hand. With a few notable exceptions, the official sessions were devoted to repetitious speeches containing the traditional homilies of Marxist-Leninist jargon. Behind this outward façade of unanimity, however, there was evidence of heated discussion that indicated considerable discontent and confusion. Most significantly, in spite of their near-monopoly of the most important official posts, the conservatives were not able to restore their old authority to silence the opposition and to demand abject obedience from them.

Although the conservatives succeeded in electing Alexei Surkov as the new first secretary of the Union and in re-affirming the validity of the doctrine of socialist realism, the liberals maintained their opposition rather than recant their "errors" or remain silent.

Valentin Ovechkin and Grigory Medynsky led the most recalcitrant liberals in openly defending the reformers' cause. Ovechkin's address was a direct, often sarcastic, attack on the speeches of Surkov and Simyonov. The latter's comments, he caustically noted, were "moderately critical, moderately self-critical, moderately bold, and moderately cautious." More important than these two orations, Ovechkin said, was the "anxiety" of genuine creative writers over the appearance of masses of "mediocre, dull-gray little books." This dullness, he contended, could be directly attributed to the bureaucratic orientations of the "middle generation" of Soviet writers who held most of the administrative positions in literary organs. Their influence was made possible in large measure, according to Ovechkin, by "the system of awarding Stalin Prizes." The latter remark was an open thrust at the nation's principal decision-makers.

Ehrenburg contributed to the attack on the "dull-gray books" by asking rhetorically what readers were likely to find in them. Answering himself, he said that they found "communal apartments decorated in gold . . . kolkhoz club houses resembling palatial mansions—a world of stage properties. . . ." Ehrenburg pointed out the lack of reality in such presentations. Vera Ketlinskaya also joined in the attempt of the liberals to stage a counter-offensive. "Our Union of Writers," she asserted, "resembles a ministry, with the difference that at its head are poets and novelists who have no administrative talents. . . ." The remarks of Ovechkin, Ehrenburg, and Ketlinskaya amounted to nothing short of a direct assault on official policy. They signaled the refusal of the liberals to lie down and play dead.

Besides having their moments on the platform, the liberals made some minimal, but nonetheless noteworthy, gains in the Second Congress. Anna Akhmatova, the poet who had been one of the objects of Zhdanov's campaign against "erotic" and "mystical" writers in 1946, was re-admitted to membership in the Writers' Union and participated in the sessions of the Congress. Several writers who had only recently been publicly reprimanded were elected members of the Board of the Writers' Union. Among these were Tvardovsky, Panova, and Grossman. The Congress therefore represented something of a stand-off between the rival factions. The conservatives still had the edge in terms of overall influence, but the liberals regained some of their strength since the August reprisals against them.

During 1954-1955 the political leadership of the country was still in a state of flux. After the decline of Malenkov and Molotov and the increase in the stature of Khrushchev in the first half of 1955, the Party leadership agreed to accept some of the requests of liberal-minded authors. This support was demonstrated by the unexpected rehabilitation of several writers whose works and sometimes even whose names had been shielded from the public for years. Babel, Katayev, Kirilov, Kirshon (executed during the purges of 1936-1938), Meyerhold, Yasensky, and more than a dozen others were among those whose works were restored for public consumption. Victims of the anti-semitic purge, conducted during the last years of Stalin's rule, were also rehabilitated. Even the long ban on the works of Dostoyevsky was lifted, as his complete works were published on the 75th anniversary of his death.

Another striking development of the mid-1950's, that has had a continuing impact on subsequent Soviet literature, was the vast increase in the translations of Western literature. Among the works made available were collections of Theodore Dreiser, Mark Twain, O. Henry, Thomas Mann, George Bernard Shaw, Sherwood Anderson, William Faulkner, John Steinbeck, Erskine Caldwell, Jack London, Ernest Hemingway, and numerous others. The translations were generally of excellent quality and some of the authors, especially Hemingway and London, became great popular favorites. Similar developments occurred in drama and the musical theater. *Dial M for Murder* and *Witness for the Prosecution* by Agatha Christie had two-year runs in Moscow before packed auditoriums. However, according to one scholar of Soviet literature, Marc Slonim, the principal source of Western influence came from the East European party-states, especially from Poland and Hungary. Soviet writers began to travel extensively in these countries and to meet and discuss issues with their writers. Slonim reports, "Not only in private conversations, but in public conferences, congresses, and public discussions, they were confronted with concepts that hailed creative freedom and unhampered search for new forms of expression. Even more shattering to the Russians was their hosts' low opinion of the theory and practice of socialist realism." [3]

THE TWENTIETH PARTY CONGRESS
AND THE LITERARY CONTROVERSY

If Stalin's death had been a boon to Soviet creative artists, the Twentieth Party Congress must be accorded an even more important place in the development of contemporary Russian literature. Moderates and liberals received official support from high-ranking Party dignitaries in the Congress even before the anti-Stalin campaign was publicly launched.

Mikhail Sholokhov, the honored epic novelist and member of the Central Committee of the Party, set the new tone for Soviet writers in his address to the Congress. He noted that there were 3,247 full members and 526 candidate members of the Union of Soviet Writers. These figures, he explained to the delight of the liberals, were deceptive, for they included many "dead souls." Repeating Ovechkin's charges before the Second Congress of Writers, Sholokhov said, "We must recognize that during the last twenty years we had but a handful of good, intelligent books, and huge stacks of gray rubbish." Most surprising, however, was Sholokhov's direct attack on the Writers' Union. It had been conceived as a "creative collective," he contended, but had become a bureaucratic organization that hindered rather than helped Soviet writers. He centered his criticism on Alexander Fadeyev, the former general secretary of the Union. "Why no one told him during the past fifteen years that the Writers' Union is not a military unit and definitely not a penal colony and that no writer wants to stand 'at attention' in front of Fadeyev . . . ?" The general secretary "could not be and is not an infallible artistic authority." He went on to deliver a sharp personal rebuke: "Neither as a general secretary nor as a writer has he done anything in the last fifteen years." Sholokhov proceeded to direct the same kind of barbs at the new secretary general, Alexei Surkov. Poets could not seek advice from him, he asserted, because "he fails to comprehend that an orchestra is composed of more than drums and percussion. . . ."

Sholokhov's speech indicated beyond reasonable doubt that official sanction had been given to modification of the standard interpretation of socialist realism. Even more interesting, however, was the failure to set forth any new boundaries within which writers had to operate. It was as though the Party elite had not considered the possibility that literary experimentation could take unprecedented and unsettling proportions. At the same time, there was nothing in any of the speeches to the Congress that suggested the leaders of the regime either had abandoned or would abandon their right to intervene if the occasion seemed to demand it.

With this uncertain liberty granted them, Soviet authors produced an avalanche of provocative works and some of them even set out to test the organizational stability of the Writers' Union. Most of the works were discrete in their probing of basic questions about the Soviet system itself, but many of the authors appeared to be engaged in competition with one another to see who could expose the greatest number of flaws, particularly bureaucratic ones, in the system. Furthermore, the topics which authors explored expanded considerably. Yevtushenko translated an Armenian poem about a Party official's love affair with a married woman. Semyon Kirsanov published his highly satirical ballad, "The Seven Days of the Week," in which the "organizational men" experimented with the mass production of hearts that could be substituted for human hearts as a means of controlling human emotions. Numerous other works appeared that touched upon similar problems, many of them by promising new poets and short-story writers such as Robert Rozhdestvensky, Yevgenii Vinokurov, and Vladimir Tendryakov. The change was apparent in the theater also, where new plays and new productions of nineteenth century dramas drew larger audiences than the plays produced in the Stalinist period.

In the midst of this literary activity, two publications were released that stand out above all others. These were an anthology of verse, stories, and essays entitled *Literary Moscow* and the novel, *Not By Bread Alone*, by Vladimir Dudintsev. The first volume of *Literary Moscow* appeared early in 1956. It contained poems and short stories as well as provocative critical essays that had not found publication elsewhere. Among the poems were several by Anna Akhmatova and others who had only recently been rehabilitated. In a critical analysis of Soviet drama, A. Kron claimed that the "stagnation" of the theater could be attributed to the "ignoring of the objective laws of artistic creation, the hypertrophy of editing, and the establishment of a bureaucratic hierarchy in the arts." The second volume of *Literary Moscow* appeared in 1957 and contained some of the strongest criticisms of bureaucracy and bureaucratic efforts to organize nearly every aspect of life that have yet been published in the USSR. Max Hayward, one of the foremost Western interpreters of Soviet literary developments, contends that the writers involved with *Literary Moscow* attempted to skirt the control of the Party and the Writers' Union by creating a "quasi-autonomous organization of Moscow writers." [4] While this effort did not succeed, it is noteworthy that the attempt was made.

Dudintsev's *Not By Bread Alone* attracted even wider public attention than the anthology of Moscow writers. It was published in serial form in *Novy mir* in 1956. Although the novel has many shortcomings from a literary standpoint, it provoked countless discussions and written responses throughout the country and was debated in Party and government sessions as well as in the executive board meetings of the Union of Soviet Writers. On October 27, 1956, *The Literary Gazette* reported a discussion of the novel that took place in the Central House of Literature. Noting how the crowd spilled into adjoining rooms, the presiding officer commented on how the meeting reminded him of the exciting years just after the revolution, when Soviet literature was being born. Other discussants asserted that in its description of an "ordinary little man who was battered by a series of misfortunes," the novel was "imbued with the love of mankind."

Just as the dramatic awakening in Soviet literature began to bear fruit, a succession of events beyond the control of the literary liberals dealt the renaissance a serious setback. The abortive revolution in Hungary, worsening relations with the United States, and internal challenges to Khrushchev created a much more difficult climate for the liberals, making it impossible for them to consolidate their gains.

THE CONSERVATIVE REACTION TO DE-STALINIZATION

Unrest in Poland in the summer and autumn of 1956, accompanied by the recall of Gomulka as first secretary of the Party and a liberal resurgence in Polish literature, began to provoke some second thoughts among Soviet leaders about unrestrained literary expression. The first indication of this came in August with the publication of the opening installment of a collection of Khrushchev's speeches on the role of literature and art in the Soviet system. The speeches contained a slightly modernized version of socialist realism and stressed that literature should be written to help build communism. However, no campaign against the liberals was evident until the reaction to the Hungarian revolution had set in.

The unrest in Eastern Europe helped to increase the influence of the old-guard in the higher Party organs. By tying the rebellion in Hungary and the unrest in Poland to the de-Stalinization program in the USSR, Molotov, the former foreign minister under Stalin and Malenkov, and Kaganovich, one of Stalin's stalwart friends and supporters, succeeded in staging a counter-offensive against the First Secretary and his policies. Khrushchev's proposal to decentralize the national ministries was rejected by the Party Presidium in December 1956. This move indicated the continuing power of the bureaucracy built by Stalin. The influence of the more doctrinaire Chinese communists also jumped, as they were called upon to help restore order in Eastern Europe. Relations with Western countries worsened during this interval as a result of West Germany's growing involvement in NATO, the Suez Crisis, and the fall of Soviet prestige following the suppression of the revolt in Hungary. Although Khrushchev succeeded in obtaining most of the economic reforms he wanted by going over the heads of the Party Presidium to the Central Committee in March 1957, his position remained insecure. This became dramatically evident in June 1957, when a majority of the members of the Presidium attempted to force him to resign as First Secretary. Even though he won that challenge, again by taking his case to the Central Committee, Khrushchev was not able to consolidate his victory until the fall of 1958 when he became Prime Minister of the government as well as head of the Party secretariat. During this period Khrushchev found it necessary to modify the scope of the de-Stalinization program in order to blunt the attack on his experimental policies by the conservatives in the Party hierarchy. The restoration of stability to the system and Khrushchev's continued dominance depended in large measure on concessions to the old-guard.

In the midst of these political events, the literary conservatives staged a resurgence. The restoration of conservative influence came in part as a result of the general rise of old-guard power in the Party and in part as a result of the fears of Khrushchev and his allies that unharnessed liberalization might undermine the support of the regime itself. The conservative resurgence was indicated by editorial attacks on liberal authors, especially on Dudintsev for his novel, *Not By Bread Alone*, and by the suppression of *Literary Moscow* after the publication of its second volume in 1957.

Despite the attack on Dudintsev, the author was allowed to defend himself before a plenary session of the board of the Moscow branch of the Union of Soviet Writers. He told the board:

> I remember the first days of the Patriotic War. I was lying in a trench, while an aerial battle raged overhead, with "Messerschmidts" knocking out our planes, which were considerably more numerous. At that moment something began to break inside me, for I had always heard until then that our air force was faster and better than any other.
>
> It is said that I tend to "blacken" reality. This is not true. I simply do not want to see a repetition of what I saw then. And I have a right not to want it.[5]

The publication of Dudintsev's remarks indicated that although the conservatives were on the offensive, the liberals still had sufficient support to have their views aired in the open. The extent to which Khrushchev felt compelled to support the conservative line had not yet been made clear.

Even as the dogmatists stepped up their attack, the liberals did not buckle under without protest. One of the most striking illustrations of the devotion of the liberal leaders to their pleas for greater freedom of self-expression in literature came in June 1957. After the Party censors refused to permit the publication of some material in *The Literary Gazette*, on the grounds that it was ideologically weak, Vera Panova, a popular Soviet writer, resigned as the editor of *The Breaking Wave* as a protest against unnecessary interference from the Party in literature.[6]

In August 1957, however, the tide turned decisively against the liberal-moderate faction of writers. *Kommunist*, the theoretical journal of the CPSU, published an article by Khrushchev entitled "For Closer Links between Literature and Art and the Life of the Peoples." The Party leader asserted that some writers, and there were "members of the Party among them," had not followed the correct course. "They appear to believe that it is the purpose of literature and art to seek out only shortcomings, to speak primarily about the negative aspects of life, about failures and inadequacies, overlooking everything that is positive." Khrushchev avowed that "the Party leadership has no intention of making concessions" to those who had "lost their footing." Too many writers, he charged, had produced works that were "contrary to Leninist principles concerning the approach of the Party and the State to problems of literature and life." Striking at the core of the liberals' official justification for many of their works, Khrushchev claimed that they could not introduce "bourgeois views" into Soviet literature by cloaking them under the guise of attacks on the cult of personality as represented by Joseph Stalin. In addition to such public admonitions, Khrushchev engaged in a series of chats with groups of writers in which he alternately scolded and gave them fatherly advice.

During this period of reaction, Vsevolod Kochetov emerged as one of the most prominent and articulate conservatives. Not content to confine the attack on liberal writers to essays and editorials, Kochetov wrote his novel, *The Brothers Yershov*, as a literary condemnation of opponents of socialist realism. In its stinging indictment of corrupt intelligentsia and the influence of "decadent bourgeois tendencies," the novel was blatantly anti-intellectual. The villains of the novel were thinly veiled caricatures of Soviet writers who had instigated the thaw in literary expression. Its central theme was condemnation of freedom in the creative arts. Kochetov played upon the fear of Soviet leaders of a repetition of Hungary by intimating that the unrest in Eastern Europe had been a product of liberalization. Considering the fanfare with which *The Brothers Yershov* was greeted in the official press, the novel appears to have had the direct support of at least some members of the political elite.

As conservative influence increased, another incident occurred that was, in one sense, both a result of the conservative tide and a stimulus to its further development. This was the Pasternak affair of 1958. Boris Pasternak towered above all twentieth century Russian poets as a great literary figure. Never a favorite of the political censors of literature, Pasternak nonetheless had experienced renewed eminence, especially during the thaw of 1953-1954. It was in April 1954 that Pasternak published some of the poems that were to comprise the final chapter of a novel. He noted in the preface to the poems that his novel was to be called *Doctor Zhivago* and that he hoped it would be ready for publication in 1955.

Doctor Zhivago was completed on schedule but it never appeared in the Soviet Union. The editorial board of *Novy mir,* after consulting with high political figures, declined to accept the manuscript. After a series of further frustrations and delays, Pasternak permitted his novel to be taken to an Italian publisher who had been sympathetic with leftist causes. Despite the appeals and protests of Soviet representatives and members of the Italian Communist Party, the editor refused to return the work and proceeded to prepare the manuscript for publication.

The treatment of *Doctor Zhivago* in the Western press, as a political novel with anti-Soviet overtones, was a misrepresentation of the work that had fanned the ire of Soviet officials. One of the principal reasons that the novel had been rejected by the defenders of Soviet realism was its non-political character. It was an intensely personal story that spanned the years 1905 to 1929 without contributing to the glorification of the system. It failed to meet the positive requirements of socialist realism. Most importantly, the author had permitted the work to be published abroad where its very publication had been seized upon by the Western press and turned into an international political event.

The Soviet press initially attempted to shield the public from news about Pasternak's novel and its international reception. However, the decision of the Swedish academy to award the Nobel Prize for Literature to the Russian poet made it impossible to continue to prevent the story of the whole episode from reaching the public. The Soviet censors then turned their wrath toward Pasternak himself. Officials promoted a widespread campaign against the writer that resulted in extremely brutal letters-to-editors of prominent publications, denouncing the poet as "traitor," "philistine," and "reactionary." A groundswell of citizens' groups, obviously with official encouragement, demanded Pasternak's expulsion from the country. At first, the poet had "joyfully" accepted the honor of receiving the Nobel Prize. Under the pressure of the campaign conducted against him, however, Pasternak finally declined to accept the award and wrote a moving and somewhat pathetic letter to Khrushchev in which he said "leaving my motherland would be equal to death for me. And that is why I ask you not to take this final measure. . . ." This letter, combined with the unfavorable global publicity given the Soviet leadership, won Pasternak the right to remain in the USSR and live the remaining two years of his life at his home in Peredelkino.

While the Pasternak affair served as a blunt reminder to Soviet writers that the authority of the censors not only existed but could be ruthlessly put into effect, liberal authors were far from silenced. Provocative questions were still raised by poets and young prose writers, who began to take advantage of the short story and novella forms. Yuri Kazakov, Yuri Nagibin, and Vladimir Tendryakov were among those who published probing personal, non-political prose works during this period. Others, more recalcitrant after the treatment of Pasternak, took to the underground and distributed their works in mimeograph copies. Within the succeeding years, several of these writers smuggled their manuscripts abroad, where they were published under such pen names as Abram Tertz and Nikolai Arzhak. One, Valeri Tarsis, was so bold as to use his real name, refusing to conceal his identity. The hero of *What a Gay Life!* by Tarsis was an obvious caricature of Nikita Khrushchev. On the whole, the underground writers are much more hostile to the Soviet system itself than most liberal writers, who are opposed more to the practice of control over creative endeavors than they are to the system as such. As Khrushchev himself noted, many liberals are active party members.

The conservatives, however, were apparently not content with the outcome of the Pasternak episode. In December 1958 they moved to entrench themselves further in the organizational machinery of the Writers' Union. This was accomplished by the creation of the Union of Writers of the RSFSR, a separate organization within the Union of Soviet Writers. It became known as the "Russian section" of the Union. The new organization was clearly a response to the attempt of the liberal Moscow writers to establish their own unit in 1956. The hope of the conservatives was to reduce the effectiveness of the liberal writers' colonies in Moscow and Leningrad by flooding the membership of the new organization with conventional writers from outlying regions.

By the time the conservatives had obtained their right to a new organization, however, the political scene had been restored to a

state of relative calm. Khrushchev had, for the time being, consolidated his power. Furthermore, he was interested in restoring
some of the prestige lost after Hungary and the Pasternak affair.
In particular, the Prime Minister had become interested in visiting
the United States and restoring a measure of normality to Amer-
ican-Soviet relations. In this atmosphere, he could afford to re-
appraise the literary scene and make overtures of friendship to the
liberal-moderate coalition of writers as a means of regaining the
confidence of the intelligentsia.

The first indication of the shift in outlook was not recognized as
such at the time. The Union of Soviet Writers had been scheduled
to convene their Third Congress in December. Without explanation, the meeting was postponed until the spring of 1959. Later it
became apparent that the reason for the postponement was that
the leadership wanted the Pasternak affair to die down before the
warring factions of the Writers' Union faced each other in an
open meeting. Direct Party intervention might have been required
in order to control the flow of events and the Party leaders apparently preferred not to intervene again so soon after the Pasternak affair. This in itself was a significant development. Further
indications of a cautious shift in policy came in the early months of
1959.

In May 1959, the Third Congress of Soviet Writers was held
in Moscow. Surkov delivered a long, tedious speech to the opening
session of the Congress. He cautioned the liberals against misinter-
preting the reasons for errors resulting from the Stalinist cult of
personality, and proclaimed that "the watchword" for all writers
should be "ideological struggle against revisionist (liberal) tendencies." Citing the most conservative quotations that could be
found in Khrushchev's earlier speeches and writings, Surkov defended the doctrine of socialist realism as representing the spirit of
party loyalty. Writers were also encouraged to portray the new
communist man, his "new social relations, his new qualities" in
the heroes of their books and stories. Overall, it was a rambling
speech that reduced the expectations of the delegates.

Surkov's speech set the tone for most of the remaining sessions.
As a result of the dullness, many interpreters discounted the significance of the whole meeting. In retrospect, however, it is clear
that the Third Congress was of major significance, for it charted a

new course in the relationship between literature and politics, the full impact of which was not realized until some time after the meetings. Indications of the new course came in the speeches of Tvardovsky and Khrushchev.

Tvardovsky delivered a forceful appeal for a re-evaluation of Soviet literature. Condemning the emphasis on the volume of works produced, the poet demanded that in the future "quality must take preference over quantity." "We do not need organizational measures here but the individual example of supreme artistry." Tvardovsky cautioned that such artistry "is not a responsibility one can entrust to the collective as a sort of deity. . . ." Instead, he said, "every writer must have *personal* understanding of tasks confronting literature on the threshold of communism." "The highest form of collective responsibility in our work is a genuinely understood responsibility for one's self and not for 'literature as a whole.'" The liberal leader then gave some bold advice to young writers: "Write as your conscience dictates, as your knowledge of the sector of life you have chosen permits you to write, and do not fear editors and critics beforehand." These remarks constituted a call to the literary innovators for a kind of declaration of independence.

On the last day of the Congress, Khrushchev addressed a much larger crowd of writers than had attended the previous sessions. The first part of the Prime Minister's speech was devoted to a defense of *partiinost,* the concept of party solidarity and support of party principles. He restated some tenets of socialist realism, particularly the idea of positive heroes, but he did not treat it as a matter of party principle. Instead, he suggested that the positive approach to plot and character had been too harshly criticized and deserved a second look by those who would reject it. In general, his admonitions were paternalistic rather than dogmatic and aggressive. Indeed, as the speech progressed, it became increasingly apparent that Khrushchev was reprimanding the conservatives as well as exhorting the liberals to exercise sound judgment. This was evident in his insistence on tolerance and his defense of young writers, some of whom (especially Yevtushenko) he took personal pride in encouraging. Resorting to one of his favorite oratorical devices, Khrushchev employed the metaphor to get his point across: "In order to learn to swim, you have to jump into the water and try your strength. . . . Let young writers develop their talents in their own ways."

Then the Prime Minister endorsed one of the principal requests of the liberals—the right to run their own affairs within the general context of the system. Khrushchev remarked,

> You will ask—what guarantee is there against mistakes? It is difficult to give guarantees since a writer, if he is a true Soviet writer, makes mistakes not consciously, not deliberately, but for reasons such as inadequate knowledge of life, false premises, and so forth. In order to prevent this, one must remember that writers live in a society, reflect the life of that society, that their work must be guided by the criticism of society and that they must consider this criticism.

These comments served as a reminder that the Party reserved the right to express its views on literary trends and particular literary works. But Khrushchev went on to say,

> Again, you may say—"Criticize us, control us. If a work is not correct, do not print it," but you know that it is difficult to determine immediately what to print and what not to print. The easiest thing to do would be to print nothing . . . but that would be stupid. Therefore, comrades, *do not bother the government* with the solution of such questions. (Italics added.) Decide them for yourselves in comradely fashion.

These last remarks created the general impression that Khrushchev would prefer to leave literary affairs to the writers and that his demand for ideological exactness had been watered down since the conservative reaction to Hungary had shaken his control of the Party.

The day after the Congress adjourned, the executive board of the Union of Soviet Writers met and demonstrated that they had taken Khrushchev's message seriously. The conservative first secretary of the Union, Alexei Surkov, was replaced with Konstantin Fedin, a moderate man much less given to interference in the work of the members of the Union. Although Surkov remained in the secretariat of the organization, he was joined by Alexander Tvardovsky and Fyodor Panfyorov, two liberals whom Surkov had bitterly assailed in the past. Changes were forthcoming on important editorial boards as well. Tvardovsky was re-instated as editor-in-chief of *Novy mir* and Panfyorov was also elected to the editorial board. Finally and perhaps most pleasing to the liberals, Kochetov, the author of the bitter anti-liberal *The Brothers Yershov,* was removed as editor of *The Literary Gazette* and replaced by the moderate S. S. Smirnov.

Liberal writers wasted no time in testing the meaning of Khrushchev's comments to the Congress in terms of the basic content of their manuscripts. Konstantin Paustovsky, one of the older romanticists of Soviet literature, wrote a column in *The Literary Gazette* containing a strong appeal for sincerity and honesty in literary works. Even bolder was Ehrenburg's essay in *Novy mir* that was printed under the caption "On Rereading Chekhov." Ehrenburg employed extended quotations from Chekhov to attack the doctrine of socialist realism, especially its emphasis on positive heroes. The elder statesman of Soviet journalism went so far as to characterize the chief components of the doctrine as "bourgeois." Turning his pen on the efforts of conservatives to draw caricatures of liberal writers in works of fiction, Ehrenburg noted:

> In the difficult times of the 1880's Chekhov spoke of the solidarity of the writers of that generation. Is it not time to give serious consideration to the question of solidarity among writers in our Soviet era? Savage assaults on young writers, cliquishness, and novels in which authors settle accounts with their comrade writers would be incompatible with such solidarity.

These comments suggested the author's hope for a united front of all writers as a means of better attaining concessions from the political leaders. Younger liberals must have looked on with great interest as the thrusts of Paustovsky and Ehrenburg failed to provoke any response from the officials.

The conservatives had been dealt an unexpected blow. Khrushchev had in effect defended the liberals' right to experiment and, more significantly, had given them a greater measure of influence in the literary community. Moreover the liberals had promptly demonstrated their newly found strength by pressing their case in the Writers' Union and in publications. Vera Panova expressed the meaning of this new approach to literature and politics in an interview recorded in *The Literary Gazette* on October 23, 1959. She told the interviewer:

> Sometimes you read a novel and you do not believe the author on page two, on page ten, or on page seventeen. And if there is a

sudden flash of truth on page one-hundred, you suspect even that, for it is buried under all the falsehood. *Nothing that compromises artistic truth can be tolerated in art.* (Italics added.)

The conservative reaction had been arrested—at least for the time being.

LITERATURE AND POLITICS: 1960-1962

After the Third Congress of Writers, literary controversy subsided for several years. Periodic sharp exchanges occurred between the rival factions of the Union of Soviet Writers, but the Party elite rarely intervened. Several promising new writers appeared and, as a whole, it was a period of great literary productivity. Much of the work followed the favorite themes of socialist realism, focusing on contemporary settings on collective farms and in factories. But the younger writers often approached these themes and environments with a great deal of creativity and sensitivity.

By this time the leaders of the factions in the Writers' Union had become easily identifiable. The most outspoken champion of conventional socialist realism was Vsevolod Kochetov. After hesitating for nearly six months, public officials made Kochetov editor-in-chief of the journal *October* early in 1961. Also in that year, he published his novel, *The District Party Secretary*, that was an even more open and abusive attack on intellectualism and liberalism than *The Brothers Yershov*. One of the figures in the novel was turned into a transparent take-off on the liberal poet, Yevtushenko, whom Kochetov had denounced as less than useless. Alexei Surkov, former chairman of the Union of Soviet Writers, and the young poet, Alexei Markov, joined Kochetov as principal proponents of the dogmatic, conservative faction. They had at their ready disposal two literary journals, *October* and *Literature and Life*, which they used to publish works of the orthodox socialist realist school as well as editorial barbs aimed at the liberals.

The older writers in the liberal faction, previously identified, were supported by a host of popular, talented young writers. Such young prose authors as Vasily Aksenov, Yuri Nagibin, and Vladimir Tendryakov produced imaginative and widely read short stories and short novels. Probably the most widely known writers of the new generation, however, were poets. The poetic form lent itself to greater advantage than prose in several respects. In the first place, poetry has traditionally been a favorite literary form among the Russian people. In the second place, it also provided a means of easier presentation to the public in the present milieu. Even if poems were rejected by editors, they could be read to public audiences. It was customary to read them publicly before they were published in any event. The censors therefore could not readily control this form of expression. Several young poets seized upon the public platform as a means of disseminating their ideas and their verses. Among the most successful of these were Yevgenii Yevtushenko, Andrei Voznesensky, Robert Rozhdestvensky, and Yevgenii Vinokurov. Furthermore, the young liberals had considerable influence on the editorial board of *Yunost*, a literary magazine for young people. The older liberals dominated *Novy mir*, under Tvardovsky's direction. Middle-of-the-roaders continued to control the chief literary newspaper, *The Literary Gazette*.

Of all of the younger writers, Yevtushenko appears to have captured the devotion of Soviet youth most successfully. Unlike many other new writers, his work was frequently openly political in tone. In February 1960 *Yunost* published his poem, "Consider Me a Communist." This poem is significant because it expresses the idealism and desires of many of contemporary Soviet young people, who accept communism but who have redefined it to suit their particular aspirations. Their interpretation is permeated with the idealism and humanitarianism found in a part of Marxist philosophy that is frequently overlooked by the older generation of communists. Yevtushenko proclaims "I am happy I can wage a righteous war against all lies. . . ." He declares that he is a better communist than many party members in high places who have lost their concern for and understanding of human life. To those who would compel him to accept the official views of the Party elite, he boasts in his poem, "I'll not be turned into a fawning sycophant." It is interesting that Khrushchev developed a fondness for Yevtushenko and sometimes took it upon himself to give "fatherly" advice, apparently in the hope of keeping him out of trouble.

Yevtushenko and Vasily Aksenov helped to articulate a profound division in Soviet society that became known as the fathers-sons controversy, after Turgenev's novel *Fathers and Sons*. This controversy was the result of disillusionment of the sons with the heritage given them by their parents. The Party has officially denied the existence of such a cleavage in Soviet society and has accused Yevtushenko and Aksenov of trying to create one. Despite this denial, the works of many young authors touch upon the theme. In June and July 1961 *Yunost* published a striking novel by Aksenov entitled *Ticket to the Stars*. The characters and action could comfortably fit in countless Western cities as several young people attempt to find themselves in a rapidly changing world. The sense of alienation and searching is powerful, although the novel itself falls short of being a literary masterpiece. One of the finest literary expressions of the fathers-sons conflict is found in Victor Rozov's scenario *A B C* (published as *ABVDG* in *Yunost* in September 1961). The implications of this drama were sufficiently clear and compelling to warrant an official rebuke in the Party press.

In September 1961 Yevtushenko generated another controversy with the publication of his poem, "Babi Yar," in *The Literary Gazette*. "There are no monuments at Babi Yar," the poet begins as he launches into a moving condemnation of anti-semitism. The scene of his poem is the place where tens of thousands of Ukrainian Jews were massacred by the Nazis during World War II. After recalling the cases of Dreyfus, Anne Frank, and others, Yevtushenko concludes:

> Oh, my Russian people!
>   I know you
> to be profoundly international.
> Yet often those with dirty hands
> call upon your clean name.
> I know the kindness of my land.
> How base are those anti-semites who solemnly
> proclaim themselves the 'Union of Russian People!'
> Nothing in me will let me forget this!
> Let the *International* ring out
> when the last anti-semite on earth
> will be forever buried.
>
> No Jewish blood runs in my veins
> But I am bitterly hated by every anti-semite as a Jew.
>
> And therefore,
>   I am a real Russian! [7]

"Babi Yar" openly raised the question of anti-semitism and was taken, probably quite correctly, as a direct assault on official policy and on the literary dogmatists.

Shortly after the publication of Yevtushenko's poem, the conservative journal *Literature and Life* printed a poem and an essay sharply criticizing "Babi Yar." Alexei Markov addressed Yevtushenko in verse:

> What kind of Russian are you anyway
> When you forget all about your own people. . . .

The essay reminded the public that Jews were not the only persons murdered and buried at Babi Yar. Official disavowals of the existence of anti-semitism appeared in the speeches and publications of influential individuals and newspapers in response to the poem. The answer of the public, however, indicated the strength of Yevtushenko's position. On Poetry Day in October 1961 over ten thousand people turned out and transformed the meeting into a mass demonstration for Yevtushenko, whose appearance and poetry reading overshadowed all else at the meeting. Western observers at the session reported that tears filled the eyes of many persons in the audience as the young poet recited "Babi Yar" and that the storm of applause that followed his recitation left no uncertainty as to their feelings about Yevtushenko and his work. Soon thereafter the editor of *Literature and Life* who had authorized the printing of the attacks on Yevtushenko was dismissed.

As remarkable as the Babi Yar episode was the publication in 1961 of a series of collections of experimental poetry by contemporary as well as older and formerly discredited writers. These works appeared in editions of 25,000, 50,000, and 100,000 copies. Without exception the editions were snapped up by the public in a few hours. It was becoming increasingly clear that the works of the liberal and experimental authors were finding a much greater demand from the reading public than those of the supporters of a dogmatic kind of socialist realism.

As important as these developments were, however, they served as only a small prelude to the unusual debate that occurred at the Twenty-second Party Congress in late October 1961. The Congress provided the forum for the official proclamation of the new Party Program, the first to be adopted by the CPSU since 1919. It also resumed the de-Stalinization program begun at the Twentieth Congress by announcing the symbolically significant removal of Stalin's body from the Lenin Mausoleum. The Program contained few references to literature. Part of the brief statement on arts and letters repeated the old clichés:

> Soviet literature and art, imbued with optimism and dynamic communist ideas, are great factors in ideological education and cultivate the qualities of builders of a new world in the Soviet people. They ought to be a source of joy and inspiration to millions of people, to express their will, emotions, and ideas, to enrich them ideologically and to educate them morally.

But then the Program described socialist realism with a somewhat different emphasis than had been common in the past. "In the art of socialist realism . . . bold pioneering in the artistic depiction of life goes hand in hand with the cultivation and development of the progressive traditions of world culture." "Bold pioneering" appeared to give a new slant to socialist realism by suggesting the viability of experimentation, something not found in earlier expressions of the doctrine.

The speeches of Khrushchev, Sholokhov, and Furtseva, the Minister of Culture, contained little that was new or unusual about literature. Khrushchev said almost nothing about the subject. Sholokhov appeared somewhat petulant in his speech, indicating a bit of jealousy in his jibes at "our fashionable boudoir poets" who attract great throngs of people to hear them read their verse. Madame Furtseva repeated complaints about the volume of "mediocre and downright bad works." Supporting Sholokhov's complaints that writers congregated too heavily in the capital cities of the republics, she disclosed that out of 5,400 writers in the nation, 4,000 resided in the major cities.

After this inauspicious beginning, the Congress unfolded the debate between literary factions for all to see. For the first time since Stalin's consolidation of power, a CPSU Congress contained sharply divergent speeches. While the speeches hardly met the standards of free-wheeling debate found in some meetings of Western political parties, the addresses of Gribachev, Tvardovsky, and Kochetov were recognizable counter-thrusts that made it clear that the differences between liberals and moderates and conservatives were not confined to party versus non-party members but that they had found their way into the highest circles of the Party itself. The conflict had assumed an intra-Party character.

The first thrusts were made by the conservative poet and editor of *Sovetskii Soyuz*, Nikolai Gribachev. He referred to the *Literary Moscow* group of 1956 as writers who had fallen under the influence of "Western fishers for souls." Demands were made "even by communists in certain cases" for what he claimed was the "liquidation of party influence over literature." He asserted that young writers needed guidance and condemned as irresponsible the publication of "Babi Yar" in *The Literary Gazette*. The newspaper had come to smack of "unsavory sensationalism," he claimed.

But the best was yet to come. Alexander Tvardovsky, elected as a candidate member of the Central Committee of the CPSU, delivered a forceful defense of liberalism in literary policy. He cloaked his appeal for a liberal spirit behind the shield of fighting the cult of personality, condemned by the Twentieth Party Congress. That Congress, Tvardovsky said, had engendered "a period of spiritual renovation . . . of liberation from all kinds of constraint and inhibitions firmly implanted upon it by the power of the pervading anti-humanistic character of the cult of personality." He challenged the dogmatists by declaring that "some remnants of the way of thought belonging to the days of the cult of personality, of its habits in the practice of literature, in the way of writing . . . still survive." Tvardovsky complained of the "lack of living depth and truth" in contemporary literature. "There is no cult of personality," he noted to make clear that he was not implicating the existing party leadership in his charges, "but its inertia, its surviving echoes still linger unfortunately in our literature and in our press generally."

The poet-editor went on to attack one of the basic tenets of orthodox socialist realism by asserting, "one cannot ignore such examples as a tone of unrestrained braggadocio that crops up in our press from time to time, striving to visualize life as all Sundays and rosy figures, and somehow to divert one's view from the other days of the week that are filled with labor, worries, and needs." Writers had the right and duty to be concerned with "the whole complexity of life" and not merely with the productive aspects of it. Characters in good literary works require "human charm," Tvardovsky said, for they could not be realistically depicted as machines perfunctorily performing their tasks for the glory of some sacred purpose. In rebuttal to Furtseva and Sholokhov, he declared that the congregation of writers in the cities was good rather than bad because it gave them opportunities to exchange ideas and to criticize each other's work as it was being developed. Finally, Tvardovsky singled out three writers for special praise and cited their works as examples of exceptional literature. These were Valentin Ovechkin, Efim Dorosh, and Vladimir Fomenko, all of whom had written highly realistic novels of rural life in modern Russia.

Tvardovsky's speech was well-received by the delegates and was the subject of much discussion. It was almost as an afterthought that the program officials invited Kochetov to address the Congress two days later in order to allow the conservatives to respond to Tvardovsky. The leader of the dogmatists first turned his attack on the older liberals such as Ehrenburg and Olga Bergoltz, who had been writing their memoirs. "Truth compels us to note," he said, "that there are gloomy writers of memoirs among authors who look more to the past than to the present or future and, as a result of such distorted viewpoints, who dig into the rubble of their poor memories in order to drag into the open long dead corpses and to present them as still containing life." Turning to the young liberals, Kochetov sarcastically commented, "Truth compels us to say that there are on the literary scene some fledglings who are even too young to have any yellow down but who are furiously trying to pass themselves off as dangerous fighting cocks." Then, in an attempt to counter the liberals' contentions that little good literature was being produced, he listed 44 authors who had published "good" works, carefully omitting any of those named by Tvardovsky. Representatives to the Congress from other party-states reported that Kochetov's remarks were occasionally hissed or ridiculed with derisive laughter. But a cool reception did not prevent him from launching into the most unusual section of his speech—a direct assault on the Union of Soviet Writers itself. "To be conscientiously honest," he asserted, "it should be said that the leaders of the Union of Soviet Writers ought to have told the Congress about the state of our literary affairs. But, we have to recognize the deplorable fact that they have, to use a military metaphor, lost the capacity of giving battle . . .

and need to undergo extensive reform." Kochetov claimed that the officials of the Writers' Union had "consigned the burning questions in our ideological and creative life to limbo" or else they would not oppose the sound doctrine of socialist realism so strongly. These charges were tantamount to a demand of a purge of the board and secretariat of the Union.

The Congress was not called upon to approve a resolution that would have given official endorsement to either side of the argument. Nevertheless, the very fact that opposing sides of a major policy question had been presented represented something of a revolutionary step in the Soviet system. It also represented a concession to the liberals. The latter fact was made even clearer by an unusual column in *The Literary Gazette* on November 2, 1961. Alexei Surkov, formerly closely identified with the conservatives, wrote that "never before on the eve of previous congresses had such great discussion of questions relating to literature and art in the life of the people taken place. . . ." Surkov went on to say, ". . . my conception of the contemporary situation in literature and its tasks for the future is closest to that expressed in the speech of Alexander Tvardovsky. . . ." The conservatives had lost, at least for the moment, one of their prime spokesmen.

Five writers were elected by the Congress to serve on the Central Committee of the Party. A sixth could be counted if one assigned Rashidov, a candidate member of the Party Presidium and former chairman of the Uzbek Writers' Union, to this category. Among the full members were Sholokhov and Alexander Korneichuk. The candidate members included Gribachev, Surkov, and Tvardovsky. Both factions of the writers had attained representation in the higher councils of the Party.

At the same time that the liberals were making gains against the dogmatist circle of writers, the Party made clear that it reserved the right to criticize. In *Pravda*, December 27, 1961, Ilyichev, a leading ideologist of the Central Committee, pointedly singled out Aksenov and Rozov for showing sympathy toward the skepticism demonstrated by the young generation. Such criticism, however, was a long way removed from previous attempts to suppress all provocative works and to force the expulsion of non-conformist authors from the Union of Soviet Writers.

The extent to which the liberals were prepared to go in challenging the old-guard writers became dramatically evident in April 1962. Elections to the governing board of the Moscow branch of the Writers' Union were conducted by secret ballot. According to Max Hayward, several of the chief conservative spokesmen were not even nominated.[8] Among these were Kochetov and Gribachev. Even more remarkably, the head of the literary division of *Pravda* and the chairman of the conservative RSFSR Union of Writers lost their bids for re-election. In their places such literary firebrands as Yevtushenko and Voznesensky were chosen. A particularly sharp rebuff was administered to Kochetov by electing Maryamov, a critic who had brutally assailed Kochetov's recent anti-intellectual novel. The liberals demonstrated their support among Moscow's literary community so effectively that the RSFSR Union of Writers was forced to retreat to Rostov-on-the-Don for their next meeting out of fear that the liberals might capture control of any session held in Moscow.

Liberal authors took advantage of the relaxation of controls and their newly found strength by producing works on hitherto forbidden subjects. Even *Pravda* and *Izvestiia* opened their pages to stories with settings in concentration camps. Other publications and plays touched upon Stalin's tactics of terror. Khrushchev gave his personal stamp of approval to Yevtushenko's poem, "Stalin's Heirs," which was published in *Pravda*. The poet called upon the Party "to triple the guard" at Stalin's grave "so that Stalin may not rise again, and, with Stalin, the past." The most widely acclaimed work of the period was Alexander Solzhenitsyn's novel, *One Day in the Life of Ivan Denisovich,* published in *Novy mir* in the fall of 1962. Over 92,000 copies were sold within two days. The novel depicts a day in the life of its hero, a political prisoner in a labor camp during the last days of Stalin's rule. Again Khrushchev personally intervened to prevent censors from forcing the author to delete certain passages from his manuscript. *Pravda* editorially acclaimed the work a literary masterpiece and compared the author to Tolstoi. In addition to these literary events, the period brought further recognition to the young writers with the appointment of Aksenov and Yevtushenko to the editorial board of *Yunost*.

The attitudes of the new writers toward their work was indicated in answers to a questionnaire sent to them by the editors of

Voprosy literatury and published in volume nine of that journal in 1962.[9] Voznesensky, classified by some critics at the extreme left of the liberal group in Soviet literature, noted "I don't think that closeness to his literary predecessors is very good for a writer. 'Incest' leads to degeneracy." This remark could be interpreted as a suggestion that Soviet literature had not provided the new generation of writers with a very strong base from which to work. Yevtushenko touched upon literary criticism in his response to the questionnaire: "To begin with, the poet must be tender toward people, love them and understand them. But something else is there, is a second essential—the poet must be uncompromisingly strict with himself, and towards the faults of other people. I want to point out that a writer has the right to be stern and unsparing to other people only if he also knows how to be tender with them." In contrast, the response of conservatives to *Voprosy literatury* emphasized the patriotic obligations of writers to inculcate the young generation with a sense of "national pride" and a "lofty love for their native land." The stress was on "duty" and "lofty love" rather than on honesty and literary value. As Vladimir Firsov put it: "A writer in my view has an obligation to develop this feeling of responsibility to the people which deprives us of the moral right to live for ourselves, blindly kow-towing to the vogues which reach us from the West, crooning the latest bit of jazz and spitting on the beautiful songs which gush from the depths of the people's exuberant heart."

In demonstration of their support of the new poets, 14,000 people attended the Poetry Day session on November 30, 1962. This year the plaudits went to Andrei Voznesensky, the young poet who wrote in perhaps the most radical style on the most "un-socialist" subjects. Voznesensky received such a tumultuous ovation that some Western observers believed that several high officials became fearful of the popular support being given to the young liberals. In any event, the 1962 Poetry Day marked a climax for the liberal tide that had begun at the Third Congress of Soviet Writers in 1959.

THE CONSERVATIVE COUNTERATTACK

Beginning in December 1962, the trend in literary affairs once again began to turn toward the conservatives. The reasons for the shift away from the liberal position are less clear than they were in the case of the conservative resurgence after the Hungarian revolution. The Cuban missile crisis in the fall of 1962 appears to have been partly responsible for the shift toward dogmatism but the primary reasons were probably largely domestic. Khrushchev was being pressed by a group of conservative leaders in the Party elite led by his one-time protégé, Frol Kozlov. In addition, Khrushchev himself sometimes gave evidence of rather erratic tendencies and may have allowed his personal tastes to project themselves on the official evaluation of trends in the creative arts. In any event, the ability of the dogmatists to regain some of their lost prestige depended upon their success in regaining the overt support of the Party leadership.

Moscow in the fall of 1962 had become the scene of extremely experimental (by Soviet standards) art displays and small literary reading groups. The daring of experimental liberals came increasingly under attack by the conservatives. On December 1, several members of the Secretariat of the CPSU prevailed upon Khrushchev to accompany them to a display of the works of one of the more avant-garde painters in the USSR. Some observers believe that they did so with the hope that he would react violently to what he saw. If this was the case, they got their wish.

On December 2, *Pravda* published an incomplete account of Khrushchev's remarks at the exhibition. According to British sources, the *Pravda* account omitted the harshest and most profane comments. These sources indicate that Khrushchev reacted very strongly to the paintings of the modern artist Zheltovsky. He declared that the paintings looked like the result of a diarrhea epidemic. The state supported artists to create real art, he declared, adding that "We aren't going to pay a kopeck for pictures painted by jackasses." The longer he looked at the works in the gallery, the more vituperative and personal he became in his criticism. "Are you a pederast or a normal man?" Khrushchev shouted. "Do you want to live abroad? Well, then go; we'll take you to the border free of charge." Getting back to the question of state support of artists, the Prime Minister declared, "The people and the government have taken much trouble with you, and you pay them back with this - - - -" [10]

Khrushchev's explosion at the Central Exhibition Hall set off a chain reaction of conservative attacks on modern art and its exponents. An arch-dogmatist was made chairman of the Academy of Fine Arts to help "collect" the situation among painters and sculptors. Aside from criticisms of Yevtushenko for having his autobiography published abroad without permission and of Solzhenitsyn for his book about Ivan Denisovich, however, the conservative reaction was initially centered on art rather than on literature. But the liberal community of creative persons demonstrated remarkable solidarity and awareness of the inter-relationship of writers, artists, sculptors, and musicians. Part of this solidarity came from the basic similarity of creative spirit required for each of these endeavors. Part of it, however, resulted from personal relationships that the state itself had fostered. The Writers' Union, the Union of Soviet Artists, and the Composers' Union had built apartment projects in the same vicinity of Moscow, resulting in a Soviet version of Greenwich Village. The ties among the community of all kinds of artists had been strengthened and the liberals were convinced that their strength lay in the maintenance of a sense of common purpose and mutual support.

The demonstration of this sense of community and common interest became manifest in a series of letters in which the liberals deliberately placed themselves in the on-going battle against modern art. Seventeen prominent figures in Soviet art and science signed a letter to Khrushchev pleading for a halt to the swing toward dogmatism, which they asserted as "alien to the whole spirit of our times." Among the signatories of this letter were writers such as Ilya Ehrenburg and Konstantin Simonov, composers such as Dmitri Shostakovich, movie directors such as Mikhail Romm, and scientists such as Nikolai Semyonov and Igor Temm, both of whom had won Nobel Prizes. Several modern painters wrote a letter asserting their right to experiment in the development of "socialist art." Another letter was written to Khrushchev by other renowned creative writers and artists that went so far as to demand the "peaceful co-existence of all trends in the arts." The precise disposition of this letter is not yet known. Some reports indicate that it was withdrawn under pressure. It has been established that one of the persons to sign the letter was Alexei Surkov, the former

champion of socialist realism whose conversion to the liberal position after the Twenty-second Party Congress had apparently been
genuine.

In response to the unrest that was developing, a meeting of
Party leaders and several hundred representatives of the arts and
literature was held on December 17, 1962, at the Pioneer Palace.
The news media only published the lengthy speech delivered by
Ilyichev. Khrushchev's remarks were never officially released. On
the other hand, some of the writers typed copies of several exchanges that took place between Khrushchev and members of the
literary community. These type-script reports were widely circulated in Moscow and Leningrad and several versions reached the
West. One of the reports carried the following exchange after
Yevtushenko recited the last lines of "Babi Yar."

> *Khrushchev:* Comrade Yevtushenko, this poem has no place here.
> *Yevtushenko:* Respected Nikita Sergeevich, I especially selected
> this poem and with a definite purpose in mind. We all know that
> no one has done more than you in the liquidation of the negative
> consequences of the Stalinist cult of personality and we are all very
> grateful to you for this. However, one problem yet remains which
> is also a negative consequence of those times, but which today has
> not yet been resolved. This is the problem of anti-Semitism.
> *Khrushchev:* That isn't a problem.
> *Yevtushenko:* It is a problem, Nikita Sergeevich. It cannot be
> denied and it cannot be suppressed.
> (The poet went on to discuss anti-semitism and then changed the
> subject to a defense of the modern sculpture of Neizvestny, whom
> Khrushchev had sharply criticized.) He (Neizvestny) came back
> from the war with fourteen bullets in his body. I hope that he will
> live many more years and produce more fine works of art.
> *Khrushchev:* The grave straightens out the hump-backed.
> *Yevtushenko:* I hope, Comrade Khrushchev, we have outlived the
> time when the grave was used as a means of correction.

The audience reportedly sat in stunned silence for a moment and
then began to applaud enthusiastically. Khrushchev joined in the
applause.

One reason for Khrushchev's ambivalent behavior at the meeting was that the burden of criticism had been passed to Ilyichev.
In fact, from the December meeting through the June 1963 Plenum
of the Central Committee, it was Ilyichev that carried the attack.
Khrushchev's speech of December 17 was never printed. Further-

more, he did not deliver the main address at the Central Committee session on ideological questions. Some scholars have speculated that the First Secretary was under serious pressure from Kozlov and the more conservative members of the Party hierarchy. Kozlov himself reportedly suffered a stroke in the midst of a heated debate in the spring of 1963, but it appears that Khrushchev still had to move cautiously in order to avoid compelling the old-guard members of the Party elite to form a tactical coalition with middle-of-the-road leaders. Such a coalition might be effectively deployed against him. The existence of this struggle within the Party may account for different impressions created by his behavior between December 1962 and June 1963. Khrushchev undoubtedly was responsible for initiating the campaign of criticism at the Central Exhibition Hall. On the other hand, he did not personally lead the attack on the liberal group of writers. It is especially significant that he played only a minor role in the Central Committee session, where it is customary for the First Secretary to direct the proceedings.

Ilyichev's speech on December 17 was relatively mild. He defended the principles of socialist realism, but emphasized that this did not prevent artists and writers from using different approaches and developing new forms of expression. On December 26, he reaffirmed this line, but went on to criticize Yevtushenko and Voznesensky by name. In addition, Ilyichev intoned a more conservative view than he had a week before. Calling for an end to "distortions and abnormalities," he endorsed an atmosphere of "intolerance toward manifestations of foreign ideology" and toward "formalist tricks in art." He also repeated the favorite conservative charge that too many liberal writers seemed to go out of their way to express themselves in abstract ways that were difficult for the average citizen to comprehend.

Events in January 1963 indicated the basic indecision over the arts that existed in high circles. Conservatives took up the criticism of modern art and began to apply it to literature, music, motion pictures, and other forms of expression. Seven members of the editorial board of The Literary Gazette were dismissed and replaced with conservatives. On the other hand, Yevtushenko was permitted to take off on another trip to Western Europe and several new works by liberals appeared in print. One of the most unusual of these was Fyodor Abramov's novel, *Around and About* (published in the West under the title *The New Life*). This book probed into peasant life and raised questions about the efficiency of the collective farm as a practical organizational instrument. It was clear that despite the abuse of them and their works, the liberals felt sufficiently secure to go on producing their manuscripts. Moreover, their works were usually published.

Even as new works by liberals continued to appear in print, a coordinated editorial attack on freedom in literature was stepped up by the conservative writers and by the Party leaders. Late in January 1963 Mikhail Sholokhov and V. V. Yermilov wrote articles for *Pravda* endorsing the campaign against literature that allegedly did not serve the interests of the people. Yermilov was particularly vehement in his criticism of Ehrenburg. The latter's memoirs had intimated that people had known in the 1920's that Stalin was developing the cult of personality and that no one spoke out against his excesses. This was contrary to the official interpretation that Stalin had not abused his power until after 1934 and that even then no one was aware of his method of terror. Yermilov claimed that the reasons for the silence of prominent people during the twenties and thirties was just as the official version proclaimed—no one knew. If Ehrenburg had known of these things then, he should have spoken up, according to Yermilov. Ehrenburg replied in a column on February 6, asserting that the essence of the attack on him concerned his personal courage and not his ability as a writer. Furthermore, he said, those who did speak out against arrests on framed charges did not live to tell about it. "Not once did I read an article of protest" in the press, the journalist declared.

Izvestiia joined the campaign of criticism on January 31 with attacks on two writers and on *Yunost* and *Novy mir,* which had recently published their latest works. One of the subjects of the editorial was Voznesensky, who had published some of his most unorthodox verse in the January issue of *Yunost*. The other was Alexander Yashin whose story printed in *Novy mir* assertedly defamed life in the author's boyhood community. Alexander Tvardovsky and Boris Polevoi, the editors of the two journals, were condemned for having permitted the works to appear.

In March the conservative offensive reached its most savage

proportions. Another meeting of Party leaders and creative artists, similar to the one in December, was held on March 7. Ilyichev opened the gathering with an address defending the right of the Party to identify the errors of those with "mistaken views." The speech contained a sharp attack on Ehrenburg, repeating the charges previously hurled by Yermilov. Pointing out that Ehrenburg had publicly praised Stalin also, he noted that "everyone" had done so. "We believed and we wrote. You, it now seems, did not believe but wrote anyway. That is different!"

The extent to which Ehrenburg had touched upon a sore point among the Soviet elite was even more forcefully stated in Khrushchev's speech. The Prime Minister, who had not had much to say about the controversy over freedom of expression since December, appeared to take Ehrenburg's remarks as a personal affront amounting to asking "where were you?" during Stalin's abuse of Soviet power. Khrushchev assailed the journalist and put himself in the position of not knowing what Stalin had been up to and at the same time of having helped the victims of Stalinist error. On the other hand, Khrushchev's comments about Yevtushenko were strangely equivocal. The controversial poet had authorized the publication of his autobiography in France on his recent trip to Paris. He had done so without even submitting it to a Soviet publishing house first. Yevtushenko must have been aware that such behavior had provoked the severest reaction from the Soviet regime in the past. It is possible that he took this step with the confidence that his friendship with high officials and his popularity with the public would protect him from the kind of treatment given Pasternak. Khrushchev both praised and criticized him, indicating his own indecision about what should be done about his daring breach of protocol.

Other conservative spokesmen were less equivocal in their approach to the young liberals. The press mounted a series of volleys during the remainder of the month that brought great pressure on them. Ernst Neizvestny felt compelled to make a public confession of his errors that was published in *Pravda* on March 15. On March 29, Voznesensky and Yevtushenko recanted errors they had committed. Voznesensky's recantation was an artfully worded statement in which he declined to capitulate but merely agreed to "work" as never before. Yevtushenko's statement is more difficult to evaluate. *Pravda* printed only that portion of it which conformed to the demands of the conservatives. He admitted to making "an irreparable mistake" in permitting his autobiography to be published in France. ". . . I fully understand and realize my error and shall attempt to correct it in all my future work," he announced. But the omission of the remainder of Yevtushenko's remarks falsely led many readers, both in the Soviet Union and in the West, to conclude that the young poet had "sold out" the liberal group. It is not known precisely what the unpublished part of his statement included but some sources indicate that he not only defended himself but condemned the efforts of bureaucrats and literary dogmatists for setting themselves up as supreme censors of the creative arts. The same sources contain accounts of a spirited defense of Neizvestny by the poet. In any event, whatever Yevtushenko had said failed to appease his critics. The day after he recanted, the newspaper of the Young Communist League condemned his autobiography while citing quotations from it that created a greatly distorted impression of its actual content. Finally, on April 3, Aksenov was compelled to join Voznesensky and Yevtushenko in a public confession of errors. Together these events constituted a big step backward for creative freedom and recalled some of the episodes of the Zhdanov period, only this time without the labor camps and mass expulsions from the Union of Soviet Writers.

As spring came, however, the liberals received unexpected but greatly welcomed support from foreign sources. In response to the fears of Polish artists and writers that a similar campaign would be launched there, Polish communist leaders made it plain that socialist realism was not on their agenda. The head of the influential Italian Communist Party repudiated the Soviet concept of controls over literature and the arts as unnecessary and totally alien to the spirit of Italian communism. Cuban communists not only criticized the Soviet drive but actively defended Yevtushenko, who had become something of a national hero in Cuba. Other national parties remained silent, although some individual members spoke out against the conservative trend in the USSR. The days of abject obedience from other communist parties had long since disappeared. Now they were making it clear that if the CPSU expected their support in the struggle against the Chinese, the parties in Western Europe and even in some of the party-states of Eastern Europe expected better things from Soviet behavior.

Khrushchev moved to a more moderate stance in a speech delivered on April 24. While the Party elite might disapprove of some literary trends, he noted, the Party had no intention of using the methods of coercion demanded by the dogmatists. Khrushchev implied that forced confessions, exiles to Siberia, and expulsions from the Writers' Union would be employed only in extreme cases and that the Party preferred to and intended to rely upon the writer's conscience and on public pressure to correct any mistakes. In defense of the liberals, he said they had the right "to criticize our shortcomings." After these comments the intensity of the campaign against the "literary left" diminished considerably.

Yevtushenko continued to receive the brunt of the criticism, but now it was largely in the form of efforts to generate public dissatisfaction with him. *Izvestiia* printed a letter allegedly from two West Germans on May 7, asking Yevtushenko why he had spent his time with "Hitlerites" rather than with victims of Nazism during his January visit to the FGR. Popular national heroes, such as Yuri Gagarin, were called upon to chastise the poet verbally, unquestionably with the hope of transferring some of their personal prestige to the general position taken by the Party leadership.

Another sign that the pressure was slackening came on May 12, with the publication in *Pravda* of an interview of Tvardovsky by Henry Shapiro of the UPI. Tvardovsky was candid in his comments. The "distinguishing characteristics" of socialist realism, he said, had not changed as rapidly as other areas of Soviet life. Contemporary literature, according to Tvardovsky, should be marked by "profound humanism, truthfulness in the portrayal of life . . . , loyalty to the advanced ideas of the age." He defended Solzhenitsyn's novel, *One Day in the Life of Ivan Denisovich,* as well as his decision to publish Alexander Yashin's story, "Vologda Wedding." Both of these works had come under sharp attack from the dogmatists. The author also supported the idea of extensive examination of Western literature by Soviet writers. In conclusion, he indicated that the publishing schedule of *Novy mir* had not been altered by the recent attacks on some of its contributors.

On June 18, the long awaited plenum of the Central Committee met to deal with ideological questions. Ilyichev gave the principal address. Not only did he reaffirm the doctrine of socialist realism, the conservative party-spokesman recommended the consolidation of all the unions of writers, artists, composers and related arts into a single giant organization. The intention of the proposal was obviously to strengthen the conservatives by absorbing the liberal Moscow and Leningrad writers groups into an organ that would be dominated by much more traditional members of non-literary unions. Such a reorganization could conceivably reduce the ability of the liberal writers to demonstrate their solidarity and, in any case, would reduce their chances of winning control of the secretariat and executive board of a consolidated union. In addition, Ilyichev asked the editors of *Novy mir* and *Yunost* to explain and justify their policies.

The remainder of the plenum session suggested that there had been little planning for the meeting. Several speeches followed the one by Ilyichev, some of them endorsing his proposal for a single union and others remaining silent on the point. The First Secretary (Khrushchev), who did not appear until late in the course of the session, gave an elaborate defense of de-Stalinization, denying that it had sparked the controversy between fathers and sons. His remarks hinted that he had been under attack for condemning Stalin too vociferously. Very little of his speech was devoted to literature and ideological problems. After singling out the head of the Writers' Union and Sholokhov for praise, Khrushchev paid a special tribute to Tvardovsky. This was especially interesting in that Ilyichev had called upon Tvardovsky to explain his "errors" as editor-in-chief of *Novy mir*. Even more significantly, he failed to endorse Ilyichev's scheme of consolidating all the unions. Separate unions were all right, he said, if they maintained proper respect for the Party.

There were other signs that a more moderate course was being adopted as well. Madame Furtseva told the plenum that cultural contacts with the West should not be deprecated and should be continued. One of the liberal motion picture directors addressed the delegates, but none of the prominent conservative writers appeared on the platform. In general, no real consensus was evident in the principal speeches delivered at the session. This lack of agreement was made more apparent by the failure of the plenum to approve a resolution to implement the recommendations of Ilyichev.

The crackdown on liberals begun in December ended with the conclusion of the June plenum of the Central Committee. The conservatives had succeeded in forcing public recantations of several writers and artists. On the other hand, the significance of what was not done cannot be overlooked. No writer was expelled from the Union of Soviet Writers and some, such as Nekrasov, had refused to recant their "errors" but were not subjected to repressive measures. There was no evidence of expulsions from either the Komsomols or the CPSU, as had occurred during earlier conservative campaigns. Perhaps most significantly, the conservatives had limited their attacks to a select group of individuals. The great majority of liberals had not become directly involved. Moreover, all of the liberals, including Yevtushenko and Aksenov, maintained their positions on the editorial boards of the leading journals. By Western standards, the whole episode may have been reprehensible, but by Soviet standards the six-month wave of conservatism had been rather mild.

Evidence that the conservative campaign had lost its momentum came shortly after the Central Committee adjourned. A new story by Solzhenitsyn appeared in *Novy mir* under the title, "For the Good of the Cause." The story was a bold assault on bureaucracy and the inability of some bureaucrats to adjust to change and to recognize the importance of human beings. In August, one of the most interesting political poems of the Soviet period was published in *Izvestiia*. The poem was by Alexander Tvardovsky, who had spent several years writing it. The hero, Vasily Terkin, was a character resurrected from the poet's World War II work. Tvardovsky entitled it "Vasily Terkin in the Other World." Terkin died and was transported to a purgatory-like other world. There he was confronted time and again with an overpowering bureaucracy, including secret police, censorship, and petty administrators with an unduly enlarged sense of power. Terkin's problems in dealing with the bureaucrats is easily recognizable as a sharp satire on the Soviet bureaucracy. Khrushchev was so delighted with the poem that he had the poet read it to a group of high-ranking state officials at his summer residence at Gagry.

Ilya Ehrenburg surged back into the limelight despite the displeasure he had evoked in the spring for having pointed out the culpability of the Soviet leadership for their participation, at least by silent consent, in the Stalinist purges. Addressing a meeting of the European Writers' Association in August 1963, he discussed some of the principal problems of Soviet literature and Western conceptions of that literature. Ehrenburg claimed, probably quite correctly, that too many comments had been made in the Western press about Soviet authors and their works on the basis of secondary sources. In regard to the content and direction of contemporary Soviet works, he repeated one of his favorite themes—"art does not repeat that which is clear to science—art reveals the world of the emotions." "It is unnecessary to be afraid of experiments," he asserted, ". . . and the right of experimentation to exist in literature must not be denied." The noted journalist was somewhat ambivalent, however, when it came to the question of "writing to order" for the state or Party. "Some of our guests," he said, "are wrong when they think that writers with civic passion . . . cannot create truly artistic works." The principal reason for the prevalence of poor prose and poetry, he contended, was not because the authors "are bound to socialist ideology but because the Lord God has not granted them talent." The elder writer's sharp tongue and pen had not been noticeably dulled by the verbal abuse directed at him earlier in the year.

At the same time that the liberals were defending their views and pouring forth new works, the conservatives continued their critical blasts, though at a much-subdued level. In January 1964 *Literary Russia,* a new periodical replacing *Literature and Life,* attempted to fan up opposition to Solzhenitsyn for his new work, "Matryana's House." The author had examined the destructive capabilities of persons blindly committed to the "righteousness" of their cause, a theme that contained some obvious implications for a system where ideological correctness served as a fundamental instrument of control. *October* attacked the influence of American drama on the Soviet theater, complaining that it submerged the evidence of class contradictions in bourgeois society. As a whole, however, the conservative criticisms were mild in comparison with their viciousness in the first half of 1963.

The remainder of Khrushchev's tenure in office was a period of relative tranquility for the liberal writers and artists. The degree of freedom that they had enjoyed in 1961 and most of 1962 was probably not fully regained, but the conservative offensive was definitely halted. The recovery of the USSR from the loss of prestige suffered immediately after the Cuban crisis and the signing of the Test-ban Treaty in the summer of 1963 had restored a sense of stability in the moderate-liberal coalition of the Party elite. The breaking into the open of the Sino-Soviet controversy and pressure from communist parties in Europe and Cuba helped to restore the confidence of the Soviet leadership in a moderate course. Of equal importance was the responsible behavior of the liberals during the period of conservative ascendency. Under the effective leadership of Tvardovsky, they carefully avoided giving the impression that they were opposed to the system and the vanguard role of the Party. Instead, they attempted to cultivate an image of themselves as creative critics, faithful Soviet citizens who wanted to overcome the shortcomings and failures they found to exist. In short, they tried to persuade others that they were better Russians and communists than the dogmatists, who merely wanted to cover up the problems of the system rather than strive to overcome them.

LITERATURE AND POLITICS AFTER KHRUSHCHEV

After Nikita Khrushchev was ousted from both of his powerful posts in October 1964, the relationship between the factions of the Writers' Union and the ruling elite underwent no serious change. The new leadership took steps to calm the anxiety of the liberals by granting special recognition to several writers in the Leningrad writers' group and by removing Ilyichev from his position in the Party secretariat. No important changes were made on the editorial boards of the literary publications.

Following a period of hesitation in which the members of the literary community cautiously watched to see what the attitude of the new regime would be, writers and their journals resumed the publication of experimental literature. Andrei Voznesensky was one of the most productive, including in his new works a poem entitled "Neizvestny—a Requiem" in honor of the maligned sculptor who had been singled out for criticism by Khrushchev and Ilyichev. Yevtushenko also published some new poems, some of them banal in their patriotism and others asking more searching questions than ever before. His poem, "Bratsk Hydroelectric Station," provoked another controversy and even received the attention of *Kommunist,* the major theoretical journal of the Party. "The poets' labor inspires sincere respect," said the critic, even though its content was not deemed to be in the best traditions of Soviet verse. In June 1965, *Novy mir* printed "Seven in a House" by Vitaly Semin that was a straight-forward attack on bureaucracy. It was not until August that *Pravda* got around to criticizing the work for making the bureaucracy appear too "all-powerful."

The exchange of barbs between members of the different factions of the Union of Soviet Writers continued also. S. S. Smirnov sharply assailed the conservative periodical *October.* The editors of the magazine replied in their June issue, protesting that Smirnov had unfairly called their publication practices "a throwback to the bludgeon" and their whole organization a "hotbed of cliquishness in Soviet literature." The editors of *Izvestiia* resorted to the old letter-to-the-editor technique as a means of chastising an author. Irate letters from taxi-drivers were published along with a note from the editor in regard to the portrayal of taxi drivers by Vasily Aksenov in a story that appeared in *Yunost.*

One of the most amazing developments in the literary controversy came on September 9, 1965, with the publication of an editorial in *Pravda* criticizing *Izvestiia* and *Village Life* for having attacked young writers for no good reason. Rumyantsev, the editor of *Pravda,* specifically praised Yevtushenko, Voznesensky, and Rozhdestvesky and defended the story by Aksenov that had been disparaged by *Izvestiia.* He declared that there had been over-reliance on the "positive hero" as the mark of artistic quality. Rumyantsev wrote: "It is wrong to oversimplify the essence of socialist realism. Socialist realism does not dictate to the artist rigid standards in the choice of themes, in deciding on genre, style and form but permits the broadest possible initiative within the framework of the struggle for communism." Taking up the thesis of the liberal writers, the editor declared, "Keeping silent about shortcomings or blurring them tenaciously, rather than exposing them passionately in order to eliminate them—it is this that gives rise to nihilism, especially among certain young people." Rumyantsev thereby turned the conservative charge of nihilism against those who used the term, asserting that they were the ones responsible for creating doubts about Soviet society and Soviet goals by denying the obvious and proclaiming the obviously false.

Rumyantsev was later removed as editor of *Pravda*. However, it is doubtful that he was dismissed for voicing the charges against conservative writers and censors since all that he wrote had been expressed before. Rather, his downfall appears to have stemmed largely from his explicit criticism of *Izvestiia*. For the party press to attack the government press openly was unheard of, especially at a time when the leadership of the country was still in a state of flux and the balance between Party and state was precarious. Even though he lost this round, it is highly unlikely that Rumyantsev ordered the editorial to be printed without the prior endorsement of high Party figures, probably of Brezhnev himself. The very fact that it was done at all represented something of a milestone in the history of Soviet journalism.

The new regime was faced with one of the most controversial literary events in the post-Stalin period with the discovery of the identities of two of the most famous underground writers. These were Andrei Sinyavsky, who wrote under the pseudonym of Abram Tertz, and Yuri Daniel, who published his works in the West as Nikolai Arzhak. As Abram Tertz, Sinyavsky had written some of the sharpest anti-Soviet works in print and at the same time some of the finest literature in contemporary Russia. His essay *What Is Socialist Realism?* and his novel *The Trial Begins* are moving indictments of the Soviet regime, filled with sardonic humor and pathos. Daniel's most noted work in the West is *Moscow Speaks,* in which the Soviet leaders authorize "a day of open killing" so that every citizen is free to murder any other. In general the works of Daniel and most other underground writers have been inferior to those of Sinyavsky from a literary standpoint.

Sinyavsky and Daniel were arrested in the fall of 1965 for "ideological espionage," "high treason," and engaging in "psychological warfare against the Soviet Union." Their trial in February 1966 created a great controversy in the USSR as well as in the West. One of the most remarkable episodes associated with their ordeal was the "stand-in" demonstration of four to five dozen students, mostly from Moscow State University, who publicly displayed their opposition to the arrest and trial outside the courtroom. In addition, appeals were made to Sholokhov, recent winner

of the Nobel Prize for Literature, and to the Union of Soviet
Writers by Western literary figures in behalf of the two accused
men. Even as the trial opened, however, it was evident that the
state had determined to secure the conviction of Sinyavsky and
Daniel.

On February 10, 1966, the trial of the two accused writers began in the Moscow Province Court. Lev Nikolayevich Smirnov was
the presiding judge and O. P. Temushkin the State Prosecutor.
Two members of the Union of Soviet Writers served as public ac-
cusers. Two lawyers, E. M. Kogan and M. M. Kisenishsky, were
counsel for the defense. Sinyavsky and Daniel were charged with
violation of Part I, Article 70 of the Russian Republic Criminal
Code. This section of the Article reads:

> Agitation or propaganda conducted for the purpose of undermining
> or weakening Soviet rule, or commission of individual particularly
> dangerous crimes against the state, the circulation for this purpose
> of fabrications that defame the Soviet state system or the socialist
> system, as well as circulation, preparation, or possession of such
> literature for this purpose, is punishable by deprivation of freedom
> for six months to seven years, with or without exile for two to five
> years, or by exile from two to five years.[11]

The prosecution demanded that the maximum penalty be assessed.

The trial began with the identification of Sinyavsky as Tertz and
Daniel as Arzhak. The two authors admitted the accuracy of the
identification but refused to plead guilty to the charges "in whole
or in part." Sinyavsky confirmed that he had smuggled his work
out of the Soviet Union beginning in 1956 with the assistance of
the daughter of a former naval attaché of the French embassy.
Daniel's career as an underground writer began later with the help
of Sinyavsky. Most of their works were first published in *Kultura,*
a Paris publication of Polish refugees. Other facts brought out at
the beginning of the trial confirmed that Sinyavsky worked as a
literary critic and Daniel as a translator of poetry. Sinyavsky was
a member of the Writers' Union and neither was a member of the
Party.

The major point that the prosecution felt obligated to establish
was that both authors had deliberately set out to undermine Soviet
authority both domestically and internationally. Only by proving
this point could Part I, Article 70 of the Criminal Code be legally

invoked. The prosecution therefore insisted that "the two deliberately and secretly sent our enemies works that, of course, evoked a hostile attitude toward Soviet rule, served as ammunition for ideological subversion against our country, damaged the prestige of the Soviet state, and even contained direct appeals for reprisals against the Soviet people and the leaders of the state." [12] In short, the state contended that their works alone identified them as enemies of the Soviet government. This was the same tack taken by *Izvestiia* in previous editorials, which referred to the writers as "two renegades" guilty of "duplicity and shamelessness" by directing "dirty libels against their homeland, the Party and the Soviet system and having them published abroad." [13]

The defense contended that the works could not fairly be evaluated as political pieces but could be accurately interpreted only when considered as literature. Both writers asserted that they had sent their works abroad to be published because of their conviction that the dominant literary views in the USSR would not accept their styles and subject matter. Both contended that the content of their stories were phantasmagoric and they had not intended them to be taken literally. The principal point of the defense came to be that the works of Sinyavsky and Daniel had to be treated as forms of literary hyperbole and that neither the actions nor the words of the characters could justly be taken as the views personally held by the authors.

In response to the prosecution's charge of libel, Sinyavsky argued, "I am not a political writer. My works reflect my attitudes about the world, not politics." [14] He further objected to the manner in which the prosecution took passages of his work out of context so as to distort his intention of conveying a sense of irony and hyperbole. In defense, Sinyavsky pointed out that he was a true patriot of Russia for "even the West calls me a Slavophile."

Daniel was even more vociferous than Sinyavsky in his denial that libel and slander had been committed. The state contended that the legal definition of slander was "maliciously circulating fabrications" while Daniel argued that "slander is something you can make people believe, at least theoretically." [15] But the prosecution refused to accept the works of either writer as having been intended as fantasies and persisted in treating the dialogue of the leading characters as the personal commentaries of the authors.

The state repeatedly made assertions that the men were not on trial for their literary beliefs and styles but for criminal activities. Their guilt in violating Part I, Article 70 of the Criminal Code legally depended upon the ability of the prosecution to establish that the words of their characters were their words.

Although it is not a violation of the criminal code to publish words abroad, the state used as supporting evidence for their charge of libel and slander that the works of Sinyavsky and Daniel had been published by enemies of the Soviet state and had been broadcast from Western Europe into the USSR. The prosecution also made much of the fact that a preface to one of Sinyavsky's books had been written by B. Filippov, an East European refugee of strong anti-communist feelings. Daniel, when faced with a similar charge, answered that neither he nor Sinyavsky knew the place of publication and had no knowledge that prefaces would be attached to their works. "We deeply regret that our works have been detrimentally exploited by reactionary forces," Daniel explained, "and that thereby we have caused harm to our country. We did not wish this. We had no ill intentions. . . ." [16] The state did not find this expression of regret persuasive.

Throughout the course of the trial the state and the defense held quite different views on the nature of literature. Daniel contended that the truth of artistic perceptions should be the basis of judgment. He insisted that it was the duty of a writer to be true to himself, using his conscience as his principal guide. Sinyavsky supplemented this contention by attacking the basis on which the prosecution had drawn its conclusions. "The viewpoint of the prosecution," he charged, "is that literature is a form of propaganda and there are only two kinds of propaganda: pro-Soviet and anti-Soviet." This view was too simplistic for accuracy, he claimed. "If literature is simply un-Soviet, it means that it is anti-Soviet. It is a poor business if writers are judged and categorized by such standards." [17]

The prosecution, however, refused to be drawn into an argument over the nature of literary expression. While insisting that Soviet literature has an educational function to perform under the guidance of the Party, the state stood by its contention that it was the political nature of the works of Sinyavsky and Daniel that was crucial. In the first place, these works did not meet the standard of contributing to the development of a communist society as Soviet literature was expected to do. In the second place, they provided aid and comfort to the enemies of the Soviet nation by casting aspersions on Soviet society and Soviet leaders. They did not meet the criterion imposed by the advocates of orthodox socialist realism to unveil "revolutionary truth" as distinct from factual truth.

Sinyavsky was adamant in his conviction that literature should not be judged by its utility to the purposes of the Party. To him the writer has a commitment to express what he believes he truly comprehends. No one has a right to impose any extraneous rules on how or what he should write. This is a central message of *On Socialist Realism,* where he sets forth the proposition that the Purpose had become a generating force in communist society. The Purpose does not tolerate any other standards, for it embodies the ultimate truth by which all else must be judged. In the name of the Purpose, "we built new prisons" so that all prisons would eventually disappear. "So that all frontiers should fall, we surrounded ourselves with a Chinese Wall. So that work should become a rest and a pleasure, we introduced forced labor. So that not one drop of blood be shed any more, we killed and killed and killed." [18] The Purpose, of course, has a striking resemblance to Soviet communism. However, rather than rejecting the goal of communism, Sinyavsky argues that it is the methods that had corrupted the pursuers of the Purpose. The West, he said, had nothing comparable to the goal to give the world. But he continued to insist that his work was not political. He justified his claim on the grounds that he was concerned with the morality of purpose in the sense of ends-means relationships and this was an ethical problem rather than a political one. The prosecution denied that the ethical could be so neatly separated from the political and used *On Socialist Realism* heavily against him.

Toward the end of the trial the state turned its attention to explaining how it had been possible for such traitors as Daniel and Sinyavsky to thrive in the Soviet environment. This explanation was primarily for public consumption and was emphasized in the Soviet press. *Izvestiia* charged them with "extreme ideological licentiousness and moral degradation." [19] Sinyavsky was labeled a liar on the grounds that his fantasies and his conception of the

Purpose were obvious and unmitigated falsehoods. Daniel was treated as a weakling who pretended he did not know what slander was and how opponents of the Soviet Union could make use of his distortions. Moral degeneracy had made them susceptible to being hired by Western agents to conduct ideological warfare against their own country. The court went on to point out that such deviants had been permitted to develop because Soviet citizens had failed to behave responsibly. Citizens had aided Sinyavsky in making contact with the daughter of the French attaché, had burned manuscripts before the authorities could locate them, and had published only mild criticism of the domestically published works of Sinyavsky.

The four-day trial was conducted before a courtroom filled with carefully chosen observers. Only selected passages of the records were made public in the Soviet Union. To the end, despite widespread protests from both Western and communist countries, the state demanded that the judge impose the maximum sentence. As expected, the defendants were found guilty. Sinyavsky was sentenced to seven years in a "strict-regimen correction-labor colony" and Daniel received a five year sentence to a colony "of the same regimen." Sinyavsky was expelled from membership in the Union of Soviet Writers. The principal newspapers in the USSR uniformly congratulated the court and the prosecution for dealing a blow to subversion and treason.

In the midst of the trial, Valery Tarsis was projected into the news by the decision of the government to grant him a visa to lecture in Great Britain. Tarsis was the only anti-Soviet writer who had dared to publish works abroad under his real name. In August 1962 he had been confined to an asylum for the mentally ill, a revival of the old tsarist method of dealing with literary opponents. Released in March 1963, Tarsis resigned from the Party and the Writers' Union, but continued his literary career by sending his works abroad. He allegedly collected a small fortune in foreign currency. His most famous work, *Ward Seven,* is based upon his experiences in the mental institution and contends that the only free people in the USSR are those who have been judged mentally ill. The reason for the unexpected decision to permit him to leave the country was probably twofold: partly to discredit Sinyavsky and Daniel, since Tarsis scorned them for having used pseudonyms, and partly because the Soviet authorities believed he would soon discredit himself in the West. Soon after Tarsis had begun his work in Great Britain, the Soviet government rescinded his citizenship.

The New York Times reported on March 17, 1966, that forty prominent liberal intellectuals signed a petition to the government that protested the conviction and sentencing of Sinyavsky and Daniel. Among the signatories of this document were Yevtushenko, who had just been authorized to tour Australia, and Solzhenitsyn. There was also an unconfirmed report that Voznesensky, who had recently been granted permission to tour the United States, was among the signers of the petition. In addition, a delegation of Czech writers went to Moscow to demand a full explanation of the trial and the French Communist Party approved an 18-page resolution demanding that freedom of expression and freedom of religion be part of the basic party program.

Even before the conviction of the two writers, Soviet officials took steps to quell some of the fears of the liberals by attempting to make it clear that Sinyavsky and Daniel were being prosecuted because of their publishing avowedly anti-Soviet works in the Western press. This was beyond the limit of toleration for the Party leaders. As a means of reassuring the liberals that "constructively critical" works were acceptable by loyal citizens, Yevtushenko and Voznesensky were among those nominated for the Lenin Prize for Literature. The Komsomol organization placed Yevtushenko's name in the hat, which was unusual since he had been expelled from its membership in 1957. Only Voznesensky of the two, however, continued to be considered in the final rounds of the highly selective process. Voznesensky's poetry, according to most Western literary critics, has greater poetic merit than that of Yevtushenko, but his style and subject matter is much further removed from socialist realism. The special treatment accorded the poet was a gesture of recognition by the new regime and was probably intended to reduce the anxieties of the liberal faction of writers. Ultimately, however, no Prize for Literature was granted for 1966.

Some evidence appeared that suggested the Soviet leaders hoped that the trial would set an example to Soviet writers and then be quickly forgotten. On February 22 *Pravda* printed an editorial that attempted to disassociate itself from the quarrel over the content of the works of Sinyavsky and Daniel and allay some of the fears of the liberal authors. Certain people, the article claimed, had become "disoriented" about the trial. It attempted to overcome the fear that the creative freedom of artists was in danger, pointing out that Sinyavsky and Daniel had been tried on criminal charges, not for literary factors. Throughout the spring of 1966, this kind of ambivalence was evident in official statements. Some conservative attacks on liberal writing were made, some liberal publications were released. Tvardovsky was not returned to the Central Committee, but was allowed to keep his post as editor of *Novy mir*. The new leadership appeared to be undecided about what kind of literary policy to endorse.

CONCLUSION

The political conflict over literature reflects a fundamental division between the modernists and the old-guard bureaucrats and ideologues whose outlook and values are largely inherited from the Stalinist period. The continuing controversy over the role of literature in the system is the most open manifestation of the division that exists in virtually every important area of public policy in the Soviet system. These divisions tend to cluster primarily around competing functional interests in Soviet society, such as heavy industry, light industry, and their various subdivisions. Some of the differences appear to result from personality conflicts as well as from programmatic orientations. The shifts in alignments among conservative, moderate, and innovationist coalitions have prevented Stalin's successors from attaining the power to purge his opponents indiscriminately, a power that seems essential for a full-fledged personal dictatorship to be established. In the absence of such a secure leadership role, it has been necessary for the principal leader or leaders to make compromises in order to ward off challenges. The changing relationship in literary-political affairs has often emanated from changes in the composition of the dominant coalition. Such changes, in turn, have been the product of conflicts over policy questions. What distinguishes the conflict over literature and the arts from conflicts over other policy problems is the relative openness with which the debate has been conducted.

The ability of the liberal-moderate coalition of writers to defend itself and to maintain some measure of independence has been a product of several factors. Since the present regime is committed to a position of hostility toward the use of terror as an instrument of control, the leadership has found it expedient to defer to the general public to some degree as a means of maintaining support. The prestige and popularity of some men of letters have given them a certain leverage against excessive restraints imposed from on high. To be sure, this leverage must be employed cautiously, but nevertheless it appears to be a safe assumption that the political elite does not want to alienate any significant portion of the intelligentsia. The support given writers and other creative artists by members of the scientific community has undoubtedly bolstered the bargaining power of the liberals. While it is conceivable that the political leaders could get along without the assistance of creative artists, it is more certain that the alienation of any significant number of scientists would constitute a serious threat to the ability of the system to continue to make rapid scientific and technological advances.

Another major factor in the status of reformist authors is the association of many of them with the Party. Political-literary conflict in the post-Stalin period has never been a simple question of a united Party versus non-Party "revisionists." Indeed, as the Party has co-opted prominent figures and representatives of groups with vested interests into its membership, the higher levels of the Party have become the scene of much of the debate over public policy. Many of the liberal authors are Party activists and some of them hold important posts in Party organizations. Nekrasov, Nilin, Ovechkin, Panova, Tvardovsky, Tendryakov, and many more liberals are CPSU members. Others such as Akhmadulina, Yevtushenko, and Voznesensky are or have been members of the Komsomols or other Party-sponsored organizations. This status has given the liberal faction direct access to the Central Committee and indirect access to the Presidium and Secretariat of the Party.

In addition to prestige with the general public and representation in the CPSU, the liberals have the asset of solidarity in their ranks. The high degree of solidarity has made it possible for writers and editors to take risks. This factor is buttressed by the disinclination of the public decision-makers to treat literary "mistakes" as crimes. Support of communists in Western Europe, Cuba, and

some of the East European party-states has given the Soviet liberals a kind of international solidarity with their counterparts in
other countries. The competition between the USSR and the People's Republic of China for the allegiance of other communist
parties has made such international attitudes difficult to ignore.

In spite of these factors of strength, the liberal authors must
remain aware of actual and potential restraints. Although the
Party elite has declined to give open and continuous endorsement
to the views of either faction in the Union of Soviet Writers, the
politically astute members of the reformist group have recognized
the need for caution. Any extreme demand on their part is likely to
alienate the moderates in the Party hierarchy and turn the powerful wheels of the state against them. To date, however, the Party
elite has chosen to keep the conservatives alive and in a sufficient
number of important positions to enable them to serve as the
principal check on the liberals. Thus, far from pressing for a resolution of the literary controversy, the Party has endorsed its continuing existence. Furthermore, both factions are restrained by the
tendency of the public policy-makers to hold each group collectively responsible for the behavior of its members. As a control
device, collective responsibility serves to remind each writer that
what he does and says may well affect the status of all the members of his faction.

Following a policy of what might be termed "gradualism," the
reformist writers have made significant strides since the death of
Stalin. By rarely submitting to pressure to recant, they have coun-
ter-attacked the concerted campaigns of criticisms against them
and openly challenged some of the traditional forms of control.
During periods of intense pressure, the great majority of liberals
have preferred to adopt a policy of silent dissent. That they have
done so with impunity suggests that considerable progress has been
made since Zhdanov's program of enforced conformity in the arts
and letters. Since they learned from the experience of March, 1963,
that recantations and submission tend to increase rather than reduce the pressures on them, it is probable that liberal authors will
not repeat that mistake in strategy except perhaps in the unlikely
event of a wholesale return to Stalinism.

In general it can be concluded that there has been a gradual
broadening of the concept of socialist realism and a shift away

from dogmatism in the post-Stalin era. Fluctuations in policy are apt to continue, at least until Khrushchev's successors have had an opportunity to resolve the leadership question. In a broad context, the political-literary controversy has been the most open manifestation of the much more encompassing debate of policy that has been taking place behind the scenes. It is conceivable that the conflict over literature and the arts will set the pattern for the future transferal of major policy debate to a somewhat more open stage than it has occupied heretofore in the Soviet system.

NOTES

1. Translation by the author of the case study.
2. Marc Slonim, *Soviet Russian Literature: Writers and Problems,* p. 281.
3. *Ibid.,* p. 308.
4. Max Hayward, "Conflict and Change in Literature," *Survey,* No. 46 (January 1963), p. 10.
5. From *A History of Soviet Literature* by Vera Alexandrova, translated by Mirra Ginsburg. Copyright © 1963 by Vera Alexandrova-Schwarz. Reprinted by permission of Doubleday & Company, Inc.
6. Robert Conquest, *Common Sense About Russia,* p. 155.
7. Translation by the author of the case study.
8. Max Hayward and Leopold Labedz, *Literature and Revolution in Soviet Russia, 1917-1962,* pp. 225-226.
9. Document, "The Old and the Young in Literature," *Survey,* No. 46 (January 1963), pp. 23-30.
10. *Encounter,* April 1963.
11. *The New York Times Magazine,* April 17, 1966, p. 20, © 1966 by the New York Times Company. Reprinted by permission.
12. *Izvestiia,* February 11, 1966. *Current Digest of the Soviet Press,* Vol. XVIII, No. 6, p. 4.
13. *Izvestiia,* January 13, 1966.
14. *The New York Times Magazine,* April 17, 1966, p. 120.
15. *Ibid.,* p. 116.
16. *Ibid.,* p. 127.
17. *Ibid.,* p. 123.
18. Abram Tertz, *On Socialist Realism,* New York: Pantheon Books, 1960, p. 38.
19. *Izvestiia,* February 13, 1966.

BIBLIOGRAPHY

Vera Alexandrova. *A History of Soviet Literature.* New York: Doubleday and Company, 1963.

Harriet Borland. *Soviet Literary Theory and Practice during the First Five-Year Plan, 1928-32*. New York: King's Crown Press, 1950.

Max Hayward. *On Trial: The Soviet State versus Abram Tertz and Nikolai Arzhak*. New York: Harper, 1966.

Max Hayward and Leopold Labedz. *Literature and Revolution in Soviet Russia, 1917-1962*. London: Oxford University Press, 1963.

Priscilla Johnson. "The Regime and the Intellectuals." *Problems of Communism, Special Supplement*, September-October, 1963.

Priscilla Johnson and Leopold Labedz. *Khrushchev and the Arts*, Cambridge: MIT Press, 1965.

Marc Slonim. *Soviet Russian Literature*. New York: Oxford University Press, 1964.

Survey, A Journal of Soviet and East European Studies. The entire issue, No. 46, January 1963, is devoted to the arts and letters.

Abram Tertz. *On Socialist Realism*. New York: Pantheon Books, 1960.

Thomas P. Whitney (translator and author of introduction). *The New Writing in Russia*. Ann Arbor: The University of Michigan Press, 1964.